A Tragedy of Lives

women in prison in Zimbabwe

edited by

Chiedza Musengezi

and

Irene Staunton

WEAVER
W
-PRESS-

A Tragedy of Lives

Published by Weaver Press, PO Box A1922, Avondale, Harare. 2003

Typeset by Fontline Electronic Publishing (Pvt) Ltd., Harare
Cover design by Danes Design, Harare
Printed by Bardwell Printers, Harare

ISBN: 1 77922 017 0

Contents

Acknowledgements

A *Tragedy of Lives: women in prison in Zimbabwe* could not have been researched and published without the support and advice of many experts, friends and colleagues.

First and foremost Zimbabwe Women Writers and Weaver Press would like to give very special thanks to the women who have been to prison for sharing their lives and experiences with us. This book would not have been possible without them.

We would also like to thank the division of Gender Equality Support Project of the Canadian International Development Agency, for not only generously funding the research and supporting the publication but for their consistent encouragement and their recognition of the significance of these women's voices. Our special thanks in this respect go to Ronald Mutasa and Muriel Nqwababa.

Thirdly, we would like to express our appreciation to the following: members and former members of the Zimbabwe Prison Service: Commissioner of Prison Services, Major General Paradzayi Zimondi, former Chief Superintendent, Mabel Chinyamurindi, Mbuya F. Mukawu and Mbuya Chikohomero of, respectively, Chikurubi and Mutare Female Prisons; Director of Zimbabwe Prison Fellowship, Peter Mandiyanike, the former director of Zimbabwe Association of Crime Prevention and Rehabilitation of the Criminal Offender, Samuel Myambo; Acting Chief Magistrate, Mr S. Kudya and Jill N. Samakayi-Makarati of the Ministry of Justice; Director of the Women's Law Centre at the University of Zimbabwe, Julie Stewart, former Education Officer at the Legal Resources Foundation, Mary Ndlovu, and Linda Chipunza of the Department of Linguistics at the University of Zimbabwe for their co-operation and assistance and for attending our meetings and offering their counsel.

Keresia Chateuka, Plaxedes Kaseke, Marina Churu and Florence Makoni for their extensive travel to locate former women prison inmates.

Particular gratitude must be shown to Tracy Mutarisi of Fontline for her care and patience in typesetting *A Tragedy of Lives*.

Finally, we would like to express our particular thanks to the Board and members of Zimbabwe Women Writers who helped us in so many ways besides interviewing the women as part of this project.

Notes on Contributors

Jill N. Samakayi-Makarati holds a Bachelor of Laws (LL.B) degree; a Post-graduate Diploma in Women's Law and is in the process of obtaining a Masters in Women's Law. She is a researcher and has conducted research on the rights of female prisoners, with a bias toward their peculiarities, as women. Her interest in the rights of prisoners dates back to 1994, when she conducted a research on the administration of Justice in Zambia, for the graduate dissertation. She is currently employed by the State in the Ministry of Justice, Legal and Parliamentary Affairs and she is the gender-focal person for the Ministry.

Julie Stewart is a Professor of Law at the University of Zimbabwe. She is currently Director of the Southern and Eastern African Regional Centre for Women's Law which runs a Masters Programme in Women's Law. Her research interests cover women and their experiences with justice delivery systems, customary law, family law and inheritance law. Her interest in these issues has taken her work into the realms of exploring sex and gender and their significance in law and law reform. Unpacking the importance of gender and sex has given rise to research on girls and menstruation in school and the potential effect that lack of management of female natural biological functions can have on her future life and career choices. Julie has published widely in all the above areas. Working on the stories of the women in prison made her realise that if she was ever imprisoned she would be permanently on extra punishment and at risk of constantly extending her sentence – she is not a submissive character.

Amy Tsanga (Dr) is a lecturer in law and the Deputy Director at the Southern and Eastern African Regional Centre for Women's Law Center, University of Zimbabwe. She is the author of *Taking Law To The People: Gender, Law Reform And Community Legal Education In Zimbabwe*, a book which analyses the need for community legal education to be informed by the realities within which people live.

Notes on Interviewers

Keresia Chateuka was born in 1965, grew up in Sanyati and went to Sanyati Secondary School. Keresia worked for Zimbabwe Publishing House for ten years before joining Zimbabwe Women Writers where she is currently employed as a Field Officer. She has written several short stories and poems that have been published by Zimbabwe Women Writers.

Audrey Chihota was born in 1974 and is a journalist by profession. She worked for *The Chronicle* for two years before joining Zimbabwe Broadcasting Corporation where she worked for four years in different departments: news, children's programmes and special features. She is currently employed by Southern Africa HIV/Aids Information Dissemination Service (SAfAIDS) a regional NGO as a media officer. She contributed to ZWW anthologies and newsletters.

Linda Chipunza holds a MA degree in English as second language from the University of Edinburgh, UK. She is a teacher, teacher-trainer and lecturer of long standing. She writes poetry and critiques the visual art. She lectures at the University of Zimbabwe in the Department of Linguistics and is passionate about women's issues.

Paidamoyo Magaya was born in 1981. She is a BA Honours, English and Communications student at Midlands State University. She was an intern with Zimbabwe Women Writers from August 2002 to July 2003.

Tawona Mtshiya was born and raised in Bulawayo 56 years ago. She is married and has blessed with three children. She holds a B.A. degree in Liberal Arts from Bellingham, Washington. She is a co-founder and member of the board for Zimbabwe Women Writers. Her poetry is published in ZWW collections. She is a Christian activist.

Shumirai Mukasi was born in Gweru in 1949 and grew up in Gweru. She is married and is a mother of five and a grandmother of two. She is primary school teacher and enjoys reading and writing. She is a member of ZWW and writes short stories and poems. She runs a young writers' club at her school in Harare.

Sukoluhle Ncube was born in 1977 and grew up in Filabusi. She went to Singwango Secondary School and is currently employed by Zimbabwe Women Writers as an administrator.

Chiedza Musengezi is a founding member and director of Zimbabwe Women Writers. She co-edited compilations of women's voices: *Women of Resilience*, *Women Writing Africa* (The Southern Region). Her short stories and poetry have been anthologised locally and internationally.

Virginia Phiri was born and bred in Bulawayo but now works and lives in Harare. She is an accountant by profession. Her works include fiction, non-fiction, poetry and art criticism. Virginia is an African Orchid expert with special emphasis on Zimbabwean orchids.

Irene Staunton is the publisher at Weaver Press. She has researched and edited an number of oral histories including *Mothers of the Revolution* and *Children in our Midst: the voices of farmworkers children*.

Mary Olivia Tandon is an attorney at Law and was on the Bench in the High Court of Uganda 1964-1970. She was a lecturer in Law at the University of Dar es Salaam, Tanzania before she came to Zimbabwe, where she worked for three years as a Legal Advisor with the Ministry of Legal and Parliamentary Affairs. She also worked for twelve years in Rural Development in Zimbabwe and Southern Africa. Presently she is an activist in Women and Human Rights. She is chairperson of Women's Action Group and Vice-Chair of Zimbabwe Women Writers, and also sits on the Board of Trustees of several NGOs. Her other current interests are literature, poetry writing and reading.

Glossary

chibage – maize, mealie-cob

chikokiyana – a strong illegal alcoholic brew

chimurenga – freedom; the chimurenga – the war of liberation

dhaka – mbanje – marihuana: arguably now a soft drug which should be legalised. Traditionally smoked in areas of Zimbabwe such as Binga. Classified under Zimbabwean (and formerly Rhodesian) law as a 'dangerous drug'.

ET – emergency taxi: usually a … car or a small bus i.e. rather than a big sixty-seater bus

freezit(s) – frozen fruit juices; an inexpensive ice-lolly

gadhi – guard

gogo – grandmother

high-density – euphemism for 'location' : poor working class housing areas

hondo yeminda – war for the land; a government/ZANU(PF) slogan for the seizure of all white-owned farms over the period 2000-2004

hure – whore

jere – jail

kachasu – a strong illegal alcoholic brew

lobola – bride-price

mahewu – home-brewed beer

mbanje – dhaka – marihuana: arguably now a soft-drug which should be legalised. Traditionally smoked in areas of Zimbabwe such as Binga. Classified under Zimbabwean (and formerly Rhodesian) law as a 'dangerous drug'.

munyai – marriage broker

ngozi – the spirit of a person who has died under unfortunate circumstances. An ngozi will haunt the person responsible for the death of the victim, until such a time as reparation is paid.

nhingi – nothing/ no one

nipa – nips, shots of alcohol

pata-pata – flat slip-on shoes

rapoko – millet

Scud – traditional beer manufactured and sold in a carton which resembles the shape of a the scud missile

sekuru – grandfather, old(er) man

sisi – sister. Sometimes literally, but more often used as a friendly honorific

voetsek – rude expletive meaning 'get away'

Commonly used honorifics

Mai – Mrs

mbuya (Karanga dialect) – woman, usually an older married woman, mother-in-law, grandmother; also used simply as an honorific

ambuya (Zezuru dialect) – woman, usually an older married woman, mother-in-law, grandmother; also used simply as an honorific

vanambuya – several women (see above) or the vana may be used as an honorific signifying respect

vanambuya gadhi – the women guards

Acronyms

CABS – Central African Building Society

CID – Criminal Investigation Dept – a department within the police force

CIO – Central Intelligence Office

FRELIMO – Front for the Liberation of Mozambique

POSB – Post Office Savings Bank

PTC – Post and Telecommunications

ZACRO – Zimbabwe Association for the Care and Rehabilitation of Offenders

ZINATHA – Zimbabwe Traditional Healer's Association

ZJC – Zimbabwe Junior Certificate: an exam taken at the end of Form 2, passing enabled you to go on to do your O-level

A note re money

The value of the money which several women refer to during their interviews will vary according to the year within which the reference is made.

At independence in 1980 the value of the Z$1 was more than equal to the £1. Its value dropped slowly over the next decade, falling dramatically in November 1996 to Z$56 to US$1 and has continued to fall since then.

The current (October: 2003) official exchange rate is Z$800 to US$1; the unofficial equivalent is Z$5000 to US$1.

Foreword

The development of this title was an initiative taken by the Zimbabwe Women Writers on the advice of the Zimbabwe Association for the Care and Rehabilitation of Offenders who work with former women prisoners. It has been a project that has taken many months. Many women, former prisoners, have returned to lives in society in which they have again to struggle to survive. A few have returned to stable homes and the support of their friends and relatives, many did not. Finding them both to interview and to do follow-up work was rarely easy. Few are at the end of a telephone, few have permanent homes, and much had to be done by taking a bus to a certain town or village and then setting out to look for the woman we needed, who by then may have gone to work in the fields, or to buy goods to sell somewhere else. Every effort has, however, been made to check each story with each interviewee.

Constantly the interviewers were told that the woman had never been asked, and had never told her life story before. Interviews were emotional experiences as often women had to reflect back on periods of loss, suffering and trauma. Nonetheless, repeatedly we left only with a sense of their courage, fortitude, humour and resilience.

Prior to conducting interviews ZWW members who had been selected had a workshop on communication skills resourced by experts. It was felt that training was important to enable them to obtain useful information. Although at first we had arranged to carry out all the interviews in prison, the plan had to be abandoned after a couple of interviews. Prisons proved to be constraining as the interviews had to be carried out without a tape-recorder and in the presence of prison guards. A few have been included in the book and are remarkable for their absence of information on prison conditions. Interviewees spoke at ease in their homes, at ZWW offices, at Zimbabwe Prison Fellowship and in city parks.

These interviews were recorded on tape and, usually, in Shona and Ndebele. Thirty seven interviews were selected out of a total of sixty-three. They were transcribed and translated at ZWW. Experts were then commissioned to write essays that provided a context in which the narratives could be read. The names of the women have been changed to protect their privacy.

It is sometimes assumed that women who have been to prison are 'bad' women, women without a morality. This is very far from the truth. In the main women are driven to what society defines as criminal behaviour out of circumstances of emotional or economic deprivation. As you read through the book you will frequently find references to standards of morality, standards of behaviour, whether in or out of prison, where their own principles and values come into play and where the situation is found wanting. The question is: are our own minds open enough to hear these voices?

We hope that this book will help all those working within the law, or with human rights, or in education or with families who come from broken homes to look at ways in which our own systems may be improved to help the needy and vulnerable members of society, those who cannot afford lawyers to defend them; or who without an income are left with children to bring up; or those who have had no educational opportunities and have somehow to fend for themselves. We hope that we will reflect on the damage that is done to children, when their mother, often the only breadwinner, is taken away from them. Should they suffer missed opportunities? Or are we creating damaged individuals who will become caught in a cycle of deprivation, and punishment.

We are all members one of another and we cannot judge without understanding; or allow others to act for us without assuming responsibility.

Chiedza Musengezi
Irene Staunton

A Tragedy of Lives:
women in prison in Zimbabwe

Introduction

Julie Stewart

When you read these stories you will find that they really are tales of the tragedy of lives, and you are likely to be struck by the similarity of the women's backgrounds. The majority of them come from impoverished families, they have very little formal education, they are economically disadvantaged and their crimes stem from this impoverishment. A minority are opportunistic women who were relatively well off when their crimes of fraud or theft were committed. Not all the women represented in this book are the victims of circumstance, and we would do women an injustice if we painted them as helpless, swept along by a tide of events over which they had no control. After their release from prison, many women show a great resolve to make a new life, and avoid those activities that put them in prison: this suggests that they have the internal capacity to turn their lives around. Nonetheless, one cannot ignore the fact that their educational, social and economic conditions will have remained the same, if they have not deteriorated: circumstances that, ultimately, led to their crimes.

A woman like me?

Often their offences arose from being mothers, grandmothers, aunts and sisters; they responded to economic pressures, to social and cultural issues but their responses crossed the boundary between what is permissible and what is not. Agnes' explanation for being in prison is one to which many a mother and grandmother can relate. How many times might we have come close to committing a serious crime but were lucky that the results of our responses were not as tragic as hers were?

> The reason I went to prison is that I pushed my grandchild into a fire. He was fighting with another grandchild. The child's uncle reported [the incident] to the police and they arrested me. … In court I admitted my crime and I was sentenced to one month in prison.

> …I am still [after my release] living here in the village with my three grandchildren. … It is a hard life especially as there is no food. I sell some of my chickens to get money to buy food. Sometimes their parents bring a little money, a thousand dollars for example, and other times they do not bring any. I guess they do not have it.

Agnes does not seek to explain or excuse her crime because of the stress she undoubtedly suffered and clearly still suffers. Yet, as with those of so many of the women, one can but wonder whether her reaction to the fighting was simply the reaction of a highly stressed woman, who momentarily reached the end of her tether. It is trite to say 'there but for the grace of God go I,' but over and over again when you read the accounts of what lead to the crime, this is the phrase that comes to mind. 'How close,' each of us may ask ourselves, 'have I come to doing exactly the same thing?' Perhaps, committed a similar act but with different results, fortunately attracting no criminal penalties. Like Agnes, the women in prison represented here are not hardened criminals. They did not, by their own accounts, plan and carry out major or premeditated crimes. They responded to situations and circumstances. Through the very nature of being women, of having heavy un-rewarding and un-rewarded gendered roles thrust on them, they sometimes responded with violent outbursts. Many of these women were exploited as cheap labour in marriage, cast aside for other women – women who were feted and entertained, with the money the wife had earned.

Maureen's story is one that often ends in what are known in Zimbabwe as 'harvest suicides'; hers ended in arson and murder. Her husband had rules:

> His home had its own rules. No wife followed her husband to his work place. So, I had to be at the rural home while he worked in Harare.… My in-laws gave me a piece of land to farm. I cleared the land, cutting down all the trees, and then I tilled it, and planted cotton and maize seeds.

Then when my crops were harvested, I was told another rule. I had to wait for my husband to come and cash the cheques that I had been given after selling my produce. I waited for him. ... I was surprised at the amount of money he gave me, ...though I am the one who had toiled night and day in the fields. My mother-in-law celebrated over my money. 'Well,' I sighed and said to myself, 'Maybe this is what married life is supposed to be.'...

Come the next planting season, I put aside the incidents of the previous season and planted my cotton. My husband had a girlfriend in Harare. ... Nothing changed. He took my cheque, cashed it, and spent the money with his girlfriend. He came from Harare with a thin blanket, two pots and a Z$100 note. [Very little indeed.] That was all I got of the money I had laboured for. I received the goods with tears in my eyes.

My husband was at his parents' house talking and telling stories. I thought of killing myself but I realised my children would suffer. I thought of burning my husband and his parents in the house but I feared the spirit of *ngozi,* which avenges the dead man's spirit.

Then one day, the devil's force gripped me when my husband was drinking beer in his mother's kitchen. ... I thought of my plan to set the hut on fire and said to myself, 'They will think the hut was hit by lightning'. ... I lit the thatch on the door and around the hut. I heard screams inside. My in-laws' grandchildren had fallen asleep in the kitchen. ... One grandchild died in the hut. ... The surviving one spent at least a year in hospital before he recovered from the burns.

Some of them committed crimes, through fear, terror and pressure combined with lack of adequate education and understanding of the causes of their problems. Witchcraft, to many is a reality. They believe they have been bewitched: medical problems readily explained with an understanding of modern medical science are seen as the product of witchcraft.

Ellen, suffered from severe uncontrollable menstrual bleeding, she believed that she was bewitched. She believed her husband's aunt was bewitching her. She believed her husband's aunt had taken underclothing that made it possible for her to bewitch Ellen and cause the heavy bleeding. She was convinced this was the woman causing her medical problem.

I started bleeding. My husband was at work. The blood flowed down my legs. It was uncontrollable ...

I headed for the bus stop where she [the aunt] was and told her that I needed my underclothes. She kept on saying I should leave her in peace and started trying to choke me. I got angry. I started beating her. Her nephew tried to beat me as well but I overpowered them. I took a log from the garden and beat her with it. She could not walk anymore.

The aunt died. Ellen was convicted of culpable homicide. If only she had known that this was a gynaecological problem, which could be treated, these tragic events would not have taken place.

A woman's place?

Families who react in horror to a woman's crimes, and ostracise her after release may have contributed to her crime, Maria's story is all to familiar to those who deal with repeated episodes of domestic violence between couples. The silence that families impose on domestic violence, the silence of a woman's submission may, finally, lead to a fatal violent reaction to what is arguably only a response or reaction to intolerable levels of persistent provocation:

I had serious disagreements with my husband. ... He left and went to work in Chiredzi. When I visited him, I realised he did not love me anymore. We quarreled and fought frequently. He beat me up badly and sometimes he cut me with a razor blade on my arms and inner thighs. It was during one of these fights that I went outside, took a pole, and hit him with it on the head. He fell down at once and was not able to get up again. [He died.]

Throughout the whole period when we fought, I never reported him to the police. I believed in suffering in silence. This is what our elders advise, not to run away from a problem. Even if your husband beats you up, you should persevere with your marriage and not make the marriage problems public and so on.

Maria continued:

On the day of the court hearing, I said that I acted in self-defense. I lifted up my skirts to show them the fresh razor cuts on my thighs. The court officials did not seem to be interested. I was sentenced to nine years. (She served three years before being released through a presidential amnesty.)

Would she have fared better if she had defence counsel who presented a defence of provocation based on the battered women syndrome (sometimes called the slow-burn defence) or self-defence? A lawyer who understands that a woman would not fight back with fists, but might seek to end her battery by finding a weapon that boosted her strength and extended her reach? Does the law need to be reformed, so that such a defence takes female responses and reactions into account, and not simply male reactions and male responses? Is it not that the difference between men and women should be recognised and understood by the courts? Women who kill are viewed as abnormal, but often they are fighting back in desperate circumstances, and protecting their own lives as best they can. Are many of these women in prison because their potential defences were never raised or because their cases were inadequately argued and presented?

Prison is for men: women don't belong

Women in prison, very like women in general, are confined in a male organised and dominated space; women are the strangers and the marginalised within the prison system. Women make up less than three per cent of the prison population in Zimbabwe, they occupy spaces meant for male prisoners. When the women are moved into these male spaces in to which they do not fit, and very little is done to accommodate women and women's needs.

The accounts of managing menstruation and nightly experiences with urinating indicate that the arrangements for women's sanitation are makeshift and lack any real appreciation of – perhaps 'concern for' is the better phrase – women's physiology or practical sanitary needs. Men can urinate into containers with a great deal more directional accuracy than women, they can avoid the risk of physical contact with the receptacle into which they urinate. Knowledge of physiology, if applied to what is provided for the women would indicate to any caring and sensitive individual that what is provided is not just unsatisfactory, it is unhygienic and a very real health risk. Every woman who reads the accounts of urinating into cooking-oil tins in the dark in a crowded cell, or trying to deal with a sodden sanitary pad leaking menstrual blood with inadequate facilities and no

5

privacy, has to feel that this is cruel and inhuman treatment. Under the best conditions, with freely available sanitary wear, menstruation involves constant awareness and careful management to avoid embarrassment.

Women who give birth in prison, or take small children with them to prison face a system which is not child friendly; prisons are not organised for the care of children, they cannot deal with children's needs. Lock-up times are from 4.30 p.m. or thereabouts to 6.30 or 7 a.m. Children, like their mothers, are, in fact, imprisoned. Prison food is not food that provides appropriate nourishment to babies and small children, women with babies and children in prison seem to carry a double punishment, coping for themselves and fending for their children. There are no realistic concessions to individual needs and to units that would accommodate mother and child, with privacy and personal space to raise and nurture a child. Children could well be crawling in the dark around those makeshift 'toilets'.

Nothing more needs to be said.

Rehabilitation or exercises reinforcing gendered dependency

Programmes designed for the rehabilitation of these women are replicas of the assumptions about gendered roles in the wider community – vegetable gardening, typing (for the lucky ones), sewing, knitting and dressmaking. Cooking for other inmates is the role of the prisoner who is restricted to internal activities and under close supervision as is the case with those convicted of murder. The appropriateness of rehabilitative activities is highly questionable. During the time she was in Chikurubi prison, Mercy was one of only two women prisoners who had a degree, yet she seems to have been engaged in sewing, embroidery and other severely gendered activities. Was this a part of the punishment or is it indicative of the failure to think of women and women' activities beyond the restricted bounds of domesticity?

Religion

The most powerful tool that these stories describe in changing their lives is religion. The women talk about finding God, the love and concern of fellow prisoners and of sympathetic and caring guards. The religion described is Christianity, but undoubtedly other religions would have similar power and provide comfort to women in prison. Prison Fellowship, an organisation that seeks to help prisoners while in prison and to help them readjust and make a new life after prison, certainly played a central role for many of them. Somebody who cares, a helping hand, is what these organisations symbolise. The long dark nights after lock up, filled with fear or burgeoning hope, make religion an important component of the rehabilitation process.

Whose prison? Whose version?

Some years ago at a speech day at my son's boarding school the headmaster commented that the school that he administered and the school that the boys attended were two different places. He meant that the boys' stories about the school did not necessarily reflect what took place, or was understood, at an official level. One might suppose that the reverse was also the case: that the official version of what took place at the school was not necessarily the one the boys experienced. Reading about prison administration, prison life, prison discipline, prison health care, hygiene and prison activities as experienced or perceived by the (former) prisoners themselves (particularly those who were no longer in prison), and then as told by the prison authorities, one must ask — which is the authentic version of prison and the prison experience?

This book was not designed to be about prisons and prisons reform, but arguably these are issues that the prisoners, guards and other contributors raise constantly through their observations and their concerns. If the officials paint a picture of happy, content, well-nourished prisoners, of guards whose concerns focus on the needs of the prisoners and their rehabilitation, and the prisoners talk about poorly prepared, often rotten, food, abuse, name calling, dehumanising practices and physically violent punishments such as beating on the feet, constant harassment, creation of trivial offences, constant changing of rules, it is as if there are two versions of prison, one experiential, one the model or idealised prison.

The stories will make you catch your breath and ask, 'How would I cope? How would I react?' Being constantly labelled and publicly denounced by being referred to not by your own name, not even by the anonymity of a number but by the nature of your crime — 'you murderer', 'you thief', 'you child killer', seems an unlikely method for sensitive and caring rehabilitation. Unfortunately at the level of official inspection, scrutiny and action it is the prisons officers' version that tends to prevail, not least because the inmates are too afraid of reprisals to speak out. (It should be noted that the prisoners who were interviewed in prison in the presence of a guard, rarely said anything negative.)

Values and reform

Reading these accounts of prison and prison life, one wonders what new values the women learn – those who guard them offer very mixed messages. Being required to do manual chores, sewing and other activities for guards who have no right to the services, at least in the manner they are demanding them, must be extremely confusing, if not annoying, to the convicted thief or embezzler.

> I'm serving time for what you are doing but there is no one to effectively police what you are doing to me.

Similarly a woman convicted of a crime of violence – perhaps killing or injuring a partner who had threatened their lives or bodily integrity – and then beaten by a guard for a trivial or even non-existent infringement of 'unwritten' prisons codes, must wonder at the justice in 'the system':

> I attacked someone who hit me, you beat me when a fellow prisoner did wrong, in a collective punishment. You are protected, I was not.

What can be done? The importance of these stories

The women whose stories make up this book are not bad women. They, with a few feisty exceptions, don't boast about their exploits they are contrite and desperate to tell their stories so that others may learn what to avoid and how to avoid it, and not end up in prison themselves. Women, are rarely recidivists, that is those who repeatedly commit crimes, except for women who are involved in what are labelled as moral crimes, prostitution . The women in this book, according to their own accounts want to avoid any further brushes with the law

These are not bad women, they do not need to be stigmatised as former prisoners, they do not need to be labelled as bad for the rest of their lives. They are women, with hopes and dreams and futures. Their stories, however horrifying and tragic require our informed responses, they need our support to build new lives. Perhaps even more so there is a need for lobbying and support to reshape and reform the punishments systems, to ensure that women who are convicted of criminal offences are punished appropriately and more importantly receive appropriate help and assistance, as discussed later in this book, to turn their lives around.

The social and economic circumstances that led to many of the crimes described by the women need to be addressed, girls need and have a right to education, equality of opportunity, equality and equity in marriage and in access to and control over resources in marriage. Social rejection of girls and women who fall pregnant outside the bounds of socially acceptable relationships, drives many of them to seek unlawful and unsafe abortions, to kill their newly born children to avoid discovery of their pregnancies.

Women who commit infanticide are usually riven with grief and remorse, they do not need to be separated from their other children, they need social and emotional support, they are unlikely to re-offend and do not present a risk to others. Often they have committed the crime of killing their newly born child to avoid social ostracism and adverse economic consequences for their older children. It is not prison they need, but psychological counselling and opportunities to reshape their lives.

Prisoners are powerless

While in prison, prisoners are powerless. Officially they can complain to visiting justices but it is the brave woman who makes an official complaint. Even the nature of the complaint or request that can be effectively made is constrained by the gender and sex difference between the prisoner and the visiting justice. Culturally and emotionally it is very difficult for a woman to complain to a male justice about sanitary conditions that involve issues related to menstruation. This book gives them a voice but it is voice that has to be boosted and projected so that families, society, the justice delivery system as a whole and the prison system listens, responds and acts.

The work of the Zimbabwe Women Writers in collecting the stories of the women has provided a powerful lobbying tool for change not only of prisons, but of women's overall condition, for reform of approaches to punishment and for more gender sensitive construction of criminal defences. It is a vehicle that gives an opportunity for us all to respond and ask that the inhumanities in prisons be removed and that alternative forms of sentencing of women are formulated.

Fortunately, as Jill Makarati's commentary later in the book shows, changes are being made and there are current efforts to ensure that women are incarcerated only as a last resort, but they need constant support and monitoring to ensure that change really does take place.

Female Prisoners in 'Male' Prisons

Jill N. Samakayi-Makarati

Female prisoners constitute about 3.5 per cent of the entire prison population. Given this small percentage, one would expect that they would meet with fewer problems. Yet the stories recounted by both the serving and released prisoners in *A Tragedy of Lives* indicate the contrary.

What brought me into contact with Zimbabwe Women Writers was the research that I undertook on the management of menstruation in prisons, as a requirement for post-graduate studies. Thus, I will also discuss issues that emerged from my research in order to complete the picture of women's experiences in prison.

In this overview, I shall begin by examining the female prisoners' experience with inadequate or absence of sanitary facilities. These include menstrual and toilet facilities as well as those for childbirth and childcare. I shall ask how female prisoners try to cope with their absence, and the underlying issues that seem to emerge from these experiences, not least the silence with which female prisoners accept this deprivation. I shall also consider opportunities for improvement, which can be created, if the prisoners break their silence. Finally I discuss the effect of the imprecise nature of the legal and policy provisions on the operations of prisons.

Insufficient sanitary facilities

Sanitation has everything to do with the ability to remove and treat waste to ensure that the health of the public is protected. My purpose here is to examine the extent to which sanitation is managed in female prisons and how its insufficiency affects the female prisoner.

Women generally feel uncomfortable to be in public places during menstruation, even where they are adequately protected. Some go to an extent of wearing dark clothes. This choice may not be available to the woman who is detained in a remand prison awaiting trial. A prisoner I interviewed during my field research described her experience in court as:

> Very uncomfortable and you will be uptight... there will be men in court... you think they can see stains on your dress.

I also held interviews with magistrates who confirmed that most women are insecure in court, although the majority of them did not link this to menstruation. One female magistrate, however, admitted that she did suspect that some women were menstruating because they were fidgety. How this affects their performance is an issue for further research. Although, this factor is not mentioned by any of the women in this book, perhaps because they were not asked, it is important, as it is in the courtroom where the decision to imprison an offender is made.

Making do with one pad a day

These are menstrual encounters of different women during their imprisonment.

> The clinic nurse...during your period she gave you half a pad. (Marina)
>
> I never saw cotton wool...I think prisons should have cotton wool because that is what women should use. (Chipo)
>
> Women would spend the day with one pad ... (Viola)

Menstruation is a natural occurrence in women. It takes place every month for about three to five days. Ordinary women are able to manage their own menstrual requirements without necessarily involving anybody else. They simply purchase sanitary protection and dispose of it after use. No one else needs to know. However, prison life is different. Female prisoners depend on the prison system for their livelihood, including sanitary requirements. The standard practice, as recounted here, is that female prisoners request sanitary wear from prison officers when they commence their menstrual period. It is only then that they are issued with the one or half a pad, referred to above. Female prisoners find this inadequate. This, as the women explained, has forced them to find alternatives:

> We find other ways...some use newspapers by rubbing the newspapers to make them absorbent ... (Manswa)

Those with a heavy flow ask for pieces of cloth from the officers to use as pads … (Chipo)

Sometimes we would end up using tissue that would hurt our uteruses. (Viola)

It emerged from my research that prisoners pull out the cotton wool from cut pads to roll into small pieces for use as tampons. It is a way of making do with the one or half a pad for a whole day and makes them feel secure. There are, however, risks involved. The woman may fail to pull out the little ball thereby exposing herself to infection or to the possibility of her tubes being blocked to the extent of rupturing. (This information was provided by a Harare-based gynaecologist, who declined to be named.) None of the women, in this collection, spoke of this, but this problem may have occurred. What the women experienced, according to Mercy, was discomfort and pain:

I push mine quite deep to avoid embarrassment. I get stomach pains and each time I pull out the little balls I notice… clots of blood…but I have to feel secure.

Other alternatives include pieces of blankets, prison uniforms and, given the presence of nursing mothers in prison, babies' woollen hats get stolen from the washing lines. Some prisoners find bathing helpful, although this is restricted to the daytime.

'Thou shall not change your pads at night'

During my research, I discussed the problems female prisoners face in trying to cope with the inadequacy or absence of disposal facilities.

Disposal facilities are located in the ablution blocks and they consist of plastic trash bags and containers. Prisoners only dispose of their used sanitary wear during the day. What is problematic, as I observed at Chikurubi, is the inadequacy of these facilities. I noticed used cotton wool lying around them that the prisoners themselves had to clean up. Not unnaturally they experience discomfort in handling disposed sanitary wear. As Thandi, one of the women I interviewed, said:

We are provided with gloves, but they are not always clean, so we normally use sticks…but even if they were clean …just the idea of seeing and picking up somebody else's used pads makes the whole process so uncomfortable. I just feel sorry for the mental patients who do not even use gloves... they use their bare hands.

Thus the problem during the day is the management of the waste. However, once prisoners are locked up in their cells between 4.30 p.m. and 7.30 a.m., they cannot change their sanitary wear. The cells have no disposal facilities. Whatever form of sanitary wear they put on at 4.30 p.m., they must wear until the following morning. Indeed they have made it their own rule to prohibit changing sanitary wear at night for, according to Thandi:

> We feel it would be unfair to others if we expose wet pads...you know how blood smells. Where do we keep them anyway?

The obvious risk involved with prolonged use of sanitary wear is toxic shock. Neither the prisons' medical personnel, nor the prisoners themselves referred to this, but it remains a potential problem. Prisoners did, however, complain of minor infections. Thandi said:

> We get itchy rash, which normally clears off by washing with soap and applying Vaseline. We only get Betadine solution [an antiseptic] from the clinic if it is serious.

It would seem that the availability of sanitary wear during lock-up (4.30 p.m. to 7.30 a.m.) would not serve any purpose, as the prisoners would not change their pads anyway due to the lack of disposal facilities.

Menstruating without underwear

> We had no pants even during our periods. We had to use old rags, those red ones. (Jane)

Female prisoners are allowed two pairs of underpants at any given time. Mostly, these are brought from home, as confirmed by the clinic:

> The ones we offer are normally referred to as *maparashuti* (parachutes). These are baggy type of panties made from strong material, they last long and they serve the purpose. (Regina)

Initially the *maparashuti* were used, much to the discomfort of female prisoners. This has, however, been stopped due to the scourge of HIV/AIDS and other infections. As Joyce said:

It was disgusting to wear pants that were worn by someone else. I was afraid of contracting diseases… we were forced to wear them especially during menstruation.

I discovered during my research that sometimes prisoners chose not to use underwear during the night because they would have washed it for use the following day. While some then inserted the little balls of wool to avoid leakage, others chose to use full pads and slept with their legs crossed. They ended up soiling their blankets, which could remain unwashed and passed on to other prisoners. According to Priscilla:

It is unbearable. For you to get detergents or plain soap to wash those blankets… it's something else.

The restricted quantity of underwear is clearly inadequate for menstruating prisoners. The decision to put a stop to the circulation of used underwear is, however, commendable.

Limited use of toilets at night: a prisoner-created rule

Some prison cells have built-in-toilets that are flushable from inside while others can only be flushed from outside; others have no built-in-toilets at all. Beti explained her experience at Mutare Prison:

The toilet…could not be flushed from inside so inmates had to force themselves not to go to the toilet. If one of us had to use the toilet at night, it meant that all of us would suffer the bad smell until the following morning…cover[ing] it with a blanket…did not work.

On transfer to Chikurubi Female Prison, Beti had yet another experience. This time she was accommodated in a cell that did not contain a built-in-toilet. Buckets were placed in the cell for use as toilets. Prisoners at Chikurubi also avoided using the toilets. Beti confirmed that she learnt to avoid the toilet, 'For the year I slept in this cell I did not use it [the toilet].'

It emerged during my research, as also stated by Viola that the buckets were 25-litre empty cooking oil containers, cut around the mouth to create enough space for use as toilets. The handle was left to make lifting easy for those charged with the responsibility of cleaning it. Apart from the smell, the bucket could overflow and one would get splashed while using it. Those with babies had to contain with the stress of restraining them from crawling on the floor.

Manageable menstruation at Shurugwi Female Prison: the benefits of discretion

During my field research at Shurugwi, none of the prisoners I interviewed complained of inadequate sanitary wear. Prisoners got sanitary wear three times a day and were at liberty to request more, according to their needs. To supplement the prison supplies, the administration used its discretion to allow family and friends of the prisoners to provide them with sanitary wear. What was common with Chikurubi, however, was the lack of disposal facilities during the lock-up period. The self-styled rule against changing used sanitary wear also applied at Shurugwi. Those housed in cells without built-in-toilets each used a 5-litre container, because the prisoners were few in number. They did not experience the discomfort of emptying other people's waste. This also reduced the risk of infections.

Imprisonment and children: the pains of mothering

What seems problematic is the time one goes into labour. Some women expressed satisfaction with their experience, as they gave birth in hospitals.

Generally, however, as we observe through the following experiences

> Pregnant prisoners suffered the most. We would… shout for help through the window when they went into labour. The nurse would shout back to tell us that if it was a first pregnancy then she would be fine. We feared a lot for the pregnant prisoners. The nurse took long to take them to the hospital. They would humiliate them. 'Why did you bring us a pregnancy?'… Some would give birth in the cells. Others would assist with the delivery. Most of us knew nothing about being midwives but we had to help out. (Lilian)

> Pregnant inmates were supposed to be checked constantly but this was not the case. …Assistance was only available when one had already delivered. (Beti)

> Babies were delivered despite the prison clinic nurse's assertion that prison cells were not equipped to deliver babies. (Regina)

And so, not only were the babies subjected to unsafe deliveries, but the other inmates were also exposed to infection. Pregnant and nursing mother who are

16

admitted to prison also face dietary problems. There is no special diet and no special arrangements are made to ensure they receive sufficient quantities of food. Sandra was pregnant at the time of her incarceration. According to her:

> We had our supper very early, around 3 p.m. or 4 p.m. In addition we were given a tiny amount of sadza. It was not enough for me. By the next morning I would be famished and without strength.

The absence of special dietary arrangements affects the children and amounts to a form of punishment. Clearly, however, children whose mothers are incarcerated end up serving their mother's sentences be they born or in her womb. Moreover, those left at home without proper care are punished because of their mother's wrongdoing. Lilian had left her child with her maid when she was arrested, and according to her, 'The housemaid had left and my child was in the care of my landlord.' The landlord and Lilian's sister later took the child to prison to live with her mother. For our purposes, however, I will examine the life of children who are admitted to prison with their mothers, in order to assess if their lives are separated from their mothers' prison terms.

'Serving' my mother's sentence

The law allows the admission of infants into prisons with their mothers (Sec 58 of the Prisons Act: Chapter 7:11), until such time that they are weaned and relatives are willing to care for them. In the absence of such relatives or friends, children can be handed over to the Department of Social Welfare. Authorities faced with any action concerning children should ensure that the action is in the best interest of the children. Yet as Martha states:

> In prison mothers do not get special accommodation. In the cell we were mixed, those with children and those without… I shared my bed with my baby… Sometimes the baby food was not well prepared…my baby had diarrhoea and on checking the baby food I found that the porridge was lumpy and no egg had been added….

Martha's contentions were confirmed by Mercy, who was admitted to prison with a newborn baby:

> You can't say, 'Can I have warm water…for my baby, please?' When you ask, you are sometimes told, 'This is not home. You knew that you wanted

to look after your baby very well. So why did you commit a crime?'...
After two weeks my baby started to show deteriorating health, she couldn't
eat anything. She cried most of the time. I asked to see a doctor... they
couldn't let B.... see a doctor. So when my family came I asked them to
take her... After about a month... my baby passed away....

Mercy's story does not disclose the cause of the child's death. However, the baby's
deteriorating health and the non-availability of medical attention is indicative, of
the lack of consideration of the child's best interests, by prison authorities. Lilian
echoed Mercy's sentiments on the attitude of prison officers:

Children suffered the most. They did not get good medical care in time.
If you asked for help for your child they would tell you hurtful things like,
'Prison has no free medicine.'

The situation is even more difficult for mothers whose children are old enough to
understand their surroundings. Lilian's child could not continue staying with her
landlord and no one else volunteered to keep her. She was over two years old
when she joined her mother in prison. She described it as:

The worst thing for me... Children do not forget. She shocks me now
and again with her prison memories... sometimes when I am bathing
and I take long, she will stand at the bathroom door and shout, 'Mama if
you are late *ambuya gadhi* will beat you up.'

It becomes difficult for mothers to separate their prison terms from their children,
except, perhaps, when they have to perform labour away from the cells. Generally,
when this happens, the children are left in the care of elderly prisoners, who
cannot do hard physical work. At the time of my field research in 2001, it was
encouraging to notice a crèche at Chikurubi Female Prison, which had toys and
baby coats. A prisoner who had interest in the children had decorated the crèche.
This is a commendable effort by the prison authorities and the prisoners.

What is the evil behind the silence?

For a long time, prisoners have learnt to keep problems to themselves. In my
capacity as a lawyer in the Ministry of Justice, Legal and Parliamentary Affairs, I
once attended workshops where ex-prisoners related their experiences in prison

to prison officers and other stakeholders. On being asked why they did not make any complaints to senior officers or magistrates, during their prison visits, they cited harassment by the warders, which followed every time complaints were made to high-ranking officials. To them, they were better off keeping their problems to themselves. Martha relates how she was beaten for complaining about the bad quality of her baby's food:

> I went to one of the prison guards and said, 'Look *vanambuya*, look at the poor quality of food my baby is fed.' As soon as I said that they beat me up…They took turns to beat me with a baton…They said I was acting proud and important.

Even mistakes, as contended by Maureen, were met with physical harassment:

> You were made to lie flat on the ground then you were beaten under your feet. Crying or shouting *yowe-e* or *maiwe-e* was prohibited.

Martha's courage to stand up to such abuse, by threatening to report the prison officials, was soon rendered ineffective. According to her:

> I told them I was going to report them to the magistrates who come to find out from us about our living conditions…. They threatened to extend my stay in prison if I reported them. It was too serious a threat. I did not want to stay a day more than necessary. I never said a word against them from that day… However… their behavior towards me improved.

The attitude of the prison officers towards Martha only changed because she stood up against them, indicative of their fear higher of authorities.

The impact of authority is evident from the interventions that have been made by the Chief Magistrate's Office. During their visits to female prisons over the years, magistrates have observed pregnant and nursing mothers in the remand prisons. The prisoners complained to the magistrates about the lack of facilities, in prison, to sustain their requirements. Consequently, the Chief Magistrate's Office issued a directive to magistrates to remand out of custody, expecting and nursing mothers. As expressed by one official:

> Having seen these women in prison, we got concerned about the welfare of their children… Why should a baby be subjected to a prison birth or life, just because of its mother?

Although the directive did not benefit serving prisoners, it is a clear indication that problems brought to the attention of authorities stand a good chance of being considered. Prisoners themselves have brought about this commendable decision by the Chief Magistrate.

The rewards of speaking out

On completion of my research, I had made several recommendations to the Prison Service through the Ministry of Justice, Legal and Parliamentary Affairs. Among them were the recommendations that:

> A specific policy on the management of menstruation should be adopted, under which:
>
> — adequate provision of sanitary protection should be made for female prisoners
>
> — relatives of prisoners should be allowed to provide additional sanitary wear

In the past, sanitary wear was purchased as part of prison hospital supplies, for hospital use. The menstrual requirements of women in prison were taken from the hospital supplies. No sanitary wear was bought specifically for use by the female prisoners.

I have not yet established the extent to which my recommendations were adopted. However, I do know that a specific budgetary allocation has since been made for the purchase of sanitary wear; and, in addition, relatives can now provide the prisoners with sanitary wear at Chikurubi Female prison.

During my research I discovered that menstrual requirements were not provided for in the prisons' legislation. To some extent this explained the skewed management. The prison administration had made an effort to provide everything else that was provided for in the Regulations, (The Third Schedule of the Prisons: General) Regulations, 1996) such as underwear, soap and clothing. The recommendation to amend the regulations to make specific provision for sanitary wear and sanitary facilities, has not yet been considered.

National debate on the availability of sanitary wear: does the female prisoner feature?

My research results coincided with the recent critical shortage of sanitary wear at the height of Zimbabwe's economic crisis. This triggered debate as to the essential nature of sanitary wear, and whether or not it should be classified as a basic commodity. The debate, which arose in Parliament and was taken up by the media, became a matter of a national interest.

The plight of the confined woman, the prisoner, was not excluded. A forum was constituted by the Zimbabwe Women's Resource Center and Network, at which concern was raised about the shortages of sanitary wear. Stakeholders in the Women's Rights Movement formed the audience, while manufacturers of sanitary wear were invited to explain the scarcity of such commodities. I was also given an opportunity to discuss my research findings.

Thus the Prison Service also became part of the network. Consequently, one of the manufacturers pledged to donate a consignment of sanitary wear to female prisoners. This he did, as confirmed by a prison official:

> Sometime this year we had a donation of pads from Mr Steven Margolis who owns a company that manufactures pads. The donation was very much appreciated, more so because it was coming from a man. (Regina)

Female prisoners in 'male' prisons: conclusion

The experiences of female prisoners are indicative of the non-availability of facilities that are specifically designed to meet the particular needs of women. A former prison officer confirmed this contention when she stated that:

> Way back they used to keep male prisoners there... these prisons were built initially for males and were not modified for the use of female prisoners. (Mabel Chinyamurundi: former Prison Superintendent)

She attributed the absence of any effort to modify female prisons to the small number of female prisoners, compared to that of their male counterparts was because, 'Investing in a very small number of people against a big number is not the normal practice.'

Because women were accommodated into existing male-oriented structures, their requirements were measured against those of male prisoners. Their needs then became over-shadowed, as they did not apply to the male prisoners. Consequently, even today, facilities designed to meet the peculiar needs of female prisoners are either limited or absent. The overarching issue, therefore, remains that female prisoners are incarcerated in male prisons. One of the only ways in which this will change is if female (ex-)prisoners have the opportunity and choose to bravely speak out as they have done in *A Tragedy of Lives: women in prison in Zimbabwe.*

Section 1:

Reproductive rights

1

Memory*

interviewed by Chiedza Musengezi

I was born in Seke in July 1979. Both my parents are peasant farmers. They are not employed. They grow vegetables and sell them at Chikwanha or Mbare Musika in Harare. My father has two wives and his senior wife has five children, so altogether we are twelve children.

We are seven in our family and I'm the fourth child. I have two brothers: Blessing who works in town and Victor who farms in Seke. I have four sisters. We live in Sabau Village. My father built a good home for us: a three-bedroom brick house with an asbestos roof and two kitchens (rondavels) and a Blair toilet. We do not have a well of our own, although other people in the village do. We tried to dig one in the yard but it was all rock, there was no water.

Even though I grew up in a big family, I was happy. We children played together. Sometimes other village children joined us to play ball, to run and play hide and seek. I did not like arguments and quarrels. I went to primary school and I wrote my Grade 7 examinations in 1996. I did not do well. I had 24 units. I was not happy with my results and I wanted to do better. I was accepted at secondary school for Form 1. My mother worked hard in the fields and raised enough money to buy me school uniform and books. I liked school. I enjoyed Fashion and Fabrics more than any other subject, but again, I did not do well and when I was in Form 2, I dropped out.

---

* Interviewed in prison.

I ran away from home to live with my boyfriend, Ranganai, in Chitungwiza. He was a gold prospector with the ministry. I had missed my monthly period, so I thought I was pregnant. I did not know about family planning, we were not taught about it in school. I had my period in the second month but I was already living with my boyfriend by then, so I could not go back to my family. I was afraid that they would not have me back. Besides, my boyfriend did not mind me staying. We were both young and not mature. Even though I was not ready to start a family, I was happy with the new life: I was now living in the city, I ate good food, I had nice clothes. My husband was good to me. He gave me money to buy food and pocket money, about two to three dollars every day. It was a good beginning.

In December 1998 Ranganai went to my family to pay lobola. We had lived together for a year and it worried me that he had not made arrangements to pay the bride-price. I used to remind him often about it. He always replied to me softly, reminding me that he did not earn much and that it took time to save money. He said he needed to put aside at least Z$10,000 for lobola, as well as money for groceries. When he finally saved enough we did not go straight back to my parents, we approached my sister Mai Davy. She received us very well and we asked her to send a message to my father through a *munyai* that we would like to come home and we were on our way. We were let into the home together with our munyai. Everything went well and I was happy that we were now husband and wife in the eyes of my parents. They had received the lobola. I was also happy that I could now visit my parents and relatives freely and they could do the same.

When I was seven months pregnant, my husband died. I knew that was the end of my marriage. He had complained about his leg two months after I started living with him. He had cancer. I did not expect him to die so young. His uncle who lived in Chitungwiza used to come to see him when he was sick. He and I took the body for burial to Mount Darwin where his parents lived. I had met his parents before. I visited them for a month when I was four months pregnant.

After the funeral I stayed behind with them for one and half weeks. When I was eight months pregnant Ranganai's uncle and his wife took me back to my parents, so that I would be under their care in the last month of my pregnancy and during childbirth. When the labour pains started my mother took me to the nearby clinic but I was transferred to Marondera Hospital because the nurse said my baby was not sitting properly in the womb, he was upright. I gave birth to a baby boy by Caesarean section. My mother came to visit. I stayed in hospital for two weeks. Two months after being discharged from hospital Ranganai's uncle and his wife came to see the baby. They brought some groceries and they named the baby Nyasha. I gave him another name – Brandon. They went back to their home pleased that they were going to spread the news about the new baby to the rest of their family. I stayed with my parents, working the fields and selling some of the produce at Chikwanha. Sometimes I would also buy a bale of second-hand clothes to sell.

I weaned the baby at fifteen months and looked for a job in Chitungwiza. I left my baby with my mother who still had two young children of her own to look after. I got a job as a helper in a hair salon in Zengeza 2. The hair salon owner was a married woman with children and I lived in her house. Every month, after I got my wages, I would go home to see my baby. Then the owner moved to Glenview and closed down the hair salon. I was without a job. I went to stay with my sister in Zengeza 5. My sister worked as a housemaid in the low-density suburbs. She found me a job as a housemaid with an Ethiopian family in Hillside.

I shared the servant's quarters with the gardener. I used to get up early in the morning to prepare tea, eggs for breakfast, and sandwiches for the child to take to school for his lunch. There was also a young woman called Helen who was home most of the time. She did not work. When people left for work, it was time to clean the sitting and dining rooms, bedroom, toilets and bathroom. I made tea for the gardener and myself at about ten o'clock. For lunch we cooked sadza. Afternoons were for laundry and ironing. On weekends I finished work at noon on Saturday, and I started work again on Monday morning. I worked for a year, the whole of 2001. I asked to be allowed to live with my baby but my employers refused. They did not give any reason, but said they would tell when it was right for me to bring my baby to stay with me.

Then, I met Learnmore and we fell in love. I started to spend my weekends in Epworth where he lived. I slept with him. I did not practice any family planning. I had never taken family planning pills before. I used to think I should, but I never got round to doing this. Learnmore used to tell me he would like me to give him a baby. Then I used to tease him, I would say you are about to be a father because I've missed my period. He would say it was all right with him. When I fell pregnant and I told him about it he gave me Z$500 dollars to buy clothes for the baby. I bought two baby sets, a towel and some nappies. I did not tell my employer that I was pregnant but Helen knew, she had noticed some changes in me and I told her I was pregnant.

The labour pains started when I was alone in the servant's quarters. I had not registered at the clinic as I did with my first pregnancy. I gave birth alone. Helen then noticed what had happened and she phoned her father and the police. When the police arrived, the baby was already dead. The police took me to Parirenyatwa Hospital and I was discharged after three days. And after that they took me straight to Rotten Row court for trial. They said I was a baby killer. I was put in remand prison at Chikurubi where I stayed for a month. Then my brother paid a bail of Z$1,000 and I was released and I went to Chitungwiza to live with my sister. They wanted time to check if I had a criminal record. In June 2001 I was sentenced to three and half years. I was to serve six months and three years would be suspended. Before the sentence was passed, the judge asked if I had anything to add for them to consider. I told him that my father was sick, he had suffered a stroke, and that my mother was asthmatic and I had a child to look after. He then said I could do community service instead of going to jail. I was remanded further while they checked to see if my brother would let me stay with him while I did community work. They went to the address, which I gave, and they did not find anybody. Although community service is good, you need a relative who will give you somewhere to stay.

You need your relatives especially when you are in prison and in court when you are being tried. Sometimes there is need for someone to be there and say I will let her stay or I will pay the bail. Life in prison is not bad. We eat fairly well: tea with bread for breakfast and sadza with either meat or vegetables or beans. We sleep in a dormitory, 34 of us. We sing and pray.

When I finish serving my sentence I want to get a passport and travel to South Africa to buy goods for re-sale.

2

Elizabeth

interviewed by Keresia Chateuka

I am Elizabeth. I was born in Chigodora. We are eleven in our family. My father was unemployed: he farmed. He died when I was five years old. My mother died two years ago. Because I had no father for the greater part of my life, I faced great difficulties. My mother was South African and she left for her country leaving us in the care of our relatives. We were shared out among our aunt, grandmother and uncles. I went to stay with my uncle. I dropped out of school at Grade 5: my uncle said he did not have money for school fees. I started herding cattle and weeding the fields. I then went to work at Border Streams, a farm near Mozambique. While I was there, I met the man who later became my husband. He was working at the same farm. His name was Tendai. He was a policeman.

I married very young, I was running away from poverty. Unfortunately, I could not have children, so I pretended to my husband that I was pregnant to make my marriage more secure. A proper wife should have children, and make her husband a father. Besides, my husband was bothering me about a baby and I did not want my marriage to end. I was comfortable, and I had food and clothes. He was beginning to demand to know why I could not have babies. After I realised that I would lose him, I knew I had to act fast. I feigned the pregnancy to the extent of wearing maternity dresses. When my make-believe pregnancy was nine months old, I told my husband I was leaving for my sister's in Sakubva where I would deliver my baby. He did not know that I was lying. I naturally had a big body and because I lived well I was bigger.

I went to Chimanimani Clinic where I stole a new-born baby. I went to the clinic's maternity ward where I loitered around. My intention was to steal a baby to cover up for my barrenness. Chimanimani Clinic was one of those clinics where pregnant women cooked for themselves while they waited to go into labour. Women fetched water from a well, which was a distance from the clinic. Sometimes they went out to fetch firewood. When mothers went to bath and there was no adult in the ward, I quickly took a baby. With the baby in my arms, I boarded a bus to Mutare. I lived with it for a month with my sister before I took it home. She provided money to buy everything that I needed for the baby. I went back to Chimanimani, to my husband's home. The relatives there were surprised, as they had never seen me pregnant, 'We never saw this woman pregnant so where did she get the baby from?' They asked among themselves.

Unknown to me, word had spread through radio, television and newspapers that a baby had been stolen. Here, in Mutare, it was reported in the Manica Post. I think my sister, especially, was suspicious when she saw that I was not breastfeeding. I could not produce the milk. My husband provided the basics for the baby. He told me to bring the baby back to him. In Chimanimani it is believed that a baby's clothes should not be taken outside until four weeks have passed; but after the first month the baby's clothes can be put on a washing line outside the house and the baby can be taken outside the house; that is why my husband urged me to come home. I told my sister that I was leaving to join my husband. I reached home to find a pram and other basics that my husband had bought: more baby clothes, towels and baby blankets.

After a while policemen came to our homestead in Chimanimani and they told me to go with them to the station. They put me in the cells. I saw the baby's mother the following morning with her baby who looked fit and well. The mother was relieved that I did not harm the child but she was angry with me. She said to me, 'Are you sure you stole my baby?' Men from the CID arrived and ordered the young mother not to talk to me, as I was their prisoner. My husband gave the young woman all that he had bought for the baby, the pram, napkins, Lactogen, everything.

I then came to Mutare where I was sentenced to four years and eight months. Two years were suspended so I had to serve two years and eight months. I was taken to Chikurubi. I was found guilty of stealing a baby. After my sentence was passed, I was taken to prison. No one came to visit me. A certain woman from Chimanimani who had been arrested for selling mbanje told me that my husband had remarried. I realised that prison life was hard and that what I had done was disastrous for my future. I cried all the time. I think both my husband and my relatives did not visit me in prison because I had disgraced them. They were angry with me. After serving my term I returned to Chimanimani where I found my husband with another wife.

In prison I used to cry often because life in the cells was hard. At times prisoners escaped especially when we were in the garden watering plants. The remaining prisoners were beaten and we cried all the time. We used to console ourselves with prayer. Before I was in prison, I did not go to church but I converted and joined the Apostolic Faith Church. I continued with the church after my release. During public holidays, other inmates had visitors who brought them food and drink. At times I washed other prisoners' uniforms for a glass of Mazoe orange [squash]. Sometimes I ironed the uniforms in exchange for food and bathing soap. In prison we were given small cakes of soap that did not last long as we had to wash our uniforms.

Prison life is horrendous. When I see some people breaking the law, I quickly tell them to stop because prison life must be avoided at all costs.

After my release from Chikurubi, I was taken to Mutare and I was given a warrant and left for Chimanimani. When I got home, everything was upside-down. My next-door neighbours did not want to see me. They feared that I would steal their babies. They said, 'Look that criminal is back, your children will be stolen.' Not a child greeted me in the village. I thought of going back to Border Streams to work there. Then I met another man, David, and we married in 1987. David knew about my crime before paying lobola. The munyai, advised me to be open about my past so she was the one who told my new husband about my crime. David did not mind. We were madly in love. We had to look for another stand elsewhere. People could not trust me and warned my husband. Fortunately I gave birth to a baby boy. Then I realised that it was not my fault that I could not have a baby with my former husband, the policeman. He never told me that he had been married twice before and that his women did not have children with him. I was very young and he took advantage of my ignorance.

I gave birth in 1987 and I fell pregnant again in 1989 and gave birth to another baby boy. Right now I have three children and I am still praying to God that I do not go back to prison. Even now, when you [ZWW] came looking for women who had been in prison, I was afraid you would take us back to prison.

I am living with my husband. He is not employed. God had mercy on me and gave me these children. After giving birth to my first born, people passed comments like, 'Look closely at the baby and see if it is really hers, she could have stolen again.' I gave birth to two more children and decided to practice family planning as my husband is not working. We survive on farming.

Where I am staying at the moment, I do not think I will last two years. I am really having a hard time. It is stressing. My former husband learnt that I had married and had children. I later met with him to explain that I had stolen a baby because I was too young to realise the implications. I thought I had found happiness with him and did not want to destroy my marriage because of my failure to have children. My former husband seems to be sorry for not letting me know that he was the one who could not have children. Through his sister, who lives close to us, he sent a message that he would like to pay fees for our eldest child, who has dropped out of school because we could not pay the fees. I also talked to my sister. I explained to her what had happened. I rebuked her for not having visited me in prison. I warned her that next time it could be her in prison. She did not reply to my letters. She said that her husband threatened to divorce her if she made contact with me. He feared for his children. I could very well understand his feelings because everybody behaved like that towards me when I came home from prison. People were no longer free so we decided to move away from the village. Even at a funeral they would point a finger at me.

To all women who cannot have babies I urge them to be patient. If you are destined to have them you will. There is no need to steal other women's babies.

3

Barbra

interviewed by Chiedza Musengezi

I am Barbra and I was born in 1975. I am the third-born in a family of three girls and a boy. I am from a polygamous family. I grew up in the Mutare area and our homeland is Chipinge. I did my primary and my secondary education in Mutare. Due to financial constraints I stopped at Form 3. Both my parents are alive. My father is now a pensioner. He used to work at PG.

After I left school my friend invited me to play netball for Lemco. I later got a job there, where we packed tomatoes, made jam or tomato sauce. I left my job after I fell pregnant. A man called Alwin was responsible for the pregnancy. I did not go to stay with him. I went back home because he had refused to marry me. I did not know that he had a wife. When I went home my parents chased me away, but I found my way back to them. After nine months I delivered a baby boy. His name is Tawanda. At the moment he is home with my parents. He is now ten years old and is in Grade 3. His father never offered any support for the upkeep of his son. He is here in town and I never considered getting back to him.

After Tawanda, I fell pregnant again, but this time I concealed the pregnancy from my parents because I was ashamed and I feared that they would chase me out of their home. I confided in my friend who advised me to abort. Despite my fears I paid the fee for abortion to the man who was going to carry it out. On my part I really wanted to abort for again the man responsible had refused to marry me and he was also denying responsibility for the pregnancy. I also feared the wrath of my parents. So, I hid the pregnancy for seven months before I went to the man who helped me abort. The abortion was successful. The fetus was already mature. I wrapped it in a cloth. It was a girl. I kept the fetus in the house before I discarded it in the evening. My parents were not aware of what I was doing.

I went with the fetus to the river that is quite near our place. I left it near the water and returned home. There were some people who saw me discarding it. I was with one of my young brothers, who was twelve years old, and he was not aware that I wanted to throw away a baby. We stayed for a day and nothing happened. On the second day word travelled around that there was a baby that had been found dumped. I never showed any signs of ill-health that could have made people suspicious. I never fell sick so nobody suspected me of anything.

It was the people who had seen me going to the river were the ones who informed the police. They were instructed to question me. I was taken to the CID office where I confessed to what I had done – I never denied the offence. They asked for the name of the person who had given me the herbs but I told them I was solely responsible for the herbs that had made me have a miscarriage. They then asked me if I had delivered a live baby, but I told them it was dead. I stayed for a while there before I went to the police. Thus I never disclosed the name of the person who had given me the herbs. I stayed at the police station for two days and went to court on the third day.

The jail cell where I stayed was a horrendous sight. There was a toilet and some dirty blankets. I could not eat after inhaling the odour of the blankets. At times I got food from home. My mother and my sisters brought it. This incident truly shocked them. They reproached me for my silence over the issue.

When I appeared in court I was told to come again in January 1990. (This happened in December 1989.) I was out of custody. They granted me bail of Z$100. I stayed at home until the due date in January and I left for court again, this time, alone. They called me and read my offence. I admitted my crime when they asked me if I took full responsibility for it. After that, the magistrate sentenced me to twelve months. Two months were suspended since it was my first offence and I was young. I cried right there in court. Some people comforted me telling me I had received a light sentence. This was true as I expected to be sentenced to five or six years, considering the gravity of my offence. I accepted my term although I dreaded going to serve my term in Harare for I did not want to part from my parents. I served my term at Chikurubi.

The life at Chikurubi, phew! When I got there I met a friend, whom I had once seen when I was in a cell in Mutare. She motioned me to come over to her. I did so and was told what they do. We stayed in rooms with an average of about 40 prisoners per room. We got two blankets each, a jersey and a uniform. We had roll call at half past six in the morning when the guards counted us. The counting was done twice for security reasons. We had tea at 8 a.m. After tea, some went for gardening while others went for typing.

Our relationships with the prison guards varied. Some had some maternal instinct while others were bad. The latter could say bad things to you. Some guards treat you as their labourers though not all do that; some are quite friendly. The bad ones can instruct a group of prisoners to sweep their yards or to polish their shoes.

Concerning health, if you fell ill in the evening, you could call out to the guards in the office. At times they did not come. During my stay one girl died after she called for help but no one came. We realised she was dead in the morning when we got up for roll-call. In prison, we had little time to discuss our offences. Some people said the baby-dumpers never repeat their offence; they settle down and have families. It was encouraging to hear such comments. During my term in prison, only the man I was going out with visited me. He was not responsible for the pregnancy.

Two days before my release, they took me back and I was released from Mutare Prison. When they told me that I was going home, I was happy that finally I was free. When my release was getting near, I told my boyfriend when I would be out and he came to welcome me back. He had bought a pair of tennis shoes for me to wear in prison.

He later married me. He, like my parents, had not known that I was pregnant and only came to know this after I had committed the offence. I never lied to him that he was responsible for pregnancy, so I can truly admit that he really loved me.

When I got home my parents received me well. My mother encouraged me to always open up to her for she was afraid that if she were unkind to me I would commit another offence. My father did not say much. I guessed he was still angry with me. I understand he did not expect such things from me.

I later fell pregnant. My boyfriend was the father. I was escorted to his house where the welcome I received was great. I never feared he would deny paternity for he truly loved me. I am sure my in-laws knew of my crime but they never showed it. The neighbours talked about it indirectly but this never changed my relation with my in-laws. Up to now I can safely tell you that nothing has changed. I am settled all right. My husband once worked at Red Seal but now he is unemployed. Before I fell pregnant I used to go to Rusape to sell clothes. At the moment I am doing nothing. I really need some start-up cash to make my trips again.

I advise women not to abort. The thought of the fetus will haunt you all your life. Sometimes you might blame the problems you face as being caused by the spirit of the child. It is better to be the laughing stock of society than to abort. It is really shameful. Women should not abort, period. I never saw the fetus ever again. The police took it to hospital for cremation. Even its sex I got to know it through some policeman who told me.

4

Clara

interviewed by Chiedza Musengezi

My name is Clara. I was born in February 1981. I live in Goromonzi with my mother. My parents separated but my mother looked after me well. We were two in our family and one passed away. I went to school up to Form 2. I dropped out of school because my friends and I were up to no good. We were naughty, missed school, ran away from home, played around, drank beer and had sex with boys from Mutare. My mother did not like what I was doing. She really did not like it at all. I was too young, and I did not see her point. She was worried that I was showing an interest in the wrong things. She tried to beat some sense into me, I mean she beat me up a lot, but she could not stop me. I was determined to enjoy myself with my friends or so I thought then. She preferred me to go to school and to attend church. I detested both – even now I do not have a desire to go to the Salvation Army, my mother's church.

My friends influenced me. We went into pubs and drank beer that we were offered by our boyfriends. I had a boyfriend and so did my friends. I was young but I had a big body so men thought I was a grown woman. (Even now I am only 21 years old but people think I am older.) From there I got pregnant. A certain boy, not my boyfriend, was responsible. He was new to our area and I had met him at Bhora. By then I had stopped going to school, I did not care about school any more, I was enjoying life with my friends. This boy was much older than me, about 22 years old, and quite rich. I had sex with him and fell pregnant. It was a one-night affair. I did not see him after that. I did not tell my steady boyfriend that I was pregnant. I did not tell my mother because I was afraid of her. I was still young. I was eighteen. If my mother found out, it was going to be trouble for me so I decided to abort. I did not want my mother to know. I was about three months pregnant I knew what muti to use so I went into the bushes and collected some. I prepared the muti and left it standing overnight in a cup under my bed. I drank all of it the following day: that is how I got rid of the pregnancy. I threw away the fetus into a pit latrine. I never thought I would be found out.

I was bleeding heavily and I soiled my dress. My mother and some elders quickly knew what had happened. All along my mother had not noticed that I was pregnant. They took me to the police station and the police inspected my breasts to see if I could produce milk. They found out I had been pregnant, so they took me to Murehwa Hospital to have my breasts squeezed again. They had milk in them. I went back to the police station. Then they took me to Goromonzi for a court hearing. I was found guilty and they took me to Chikurubi Prison where I stayed for about three months.

It was hard for me to be in prison since I was not used to the life. With time I got used to it and I settled down. There were quite a number of us in our cell. During the afternoon we washed our plaits or plaited our hair. There are many activities that we did but there was no hard labour but bedtime was hard. The blankets were very dirty. We tried washing them, but you know how it is with blankets that have been used by too many people – we could never get them clean.

After my release I realised what I had done was really bad. Now I am married. I met my husband in Bhora and I lived with him in Harare for about two years and then I left him because he had found himself another girlfriend. In fact, she used to be a friend of mine. He had not paid lobola for me – not even a cent, so I just walked out of the house. I left all my clothes and other property behind.

I did not tell him of my prison experience. I could not bring myself to tell him. It was impossible. It bothered me a great deal withholding such important information from him. I was afraid that he would find out one day. I am still turning things over in my mind. I think I need to go to the doctor's or a qualified counsellor to help me come to terms with my past. I will try to tell my future husband that I have a load on my heart that needs lifting. Ha, it is hard. I find it hard to discuss my past with people close to me. My mother has not forgiven me. Sometimes she shouts at me blaming me for what I did. She does not have many children, so she tells me I should have let her keep the baby.

Section 2:

Domestic issues

5

Loveness

interviewed by Keresia Chateuka

My name is Loveness and I was born in 1958 in Mutare. We are two in our family, I have a brother. My parents separated. My mother re-married. Our grandparents raised us together with their other grandchildren. I only went to school up to Grade 6. I dropped out because of a leg injury. I wanted to do dressmaking but I could not, because my leg had not healed. Then I got married to Frank M. We lived together for four years. I failed to bear him children so he took me back to my grandparents. They are now late but I still live in their house. I re-married last year but my husband died in February 2003.

I went to prison in 1996 after I had separated from my first husband.

I had found myself a boyfriend when my former husband turned up one evening. He said that he had come to see how I was getting on with life. I told him that he was not welcome. Although I lived with my boyfriend he was not home, he was at work. I told Frank that I had a boyfriend and that he should leave my house. He took Z$30 and put it on the table. He said the money was for me. I refused it and he put the money back into his pocket. He went outside and then, after a short while, he came back. He was drunk. I told him that it was my bedtime and that he should leave my house. He refused and he argued with me. He beat me up and demanded that I give him back his money even though I had not taken it. I went to my neighbour to ask for help.

Some young men who lived next door came. My former husband insisted that I had stolen money from him. I explained to the young men that he was only interested in making trouble. I had not taken his money. They forced him out of my house and beat him up. He reported the matter to the police and came back to my house with a policeman. He woke me up and accused me of stealing money from my former husband and of arranging to have him beaten up. He took me to the police station where I was locked up for two days. In my statement I refused [to accept] that I had taken the money. The policeman who was taking the statement threatened to write what he pleased if I insisted that I did not steal from Frank. I went to court the following day and I paid Z$50 bail. I was remanded out of custody until 30th January when I appeared again in court and then I was remanded in custody. I was remanded two more times in prison. In March 1996 I was found guilty and was sentenced to ten months in prison. Six months were suspended and I stayed in prison for two months after a further two months were suspended.

I was in Mutare Prison for a few days and then I was transferred to Chikurubi Prison. I arrived in the evening. I was given two small threadbare blankets. I was very cold throughout the night. I was also given a dress, but it was torn, I could not move around in it because parts of my body were not covered. However, after the first night, I was given a better dress and warm blankets. I also got a piece of soap, but it was so small it did not last. I had to exchange ten slices of bread for soap, which meant that I had to go for ten days without bread at breakfast. Sometimes I also exchanged my piece of meat for toothpaste. These are some of the tricks I had to resort to in prison in order to stay clean.

In the cells, people used to fight. This usually happened in the night after we had been locked up. We had to call in the prison guards to stop the fights. Fights broke out because of gossip or if someone failed to pay a debt, like a soap debt. The first day I worked in the garden but the following day one of the prison guards asked me to crotchet doilies for her. For the rest of my stay at Chikurubi I made doilies. I did not mind because I did not have to go and work outside. Sometimes I joined the sewing group. We made uniforms for the prison guards. We did everything from designing and cutting to making buttonholes.

If you fell ill in prison you went to the clinic. I had a problem with my leg, which had been operated on several times. I used to go to the clinic whenever I felt pain.

I was released from prison in June. I went back home. From Chikurubi we were taken to Rusape in a prison truck and then to Mutare. People were friendly towards me – both my family and my neighbours.

6

Beti

interviewed by Chiedza Musengezi

My name is Beti. I was born in October 1962 and I am the second-born in a family of five girls and five boys. All the children in our family went to school up to Form 4. The five girls got married and so did three of my brothers who now live with their families in Shurugwi, Harare and Kadoma. The other two are still at home. As a teacher in Chivhu, my father used to come home during weekends so we stayed at home with our mother.

I got married in Sanyati and I have four children: three daughters and a son. The eldest is 21 years old. She is supplementing her O-levels. The second born is in Form 4, the third in Form 2 and the last one is in Grade 7. My husband died in 1997. Our life was admirable. Things only took a bad turn after he got involved with another woman. From then on, we had no peace in the home as he battered me every time he came from his girlfriend. The police knew about it – I reported him all the time. They treated the matter as domestic violence. They did not have him prosecuted. The public relations officer counselled us, although his efforts came to nothing. Instead, things got worse. My husband took to beating me and accused me of having an affair with the police public relations officer. I also tried seeking counsel from his relatives but it did not work.

One day he came home and provoked me. He said demeaning and insulting things about me. I hit back with insults that matched his. Sometimes he would leave home very late in the night and when I asked he would reply, 'I'm a free man I can leave any moment I feel like.' Sometimes he told me that I was a useless wife and that I showed no love and respect for his relatives. I would tell him what I thought about him – that there was nothing special about him and that it was his duty to love his relatives before I did. When I answered back he became more insulting. For example, he would call me a whore, a witch, a thief and any bad word that came to his mouth. This went on for a long time. I was deeply hurt by his words. In the end we fought. We used to fight a lot and each time he would beat me up badly.

On this particular day he again beat me up very badly and afterwards he packed his bags and said he was leaving. However, since it was late in the night, he then decided to sleep. I decided to get back at him. I went to the kitchen where I heated some cooking oil in a cup. I took the boiling oil to our bedroom and poured it into his ear. He writhed in agony. I ran out. I only wanted to harm him and not to kill him. I intended to harm him, not seriously, but in revenge for what he did to me, but now [that I had done it] I could not stand the physical pain he was in. I ran out of the house, but I did not go far, I stood by the bedroom wall.

My children woke up and watched in horror, they cried and ran to our neighbours to seek help. They took him to hospital. My eldest daughter who accompanied her father returned the following morning. She told me that his condition was critical. The hospital was not going to give him treatment until I gave a statement to the police. I quickly went to the police station and I was arrested. The police knew of the incident; the hospital doctor had informed them. We left for hospital to see my husband who was tossing and turning in pain. He was indeed in deep pain. After the police gave a report my husband started receiving treatment. The police took me to their station. I was put in a cell. I gave a statement and stayed in the cell for a week. I later learnt that my husband had died. On hearing this, I passed out three times. I was truly shocked that I had killed him. They told me I was going to court for causing my husband's death. I was charged with culpable homicide.

I was not allowed to attend my husband's funeral. They told me that I was going to prison for three years. This sentence was light as the police records showed we had several domestic disputes and that my husband used to beat me up. Upon my arrest I still had fresh wounds and some parts of my body were swollen. I finally served one year six months and the rest of the sentence was suspended. I was released in 1999 after serving my sentence in Shurugwi.

In prison we went for roll call in the morning. Afterwards we bathed, had tea and did our respective duties. I was lucky: I worked in the kitchen preparing meals. Some worked in the garden and watered flowers, while others cleaned the cells. We used the produce from the garden for our meals: vegetables, tomatoes, onions and beans. Although we ate well, I found life in prison unbearable; it was hard because it was so severely controlled. We lived lives of commands and instructions: '... wash now ... eat ... work in the garden ... sleep ... get up,' do this and do that. There was no respect. The prison guards addressed you by the crime you had committed. In their eyes you were a thief, a murderer, a prostitute or whatever it was that you were convicted for. I was addressed as 'the one who killed her husband'. There was not a moment when I was not reminded of my crime. It was hurtful. Prison life is hard and undignified.

However not all the guards were cruel. I quickly learnt that if you listened and obeyed whatever they said you had to do, everything worked out right for you. There was a female guard who was so fond of me that I ended up working at her house. If the guards loathed you, you were doomed for the rest of your stay. When I fell sick I told the guards. At times, they did not take people who were sick seriously. They would take you to hospital only if you were very sick. Pregnant inmates were supposed to be checked constantly but this was not the case. Some went into labour and gave birth in the cells. Assistance was only available when one had already delivered. It was impossible to prepare for the baby's arrival the way one would at home. Sometimes relatives brought baby clothes. Those who had no relatives got help from organisations whose names I cannot remember.

When I was in prison I wrote a letter to my parents. Afterwards they came to visit me whenever they could. My children only came when they had bus fare. They supported me and told me they knew that their father had abused me. They suspected that it would eventually lead me to do something drastic. During my stay in prison my children looked after themselves getting some assistance from the neighbours. They grew vegetables so they had some food. At times the neighbours assisted with bus fare for the children to visit me.

I later learnt that my husband's relatives took his body for burial in Gokwe. They collected all his personal things such as clothes; they packed them in a bag and left. That was the last time they set foot in my homestead. I did not go to see where my husband had been buried. I was afraid to do so.

Upon my release from prison many women from the neighbourhood came to console me. They urged me to put my trust in God because he forgives. They gave me hope. A few men also came but others never wanted to see me talking to their wives. They feared that I was bad influence on them. I applied to be given a piece of land and now I am going to see my plot in Village 8. That is where I am going to prepare the land for the coming planting season. My eldest daughter is working as a nurse-aid at a hospital. She assists with money: she keeps us going. I also get money through gardening, farming and the food-for-work programme. I use the money to send my children to school. My boys are well behaved they do not seem to hold a grudge against me over the death of their father. He was not a good father to them. At times he beat the whole family. I urge all women in bad marriages to leave before they get into trouble.

7

Sabena

interviewed by Linda Chipunza

My name is Sabena.* I am an inmate at Chikurubi Prison in Harare. I live in the area around Mount Mellanay Mission, a Catholic mission in Nyanga. I am a 47-year-old divorcee with six children, and I am serving a two and a half year sentence for cattle rustling.

I was married in 1975 and got divorced in 1991. My ex-husband is in prison for incest but I do not know how many years he was sentenced to [serve]. He was not a good man. He was unemployed and he drank a great deal. He was also a womaniser and he gambled heavily at a big hotel near our home, Monte Claire Hotel. I divorced him when I discovered that he was abusing one of our daughters, which is the reason he was imprisoned. This was discovered when my eldest daughter told my younger sister, that he was sexually abusing her. My sister then reported the issue to the chief, who reported the case to the police. Some say he did it to get medicine to help him win card games when he gambled. The sister, who helped to have him arrested, unfortunately passed away last year leaving behind her children.

I have six children, four boys and two girls. My eldest daughter is married and lives in Masvingo province with her husband. We have had no contact since she left to live with her husband. My second-born completed his O-level examinations a few years ago, but we did not go to inquire after his results. My third born is in

---

* Sabena sobbed throughout the interview in prison.

Grade 7. I do not know whether he will be able to write his exams this year. (You see, I have been keeping my children back in junior school, so that they do not all go to secondary school at the same time, as I would not be able to afford the fees.) One child is in Grade 4 and my youngest is two years old.

When I was arrested I lived with my four children and my mother, who is 70 years old and completely blind. I believe that my mother is taking care of my children, but since I was arrested I have had no communication with them.

Before stealing the cattle I had been working on a tomato farm in Nyanga. It was here that I met the father of my last two children. He was a driver at the farm but he died in a car accident. When we met we were happy at the beginning. The problem was that he was married, and I got little support from him. When he died all the property went to his wife and I got nothing. I have had enough of marriage and I will never get married again.

My family and I lived in resettlement area with my mother; our neighbour was a white commercial farmer. There was no fence around his farm and his cattle just wandered about, sometimes not too far from our homes. It was from this white man's farm that I stole the cattle. Everybody was doing it. I was just unlucky to get caught. In fact, I suspect that some of my neighbours reported me to the police. It was two weeks after I had stolen the cattle that the police came to my homestead one morning in January. I had been keeping the cattle in a kraal I had built to house them. I knew deep down that they would soon catch up with me, but my economic situation had forced me to do it. In 2001 I did not reap anything, as I only started planting in January, which is the end of the season: it was too late.

On the morning when the police came I was in the kitchen with my mother and my children making tea when I heard voices outside. This was followed by a loud knock on the door. When I saw it was the police, I quickly left the kitchen so that my mother, who was sitting by the fire, would not hear the commotion. My three children who were preparing to go to school saw what was going on. They cried bitterly and so did I as the police asked them to show them where I kept the stolen cattle. My youngest child was still asleep. I still imagine how my mother must have suffered as she cried out after me as I left with the police. My heart aches when I think of my children and my mother. All I managed to tell them was to go to the mission and tell the nuns what had happened to me and to seek whatever help they could. At least I had managed to give my mother some water for her to wash her face, but I had not managed to finish making the tea by the time the police arrived.

When we got to the kraal the police instructed me to drive the cattle down to the police station at Nyanga. When we got there the police booked me in. I cannot explain the horror and anguish I went through that day. I cried until I could hear strange noises and sounds in my head. When they opened the cell door the stench that hit me was enough to knock me over, this was my first time in police custody. Throughout that night I drifted in what must have been varying degrees of consciousness. I thought I had died. In fact I wished myself dead, the smell in the cell could not have been of the living. I could not even touch the filthy rags that were supposed to be blankets that were folded in a corner of the cell.

I was alone in this God-forsaken cell. I cried and cried and asked myself what I had done. I had known at the time that what I had done was wrong, but what else could I do? How was I now to raise the children that were my sole responsibility? I did not sleep. I lay awake crying and cursing myself. In the morning the warden brought me a mug of tea. There was no sugar and no bread, just tea. The cup was not very clean, but by now I was hungry, very hungry. At 8 a.m., I was taken to court where I pleaded guilty to charges of cattle rustling and soon afterwards I was transferred to Mutare Remand Prison. I was jailed in March 2002 on the charge of cattle rustling. I was handed a two and a half year sentence.

In Mutare I was relieved when they removed the heavy chains and leg irons. I had no idea how long I would be there for. Occasionally, I saw other prisoners' visitors and managed to ask about my home area, Nyanga, to find out if it was raining there. I was concerned about the crop I had planted that was intended to feed my family until the next rainy season. I could not sleep for thinking about my children and my mother. Who was fetching water for her? Who was cooking for the children? Was there any food to cook? Were they going to school? Had they managed to seek assistance from the nuns at Mount Mellenay Mission? I also wondered about the maize crop: had anybody remembered to apply the fertiliser we had been given by the government? Sometimes my head would spin.

While in prison I managed to write a letter to my mother advising her to go to the mission to seek help for her and the children. I have not received a reply. This worries me. I never said goodbye to my mother. She must be worried too, and confused.

I was in Mutare Remand Prison for four months and then I was transferred to Harare because my sentence was more than eight months long. I shall be incarcerated until September 2003.[†] I cannot wait for that day. I do not know how I am going to wait that long before I see my children and my mother again. I pray she is still around. I mourn my two late sisters every day and my only brother is also late, so now just me and my mother remain. If they were still alive I would not have to worry so much. I have lost contact with my first husband's relatives. I do not think they would want anything to do with my situation nor with me. They are my children you see, and no one wants to take on the responsibilities of another, and both my former husband's parents are late.

I pray that my children get a good education and live better lives than mine. I would not want them to suffer as I have. My eldest daughter is out there. I do not want to involve her in all this. She had a very stormy childhood and now she has put it behind her. She is married and all this may destroy her marriage. I am all right here in Harare. They look after me well. I am learning this and that, but I cannot stop worrying about what is going on back home, whether my mother will still be alive when I get out.

I asked the judge for an alternative sentence, community service, so that I may be with my family, but this was turned down. They said my crime, stock theft, was a serious one. I wish they had considered me because of my particular situation, my mother and my two-year-old. Sometimes I wonder if she will recognise me when I come out of here. I also wonder how I will be accepted back by the people in our village, and by my friends: how they will react towards me? Women at our church, what do they think?

Here I belong to a group that tends to the vegetable gardens and the prison complex. In between cleaning and gardening, I am learning how to make pillowcases. I have no friends here. I still find it hard to believe that I will be here for the next two years. I still feel the pain. I think about my situation and that of my family a lot. The women here are friendly. When I get out of this place, I shall tell others of my experiences. I never knew that stock theft could land me in here and for so long. The church people know me and I hope they will help me to get back on my feet. I plan to rear chickens and sell them in order to raise money for my children's school fees and uniforms.

[†] Sabena was, in fact, released a little earlier than she expected on an amnesty.

8

Maria

interviewed by Chiedza Musengezi

I am Maria. I was born in July 1968 in Mozambique close to the border with Zimbabwe. My mother had nine children with my father.

We had a very difficult childhood. My father lived in Dangamvura with another woman and he neglected us. We did not have enough food and clothes. This is why my mother had an affair with another man. She was caught with her lover in the house. My father was so angry with her that he told her to pack her things and leave his rural home. When my mother remarried, we went back to our father. Our mother sent us to him because she had nothing. She could not provide for us. However, he refused to look after us. He said that because our mother had had an affair, he was not sure if we were his children. He suspected that our mother could have had other affairs that resulted in children — all of us.

This is when we went to Mozambique, to our mother's parents. We stayed with them for four years. It was a hard life. No relatives gave us assistance. We all had to look for jobs such as carrying goods for people in our village, bags of maize or sugar. I started school when I was nine years old in Mozambique and I went up to Grade 3. My mother then married her lover, Emmanuel, the one she was caught with at home. He is the one who saved me in the end. My birth was registered in his name, not my father's name. We moved in with them. They were now staying in the high densities in Mutare. I started school again. I went to primary school from Grade 1 to 6. That is how far I got in school.

I fell pregnant when I was in Grade 6. I had met this man at the market where I used to help my mother at her stall. The man agreed to marry me. His name was Vhachi from Penhalonga. I gave birth to a baby girl, Memory, in 1985. Then I had a second one in 1986. I called her Theresa. When I was pregnant with the third, I had serious disagreements with my husband. The disagreements came about because I had little education, and I had no job. He was a driver with the railways. He left and went to work in Chiredzi. When I visited him, I realised that he did not love me anymore.

We quarrelled and fought frequently. He beat me up badly and sometimes he cut me with a razor blade on my arms and inner thighs. It was during one of these fights that I went outside, took a pole, and hit him with it on the head. He fell down at once and was not able to get up again.

Throughout the whole period when we fought, I never reported him to the police. I believed in suffering in silence. This is what our elders advise, not to run away from a problem. Even if your husband beats you up, you should persevere with your marriage and not make the marriage problems public and so on.

After I had hit my husband with the pole, he fell down and I went to my next-door neighbours to report what I had done. They helped me to look for a car to take him to hospital. When I went to visit him in the morning he had already died. I went back home and from there I went to my husband's rural home. I narrated what had happened. I was honest with them and I told them that he had died because I had hit him on the head with a pole.

At the funeral I was sitting by myself, my husband's relatives did not come near me. However my relatives were sympathetic. Just as we were coming home from burying him the police arrived. They took me to the police station where I gave a statement. On the day of the court hearing, I said that I acted in self-defense. I lifted up my skirts to show them the fresh razor cuts on my thighs. The court officials did not seem to be interested. I was sentenced to nine years. I went to Chiredzi Prison and was later transferred to Chikurubi Female Prison. I only served three years of my sentence: I was let out on a presidential amnesty.

When I went to jail I asked if all my children could come along with me because there was no one to look after them. I had three children and was pregnant with the fourth. They allowed only the youngest to come along, not the other two. It was my first time in prison and what surprised me was how *vanambuya gadhi* addressed prisoners. They addressed us by the nature of your crime. In my case, therefore, I was a 'murderer' and not Ellen. They used to say, 'you murderer, come here'. Or if *ambuya gadhi* was standing at a distance from me she would shout, pointing a finger in my direction, 'I want that murderer standing over there!' Then I would go to where she was. In prison, one lives a life of instructions. You are told, 'Go and clean the toilets … Go and weed the maize field …' go and do this and that. I was quite heavy with child: I could not manage heavy duties. They gave me light ones, such as, polishing the floors. When I went into labour, they took me to hospital. One *ambuya gadhi* came along with me. I was in hospital for three days. The labour pains were on and off. The hospital sent me back to prison. They thought that they could be false labour pains brought on by my fear of prison. However after only one night in prison, I went into labour again the next morning. I was taken back to the hospital and I had a baby boy. I had brought some clothes from home and *vanambuya gadhi* gave me some. The children also got milk at weekends.

For all the time I was in prison none of my relatives, both from my side of the family and my late husband's came to see me. I expected my brother, who comes after me, to come because he could afford the bus fares, unlike the rest of my brothers and sisters. However, I had a little news from home from some inmates that I met from my area, but this was after my transfer to Chikurubi. I was released from Chikurubi Prison.

I went back to my rural home. It had been ransacked. Everything had been stolen: cattle, goats, wardrobe, sofas, television. Both my daughters had dropped out of school. They worked as housemaids in the village. Now they are big girls. The eldest one is doing Form 3, the other girl only went up to Grade 4. She and the other boy dropped out of school because I failed to raise school fees. They help in people's homes here in the city. At the moment I'm staying in town with the little boy who is now four years old. I live in a small room, separate from the house. It is made out of timber. The room is so small, there's hardly any space for me to cook. A church minister is sending my eldest daughter to school. She goes to the same school as his children. At home I have three children, two boys of twelve and four and a girl who comes before the older boy. The boy has been out of school for four years now. The eldest girl, who goes to secondary school, approached her uncle, her father's brother for assistance, but she got nothing. Instead when she came back from his home she asked me how her father died. I could not face telling her what happened.

I work on the food-for-work programme. I sweep the roads and after every two weeks I get Z$1,500. It is not enough for my family. My relatives are not willing to assist. My brothers who are in a position to help do not want me to knock on their doors. Their wives are especially unfriendly to me. I think that none of my relatives have forgiven me. You would think they knew nothing of my troubled marriage. Every time I ran to them after a fight with my late husband, they would beat me up. I have scars on my head from my brother's assaults. They did not want to hear about me leaving my husband. They beat me up until I went back to him. They accused me of wanting to be a prostitute and of setting a bad example to my younger sisters because I am the eldest girl.

I once left my husband when I had two children. On this occasion we had fought because he would not let me touch him in bed. Whenever I tried to get close to him, he would get angry, really angry as if some evil spirit possessed him. He would be violent, stiffening up and throwing off my hand and hitting me against the wall. He did not want to get intimate with me at all. He used to spend most of his time with his girlfriends. Even though I have four children with him, there was no tender-loving care between us. It was more like rape, forced and quick. The situation got bad to the point where he would only provide for his children after I took them to his work place and the children would say what they wanted in his face.

After his death, the children got absolutely nothing. I think my husband's family shared out his property and pension between themselves. I did not get a thing. If you see where I live with my children you would be shocked. Sometimes I spend a week living on porridge. However I have brothers who own combis and hair salons, but they never think of helping me. If I knock at their doors, I only get a promise of help, that is all. In their eyes, I am a murderer and not worthy of help. I would not mind if it were only me, but they are denying assistance to my children. They are innocent and deserve to have a reasonable start for a better future.

When I came out of jail and went to my marriage home, my late husband's brothers and their wives said they did not want to see me anywhere near them. I had to leave the village quickly. My two-roomed house that I had built had been given to a young brother of my late husband and his wife. They would not allow me to get into the yard. They wouldn't even let me stay the night so that I could travel in the daytime with my two children. I left immediately and went to my brother's in the high densities. My brother allowed me to stay with his family for only two days, after which he gave me some money to board the bus to Mozambique with my children to go to my mother's parents. In Mozambique I explained to my aunts and uncles what had happened. They did not appreciate my situation at all. They were more worried about the bad influence I might have on their children. They gave me money to catch the next bus to the city. Then I decided to approach the churches. The minister of the Methodist Church understood my situation after I had narrated my story. The church received us and gave us a room to stay in the churchyard. The other children I had left at home, the two girls, had been chased away from home and were now working in people's homes as housemaids.

However the Methodist Church had leadership problems. It split into two groups and I was told to leave the church premises. I had to look for somewhere to stay. That is when I started to stay in the small wood house here. I approached our councillor because I needed a job. He is the one who advised me to join the food-for-work programme. The Z$1,500 I get is too little for me to buy cooking oil and mealie-meal. At the moment I assist people who are harvesting maize in the fields around the city. They pay me in kind, with a bucket of maize.

I do not have a close friend. Every time I think I have one, I find out that she is saying bad things behind my back. Now I find I cannot really talk to people from the bottom of my heart because whatever very personal information I tell them they use it against me later. No sooner do I tell a friend about my personal life than I find strangers pointing fingers at me and shouting 'murderer!'"* However,

---

* The interview she gave Zimbabwe Women Writers was apparently the first time she had told her entire story at once to someone who wanted to listen, and she cried most of the time. When ZWW returned with the story for her to fill in the gaps, she cried still more. As the interviewer said, 'She obviously talked with her tears. It is unfortunate that they cannot be turned into words.' It was also not possible to get some of the crucial dates, e.g. when she went to jail, and when she was released.

my biggest worry is my children. They need help to go to school and have a decent place to stay. They do not have birth certificates. Their father said he was going to register their births, he was still saying this until he died. His brothers do not want to see the children or me. The school where my daughter, Memory, goes to says they will try to talk to one of my brothers so that the births can be registered in his name. Even the girl in Form 3 will not be able to sit for her O-levels without a birth certificate.

I wish to start a vegetable market. Maybe I may make enough to look after my children. I need start-up cash of about Z$10,000. I have no clue where I can get that amount of money.

9

Sofia

interviewed by Keresia Chateuka

I am Sofia.* I come from Mount Darwin. I am 48 years old. I was born in 1954. In my family we are six, three boys and three girls. We had a reasonable childhood because my parents were committed farmers. They grew enough food for us and my father managed to send us all to school. But I only went up to Sub A and then I got married. (We girls were quick to get married. All three of us are settled and have our own homes.) All the boys have a modest education. The eldest is a teacher at our village school. The second one is a village headman and the third is employed.

My husband was in the liberation struggle and eventually he came back. We were very happily married. We were serious farmers, we grew maize, groundnuts and other crops for food, but we also grew some crops for cash: cotton and Virginia tobacco. We had a garden where we grew vegetables. Sometimes I exchanged vegetables for *masawu* fruit from Mozambique that we also sold. Our home is close to the border. We were never short of money.

Now I am mother of four, two of them are twins and the eldest is in Form 4. She is the one looking after the family from the time that both my husband and I were arrested. About two years before I was arrested my husband said he wanted a young woman for a second wife. I was totally against it. I did not like the idea of sharing a husband especially with the HIV virus that is now common. My husband was adamant. I pressed for the reason why [he wanted a second wife], he said

---

* This interview was conducted while Sofia was in prison.

there was need for an extra hand to help with the work since all the children were going to school. He was against paying someone to help.

My husband and I are both in prison because I used to look after my cousin, my aunt's child. Her mother had passed away. I took her when she was in Grade 4: when I was arrested in April 2000 she was seventeen years old and in Form 2. The children had alerted me that she and my husband were getting very close – like two people in love. I asked my husband about it and he admitted that he intended to marry my young cousin. One day I went to a relative's memorial service. I returned earlier than expected and found my husband in bed with her. I was extremely hurt and so angry, I went berserk, I was really mad, and the child ran away to her sister's where she reported that my husband had raped her. My husband admitted that he wanted to marry the girl but again I refused to be the co-wife with a child whom I had raised. It was also ridiculous because this child is my own aunt's daughter. My husband's relatives were actually encouraging him to marry to rest the case, probably because they knew the legal implications and they did not want him arrested.

I was not involved in the rape but this is how I came into it. When this child ran away she went to her sister's who then influenced her into lying that I had been aware of my husband's intentions to rape her.

We were just surprised when on 20th April 2000 the police turned up at our home to announce that they were taking us into custody in Bindura on allegations of rape. I tried to explain but they insisted that the courts would settle the case. We were not kept in custody. We were out on bail until the day my husband was locked up on 23rd May 2000.

On the day of the hearing we left home for Bindura. Our case was heard and my husband was told that he was to be imprisoned for ten years. I was the one who first admitted that my husband had had sex with my young cousin. I was then told that I was not going to return home until I had also received my sentence for helping my husband in raping the girl. According to the magistrate, I should have reported my husband to the police to protect the young girl. He said had my husband murdered my cousin, I would have helped him to conceal the murder. I was in shock. I never thought that what I had not done – not reporting my husband could be a crime. My husband wronged me. I was deeply hurt and asked several times whether it was indeed true that I was convicted. The court confirmed it.

I could not eat for four days because of the deep pain. I had left my children without suspecting that I could be imprisoned. One of them was not well, so I was deeply hurt. There is no one to look after them. My case was then presented and I was sentenced to six years, but three were suspended. I was then transferred to Chikurubi after having stayed briefly at Bindura Prison.

On my first day in prison I felt lost. The older inmates advised me not to be worried by a mere three-year jail term. Some of them had been in for ten years and still had more years to serve. They comforted me but it was really difficult. I used to cry and think and I became so ill that some started thinking that I had AIDS. I was hurting inside from serving a jail term for a crime that I never committed. My husband is serving his jail sentence in Chikurubi Maximum Prison. I see him from time to time. *Vanambuya gadhi* allow me to go and see him. When we meet we ask after each other's health and talk about our children.

In prison there are many things to occupy us but staying in prison is terrible, although one gradually gets accustomed to it. There are certain good things that we do. We are allowed to read books. I have already taken my Grade 7 examination. I can now sew and others learn to type. We are served well with food such that there has never been a day that I have gone without. In so far as hygiene is concerned it is just like at home, we have to see to our hygienic needs but you always find some odd people who do not care about such things. Nursing mothers sleep on their own depending on the nature of their crime. Many women are in here for crimes such as: baby dumping, abortion, theft, murder, and rape. If they are in the D-class, they have to mix with those who are not breast-feeding. The D-class is those sentenced for many years starting from ten upwards. But you can graduate to B-class or even A-class. The cells are reasonably big such that there can be six or more inmates in each cell depending on its size. We have entertainment in prison – church services, choirs – and we have interesting activities at the end of every week.

We are supplied with everything we need for sanitation although at times supplies are insufficient, but we are allowed to get such things from home when relatives come to see us fortnightly. When someone falls ill, we call the *ambuya gadhi* so that she may arrange for medical assistance. We get medical treatment from the local clinic but, if the illness is serious, we are taken to Harare or Parirenyatwa hospital.

Sometimes people suffer mental anguish to the extent that they can get physically ill. I can personally testify to that because I had a persistent headache and could not sleep because of too much thinking. My father passed away when I was here and it troubled me since he is the one who frequently visited me. My children are continuously ill, and there is also this severe drought. I hear nothing was harvested at home. If it were possible we could be released now so that we could go and fend for our families. We can put to use the skills we have learnt.

I now know crimes that are committed out of ignorance. I look forward to a stable life, like I had before my imprisonment, in spite of how people will regard me. If only they could be kind and release us because we left our children on their own. We do not know what's happening at home. Many who are released come back, especially shoplifters. Why do they come back? I don't know what would drive a person to want to come back to this place. Some who were released through the amnesty are already back. I wish they could release those of us who wish to work for our families. If only I could be given an opportunity to do community service so that I can complete my sentence. I think it is better to serve my sentence from home with my family.

The relationship with the prison guards depends on the personality of the inmates. This is what counts. Refusing to go on errands and fighting others and other issues like that is what will make someone receive some continuous beatings. There are thick heads and they are continuously beaten up, but I have never been beaten up or scolded. There are grown up women who are mischievous and stubborn.

As far as food is concerned we are given only one slice of bread and one cup of tea for breakfast. We are each given a plate of sadza for lunch and for supper. We have sadza with meat, vegetables and beans. For meat there is beef or pork and you make your choice. Cells are locked up after 4 p.m. or 5 p.m. until the following day. We get enough blankets and get additional ones if we ask and if stocks are adequate. We also get a piece of washing soap, a tissue and some toothpaste every month. On public holidays in April, August and December we are allowed to receive food from home, except alcohol. We are visited twice a month so we can receive such provisions as soap, lotion, tennis shoes and socks from home. TB patients can receive food from home from time to time. The same goes for those who are on remand. Those who bring food are asked to taste it first for security reasons. We are allowed to receive phone calls from relatives.

Vanambuya gadhi receive the calls and can telephone on our behalf if we have problems. None of my husband's relatives have ever been here to see me, because of poverty. My brother, who is a teacher, is the one who visits us and gives us whatever he can afford. He actually visits his brother-in-law, my husband, first and then comes to encourage me saying prison is a common thing. As a person who goes to church, he takes it easily, he accepts it.

After my release I will not have any problems because I have learnt many skills here in prison. I want to open a tailoring shop and teach my children dressmaking. Is there any skill we lack? – we can even fix some electrical goods such as our over-locking machine. I can make seat covers for sofas, knit and sew tracksuits and school uniforms for both boys and girls.

I want people to understand that prison life is terrible. People should guard against committing crimes out of ignorance. I personally now know that insulting, lying or fighting others are serious offences that may land someone in jail. I would like to thank my daughter in a very special way because she is the one who is holding the family together while I am here.

10

Agnes

interviewed by Keresia Chateuka

My name is Agnes. I was born in 1944 in Shurugwi. Both my parents died so I left there when I was very young. My sister took me in and I lived with her until I got married. My husband and I separated many years ago. I have no idea where he is or what he is doing.

I have twelve children, six boys and six girls, all fathered by him. Two died and the rest are living. He left a big family behind. I had a hard time raising the children by myself. Fortunately I had some cattle. I could plough the fields and grow crops. I sold some of the cattle and crops to raise money for the children's school fees. The older children went up to Grade 7, but the younger ones did well, they went up to Form 4. All my daughters are married, and now I only have grandchildren living with me.

The reason I went to prison is that I pushed my grandchild into a fire. He was fighting with another grandchild. The child's uncle reported [the incident] to the police and they arrested me. At first they took me to Kadoma and then to Chikurubi. The uncle took the child to hospital. He was badly burnt and also had a fractured arm. I stayed a week in remand prison. In court I admitted my crime and I was sentenced to one month in prison. I then went to Chikurubi in a truck because there is no women's prison in Kadoma. When I arrived there, they gave me a place to sleep.

The following morning we lined up for food. After that we would be given work to do. They gave us very blunt axes and grass cutters. Some cut down gum trees while others chopped the branches up for firewood. Some carried and stacked the wood in a shed. When we finished our work we went back to line up again for our lunch. After lunch we would go back to work. The cell was one big room with bunk beds. We slept on beds. The next morning we washed, had food and were given more work to do. We dug a big hole and shovelled out gravel. I do not know what they used it for. This went on for two weeks. The guards gave us hard work to do for two weeks. Afterwards we were given light duties like picking up paper in the yard. Towards the end of my sentence, I hardly did any work. On the day I got out of prison I was called to the office and was given back my clothes.

I think the most important thing to observe in prison is obedience. Prison guards want total obedience. Even if the prison guard asks you to go and work at her house, you have to do it. You get on well with them as long as you do not give them problems. We had enough food to eat in prison. Some people cooked when some of us were out working. We would come back from whatever work we were doing and wash. Afterwards, we would pick up a plate and queue up for our share of food. It was orderly. If you left any food on your plate you would throw it into the bin and take back the plate for washing. We also got sandals in prison. The prison guards would give you a pair. We went to the clinic to get cotton wool to use during menstruation. If you were sick you would be given medicines. All you had to do was ask.

In prison we were put into groups according to the nature of our crimes. On arrival they asked you what crime you had committed. They gave you a denim dress and told you which cell to go to. Those in remand prison had white dresses. Nobody came to visit me during the month I was in prison. Many of my relatives did not know where I was. Before I left prison they gave me a travel warrant. It allowed me to get on the bus for free. With my warrant I went to Mbare and got a bus to Kadoma. When I arrived home my grandchildren were happy to see me including the grandchild who I had pushed into the fire. He grew up under my care until he was a grown man. It is unfortunate that he died in prison. He was convicted for rape. He had sex with a deaf and dumb girl without her consent.

Nothing had changed when I got back home: the village head did not chase me away. I am still living here in the village with my three grandchildren. Two of them go to school, but the third one is sick so he stays at home. After school, one minds the cattle for the rest of the day and the other fetches water from the borehole. They are helpful around the home. They also come with me to the fields when it is time to weed or harvest.

It is a hard life, especially as there is no food. I sell some of my chickens to get money to buy food. Sometimes their parents bring a little money, a thousand dollars for example, and other times they do not bring any. I guess they do not have it. Life is quite hard for me. The grandchildren need food and soap. I have no money to have the maize ground at the mill. If only it had rained, I would sell some of the crops. There will not be a harvest this year – the sun scorched all the crops.

11

Monica

interviewed by Chiedza Musengezi

My name is Monica, I was born in April 1969 in Kwekwe. We are nine children in our family. I grew up in Zhombe. I went to Zhombe Mission for primary school. I went only up to Form 2 with my secondary education. There was no money for me to continue. My sisters went further than me because my brothers helped out with school fees. My father worked on a mine in Shurugwi while my mother stayed at home. She raised all nine of us in Zhombe.

After I dropped out of school, I got a job as a housemaid with Mr and Mrs X., who taught at the secondary school. I swept the house, shined the floors, washed clothes, and looked after their two-year-old child. When I left this job I went back home, but I soon realised that I should not be sitting around doing nothing while my mother did not have enough money to look after us. We were many and there was never enough money for all of us. So I decided to come to Harare where I stayed with my cousin while I looked for a job. Again I found a job as a housemaid at a flat in Eastlea. I worked for Mr M., who had a wife and two children. My duties were the same as before. I cleaned the house and looked after the children. This is when I met Webster. We fell in love and we got on very well. He was a security guard when I met him. He later learned to drive and got his driver's licence. He then got a job as an emergency taxi driver. He drove the small vehicles, the ones that go to Avondale from the city centre. He still holds this job today. We decided to get married so I left my job. I was not pregnant. I accompanied him to Zhombe so he could meet my parents and pay *lobola*. Although he had only a little money, my parents agreed that we could live together as husband and wife. They were soft with him. They did not want to make life difficult for us simply because Webster was not rich. We left Zhombe, my husband and I, for a new life together. I had my first child in December of same year soon after our marriage in 1988. This is how I started my married life.

We were happy until 1994, when I had my third baby, and then I faced problems in my marriage. My husband's relatives started to speak badly of me. They complained that I was a foreigner. It is true that my father came from Zambia, but they were talking as if Zambians were low people not fit to be part of their family. They complained that I did not behave like a well-brought-up woman and many other bad things. At first my husband did not worry about their complaints, but later he listened to every word they said about me and he took everything seriously. He then told me to leave with my children. So I left with my children and went back home to my mother in 1994.

I stayed with her, looking after my children and working the fields until 1996. I could then see that my mother was old – she could no longer care for my children and me. I thought it would be better to go back to Harare and find a job. I left my children with my mother and I arrived in town in September 1997. I stayed with my cousin in Highfield. I did not find a job. I found a man who was interested in me instead. He was a constable at Glen Norah Police Station. His name was Shepherd D. He did not go to Zhombe to pay *lobola*, we simply discussed and agreed to live together. I was so blinded with love that I never thought that I would face the same problems that I did in my first marriage. We lived happily together until 1999, when D. was taken ill. The doctor said he had arthritis. His feet and knees swelled, and his feet could not fit into his work shoes so he wore open sandals. He was given light duties to do. He never recovered fully; he was in and out of hospital until they asked him to resign from work. He resigned and waited to receive his pension. That was in 1999.

For the two years I lived with D. he did not pay anything to my parents towards *lobola*. By then I wanted him to marry me properly – to pay *lobola*. I used to ask him about it and he used to give excuses. He would say he was ill or had not yet received his pension. When he finally received the money he bought a car. He was always with his friends. My life changed for worse. He would never listen to what I said. If I asked for money, he would refuse. He took to beating me very badly. Whenever I tried to discuss something important, he would beat me into silence. Eventually I decided to leave him. I did not have children with him, so it was easy for me to leave. I decided against having children because when he fell sick, I became suspicious. I was not sure what was the matter with him he could have been HIV positive. However, he wanted me to have children with him. I used to tell him that I too wanted to have babies but I was failing. I lied because I did not want to have babies: our relationship was not good. I was unhappy. Sometimes he would drive off with his friends and not come home. It was not a good life at all. I had to leave. My friend from next door advised me that I should not just leave with nothing. She said I had worked hard caring for him and his three children from his first marriage and I had to find a way to compensate myself. She said I could take household goods, so that is what I did because I liked the idea too. I took sofas, a fridge, a stove and a kitchen unit and hid them with a friend. I did not take anything to my rural home. He came back to an empty house and he went to report to the police.

The police followed me home but of course they could not find the goods. They brought me back to Harare and they asked where I had put my husband's things. At first I denied that I had taken them but I soon realised that I had committed a crime. I told them what I had done and they recovered everything except the fridge, which I had sold. It is the fridge that sent me to prison. I had sold it to raise money for my bus fare and the remainder I used to buy food for my children. They arrested me for selling stolen goods. That is why I ended up in prison in March 2000.

In court, I was given bail but I could not find someone to pay it for me. No relative came on the day of the hearing: I was by myself. After my failure to pay bail, I was remanded in Chikurubi Prison. I used to go to court from Chikurubi until the day I was sentenced. I was jailed for eighteen months.

Um, as soon as I set my foot in prison ... no, when I came out of court and got into the prison truck and was now in the hands of *vanambuya gadhi*, the world seemed a different place: in my eyes it had changed. I felt as if I was no longer in Zimbabwe but in a different country altogether. I could not talk. I felt a big lump of tears in my throat. I wanted to cry out. Then I arrived at Chikurubi and they made me sit at the office. I was confused. I saw women dressed in green and yellow. I was really confused. I did not know what I was doing. They were filling in papers, and then someone threw a green dress at me and said, 'Go to remand!' Then, ah, yes, I was in prison for sure.

I went to remand section and when I looked at the women there, I felt better because I saw women of all ages, mothers with babies, old women, young women some of them the age of my eldest child. Suddenly I felt I was not alone, we were many in the same situation. I slept and woke up in the morning. The room we slept in was tiny. Prison is a big of place of small rooms. A little room this long and this wide [stretches out her arms]. How can seven people sleep in such a small place? There were seven of us. I was given four blankets.

When I entered the cell, those who were already inside greeted me warmly. I was well received. They shook hands with me. Now, I must say, that I was the one harbouring bad thoughts about them. I thought I had come to the bad place that I had heard about. I thought the one who had been very friendly wanted me for a sexual partner. I had heard that such things happen in prison so I could not relax. There was a young woman who said she and I could be friends. I agreed again because I had heard that in such places there were bosses whom nobody dared to disagree with. I had heard these stories from people who claimed to have been in prison. However no such things happened. I slept and woke up in the morning. She offered me her soap and towel to use and her Vaseline too.

Later in the day I was given my own piece of soap and towel, not a big towel but a towel all the same. It was a pleasant surprise for I did not expect prisons to supply such things. I used to think the worst of prisons. I thought them to be awful places where people lived like wild animals. When I heard my name being called out to receive soap and a towel, a new one at that, I let go bad thoughts about prisons. I began to mix with others; I became real friends with some of my inmates. We talked to each other about our problems. We comforted one another. I learnt that some of my inmates were jailed for ten years and some for twenty years. So my situation was not bad, I was going to be out soon. It was then that I realised that even though I was in prison, a bad place indeed for anyone, I would finish serving my sentence, and then I could start another life. I felt better, relaxed.

Mind you, I had lost a lot of weight in a short time. I used to look at my body when I was bathing and I could see that I had wasted away. Death did not feel far away. I had also heard ugly stories about how the *vanambuya gadhi* let you out just in time for you to die outside the prison walls. I think people who have never been inside a prison spread these stories. Meanwhile my family did not know what had happened to me. My mother did not know that I had been jailed. In prison we were given paper every month for writing letters. On my arrival I was given some because *ambuya gadhi* wanted me to write to my family. So I wrote to tell them that I was in trouble. They got my letter and I got a reply. However they had no money, so they could not visit me. My first husband visited me and he brought all the children with him.

In prison, doors were opened at 6:30 in the morning, we would then go to bath, and have our breakfast of tea and bread at 7:30 a.m. Afterwards, at about 8:30 a.m., we would be divided into different groups. Some would go to work in the vegetable garden some would go to work in the kitchen, cooking, and washing dishes. There were others who went for typing: a white woman came to teach typing. Some would sweep the prison yard and water flowers, while some would go to learn dressmaking. There were some prisoners who were not allowed outside because they were regarded as dangerous. I took up typing after passing the entrance test. I did typing up to intermediate level. I can use computers too. Finding a job has proved difficult and I think it is because I do not have O-Levels. I only have ZJC.

We had enough food in prison; we did not go hungry at all. There was plenty of sadza, a heap of it on the plate, this high [raises hand to indicate level]. The only problem is that sometimes it is not well prepared and so it does not taste good. The vegetables are not finely cut; they do not add salt and cooking oil. Sometimes the bad food would make prison life seem hard, but it is not so: there is plenty of food, if only it were cooked properly. We prepared the food ourselves, so maybe with strict supervision it could improve. The prison guards watched over us as we cooked but they would let us prepare the food badly while they watched. Sometimes the meat would just be boiled. Can you imagine eating boiled pork? Sometimes they would dish huge pieces of meat red with blood on to your plate. The appearance of such food would not tempt you to eat. I did not do any cooking: cooks were selected from those inmates who could not go outside because of the nature of their crime, murder, for instance.

When I look back at my time in prison I can also see that prison was a place for learning. I can now type; some are dressmakers. This is useful, but prison is not a good place to be. Not everybody learnt to type: we were only sixteen in the typing class and yet prison was full of women. Only a few get a chance to be trained to do something useful in the future. Prison is also not good especially for the young girls. It may harden them. They may be fearless enough to commit more crime. Sometimes the life may not seem bad especially for those from worse off situations. Nothing bad happened to me throughout my stay in prison from March 2000 to April 2001. Nobody beat me up, nobody scolded me, no guard laid a hand on me, no guard said 'voetsak!' to me. If you get along with others and make friends and you do not break any prison rules, it can be a reasonably comfortable life, but I was very unhappy.

A year in prison felt like twenty years. I thought of my children all the time. Did they have any clothes? Were they going to school? Leaving your children at home when you go to jail is very painful and worrying. There are also relatives to worry about. What did they think of me? How would they look at me from now on? I thought of all these things. I'm very grateful to the Salvation Army woman who used to take us for prayers. I found her comforting. She used to encourage me to leave all my worries to God. I used to pray in the evenings always asking God to look after my children. Sometimes, when I got a letter from home with news of the children, I would be very happy. The day my first husband visited with the children was the happiest day of my life in prison. It was a Saturday and because we did not have typing classes on weekends we were locked up in our cells. I heard someone calling out for me because I had a visitor. First I thought it was my mother but when I saw my children with their father, ah, I was happy. Their father told me that he visited the children often and he had also bought them new clothes for Christmas because it was in December. I could see it for myself. The children looked well and they were smartly dressed. I was relieved as well as pleased that this man was taking good care of his children. From then on I felt better, I stopped worrying too much about them.

In prison, too much worry can lead to illness and you can die. I saw it myself. I observed people who were not well, their condition worsened because they worried all the time. Some inmates were divorced by their husbands and they would learn about it right there at the gate when their husbands came to tell them that their marriage was over. It is difficult to cope with such things in prison. It adds another problem to the main one of being jailed. Prison is not an easy place to live in. It is important that one does not get additional problems

For those with relatives in prison, it is important to visit them to help put their minds at peace. A single visit can work wonders for a prisoner. When they visit, they should also try to bring things for everyday use like slippers, tennis shoes, a bar of soap, toothpaste, underpants, cotton wool. During the cold season socks would be useful. When you receive these things in prison, you feel loved, you feel you are not alone. If people do not visit you and you see some of your inmates coming back with armfuls of presents, then you cannot help think why your relatives do not visit. You feel rejected for the crime you committed. You think that maybe they secretly want you to suffer for your crime. It may not be true. Prison is not a place that encourages good positive thoughts, because you are not free. You are fenced in. You cannot walk as far as that durawall without being commanded to come back like a stray cow. You cannot do the things that you would like to do in life. So it is important that relatives visit, especially during public holidays like Heroes holiday and Christmas. Bring them good food if possible.

When I finally finished serving my sentence and I was told I would be released the following day. I was given back my clothes and I washed them but, all the time, I was worrying about where exactly I would go. Although I have a cousin here in Harare, I was not sure whether I would be welcome in her home. She did not visit me all the time I was in prison. I thought she did not want to see me any more. After all, I had stolen and sold somebody's property, and it was possible that she no longer felt safe with me. I also thought she probably suspected me of not being mentally balanced, I would steal again at the first opportunity. You really get confused trying to work out what people think of a person who has been to prison. You think all they see in you is a criminal. I did not know whose door I would knock at and be let in.

Nonetheless, after my release, I went to my cousin and everything I thought about her was not correct. She was the first to see me coming, and she ran towards me with outstretched hands and hugged me. She was so pleased to see me. She asked after my health and so forth. Not once did she treat me like a criminal, she was respectful towards me. She also knew how I had ended up in prison. I had married badly and I did not know the law well enough to realise the criminal act I was committing. Nobody laughed at me, only I nursed negative thoughts about myself sometimes.

When I eventually went to Zhombe, the children were very happy to see me. The eldest was doing Form 1, and the youngest was in Grade 2. When I left them again on 2nd January, they did not like it. Now I'm staying with my girlfriend in Highfield. Her name is Selina. We used to rent the same house when I was married. We were both lodgers at the same house and we became friends. I visited her after my release from jail and she invited me to come and stay with her. She is married and her husband does not mind me staying with them. He is supportive. Selina has a table at the market that she gave me. Now I stack the table with oranges, tomatoes, etc., for sale. I make little money but it is enough for me to survive.

Since I left home in January, life has not been easy, but it was equally hard at home. I needed money to send my children to school. My brothers are now married and they have families of their own. They have new responsibilities. I needed to move away and start a life of my own and my children. This is why I left them. I'm looking for a job, any job, even as housemaid. However, I still have not found one.

I came to know Prison Fellowship when I was still in prison. They visited us in prison and they connected us with people who wrote to us and sent us leaflets with information about God. They also preached to us. Baba Mandiyanike, the director of Prison Fellowship, encouraged us to report here first before we go home after jail. He said this was important because sometimes family can reject us and we would have nowhere to go. Rejection could then drive you to do something criminal like stealing and you would go back to prison. Baba is helpful in such situations: he can go to talk to your family, persuading them to take you back into the family. He can also give you shelter and food while the talks take place. I know of a young woman who got this kind of help. On arrival, Prison Fellowship would ask you where you are going and if the people are willing to let you stay. You have to give information on the form that they give you to fill in. They also encourage coming back and seeking help whenever you feel the need. Sometimes you may not have clothes or, in the case of mothers, they may find their children do not have clothes. Prison Fellowship can assist in such cases.

I found Prison Fellowship a very helpful organisation. In my case, I told Baba Mandiyanike that I had family that was eager to have me back. However, I'm considering getting a loan to start a small business. Prison Fellowship can give a small loan to help you start to live an honest life. It is easy to drift back into crime when you have nothing. My brother is against my idea though, he thinks I might fail to pay it back and get into trouble. He advised me to find a job and then save money to start my business. Should I get a loan, I will buy second-hand clothes for resale in places like Mutoko. Some people say you can get good money.

I would like to say something about young girls I saw in prison. I think they are too young to be in jail. I wonder if it is possible to separate them, let them live as a group, and give them a proper education. At the moment they do not seem to learn anything of value: some of them have absolutely no manners and use foul language. Some are disrespectful towards the older women prisoners. They totally refuse to take any advice from these older women on the grounds that they too are prisoners and have no moral right to instruct them on good behaviour. They say they would not take the advice of a thief and so forth. I'm afraid that their behaviour gets worse if they stay in prison. Some of them, in the end, seem to enjoy prison life. One young girl was released from jail on 17th January and she was back on 27th January. If only these girls could be given another form of punishment out of prison and which allows them to get some education. Mothers with babies also need a lot of help and fortunately churches and people from abroad give them cereal, peanut butter and clothes for their children.

In prison it is not easy to tell the rich from the poor at first because we all wear uniform, but you soon find out. The rich get a lot of presents, five to six pairs of tennis shoes, for instance. Their visitors come in cars, as many as four, sometimes.

I do not want to get married again. I simply want to do things for myself. I have good health and I can work. When I was a younger woman it never occurred to me that I could take care of myself. My ambition was to be provided for by a husband.

This story used to weigh heavily on my heart. Once jailed, you live in the shadow of prison all your life. Now that I have told it I feel better, the lump has lifted.

12

Maureen

interviewed by Keresia Chateuka

My name is Maureen. I was born in Chigodora under Chief Tito in September 1956. My mother comes from South Africa. We are ten in our family, six girls and four boys. Our parents managed to educate us all. My father wanted us to be educated.

My father worked in South Africa. He resigned from his job to start a business here. He had a mill and a store. My mother worked in the shops in town. She worked for TM, formerly Jaggers. So we stayed in town till I got married.

My parents are now late. My mother died in 2000 but my father died in 1972, when I had completed my Standard 6. Back in those days, attaining Standard 6 was a great achievement. We considered ourselves educated people. After my education I joined others in co-operative farming until I met my husband after he had come to visit his relatives in our rural area. His name was Richard.

We fell in love. He told me he worked in Harare. He took me to his aunt. Afterwards he paid *lobola* for me. In those days it was paid in pounds. I went to his home area to stay. His home had its own rules. No wife followed her husband to his work place. So I had to be at the rural home while he worked in Harare.

I gave birth to my first born baby girl in 1978. My in-laws gave me a piece of land to farm. I cleared the land, cutting down all the trees, and then I tilled it, and planted cotton and maize seeds. During that time my husband sometimes came at month end. At times he came when I was in the field looking very dirty and shabby. I never took notice because of that. I had accepted living in the rural areas and working in the fields.

Then when my crops were harvested, I was told another rule. I had to wait for my husband to come and cash the cheques that I had been given after selling my produce. I waited for him. My husband came. We went to cash the cheque. I was surprised at the amount of money he gave me, it was little though I am the one who had toiled day and night in the fields. My mother-in-law celebrated over my money. 'Well,' I sighed and said to myself, 'maybe this is what married life is supposed to be.'

I once packed my bags and left but I was told to return to my husband. You know, long back, the elders never considered a daughter returning home without an aunt or an elder from her husband's family. They said all complaints had to be addressed in the presence of the husband's elders.

Come the next planting season, I put aside the incidents of the previous season and planted my cotton. My husband had a girlfriend in Harare. I hoped the situation would change after the birth of my third born. Nothing changed. He took my cheque, cashed it, and spent the money with the girlfriend. He came from Harare with a thin blanket, two pots and a Z$100 note. That was all I got of the money I had laboured for. I received the goods with tears in my eyes.

My husband was at his parents' house talking and telling stories. I thought of killing myself but I realised my children would suffer. I thought of burning my husband and his parents in the house but I feared the spirit of *ngozi*, which avenges the dead man's spirit. My husband told me he was on leave and I said it was well.

Then, one day, the devil's force gripped me when my husband was drinking beer in his mother's kitchen. It was in the evening and it looked as if it would rain. I thought of my plan to set the hut on fire and I said to myself, 'They will think the hut was hit by lightning.' My children were already fast asleep. I got out of the house with my matches, and headed for the kitchen. I lit the thatch on the door and around the hut. I heard screams inside. My in-laws' grandchildren had fallen asleep in the kitchen.

I thought of running away but realised I would sell myself out, so I started walking about. And then I ran away. The fire was unquenchable. My mother-in-law was shouting, 'There are children in the hut, my son-in-law's children are in the hut.' One grandchild died in the hut. It was the daughter's child. The surviving one spent at least a year in hospital before he recovered from the burns.

I was hiding in the hill. My in-laws asked my children about my whereabouts but they did not know as they had been asleep when I left the hut. There on the hill I was in a dilemma. One part of me wanted to commit suicide. I knew I was going to be sentenced for arson and murder, and sent to jail. I was stranded. I could not think straight. I spent three days there on the hill. The police came. I could see them from the hill. I saw everything that transpired at the homestead. Then I got hungry. So I decided to give myself up. I knew I could not go to the homestead because I could be killed. I opted to visit the headman. He asked me why I had committed such a horrendous offence. I explained everything to him. He rebuked me for not having reported the matter to him. I told him I never thought about it as I had made my decision. He explained that since I was married, he was going to consult the elders of both families.

When the chief was consulted he said the story was already in the police's hands so there was nothing he could do. The police were called. I accepted that I had committed the offence. They asked the reason, I explained. The police took me to Chisumbanje, where I stayed on remand for three months before I was sentenced. Later they took me to Chiredzi. They took a statement. It was said that I had accepted my offence. I told them I had done what I did because I had suffered so much in the fields only to get peanuts at the end of the day.

I got my sentence in April 1992. I was released in May 1996. I served four years. The extras were removed. They said this was so because I had told them the truth. When I left prison I did not know that my husband had passed away.

My life in prison was very hard. Any girl old enough to be my daughter could tell me hurting words and I would cry. All my life I have never had high blood pressure but I developed it while in prison. Now I take BP tablets every day. If I skip, I will spend a night in hospital.

In the morning we got out fully dressed but at half four, lock up time, we were ordered to fully undress. We would lift our legs as they inspected us to see if we were hiding dangerous items. During your monthly periods you had to see to it that you did not mess the blankets. At times we thought of using the blanket edges to act as sanitary pads.

I cannot even mention the quality of food we received. At times we got black tea which would be stone cold. We ate beans that had aphids in them. Sometimes the cooking oil in the relish would be raw but we fought for the food. We always finished our food. If you made a small mistake you were made to lie flat on the ground then you were beaten under your feet. Crying or shouting *yowe-e* or *maiwe-e* was prohibited. Bending your legs was not allowed while you were beaten. And while this happened some female jail guards would be looking on. If you reported an illness, they first called you by the name of your offence. They could say, 'Am I the one who told you to torch your house? *Voetsek.*' You would be ordered to get your shovel and head for the garden.

Even now, when I hear prison stories I do not feel right. People can harass you for no reason, even when you are naked. Sometimes you are instructed to get up and dance when there is no music. You have to sing your own song and dance to it. You are asked the offence you committed. You say it out and you are instructed to act it out. Show the other inmates how you actually did it.

All the time in jail you will be thinking of your children. I was pregnant when I went to prison. When I was released I had already had my baby. It was another boy. When I had finished serving my sentence I thought about where I had to go. I could not go to my husband's home as I had heard he had passed away. Furthermore I knew I would not be received well. So I decided to go to my parents' home. When I reached there they took me for a visitor. They said I had my own home to look after. They assigned me a relative to accompany me back to my in-laws.

I went to the headman with the relative who had accompanied me. The headman said my story had been solved by the government, so there was nothing else to do. He told me to go back to my family and look after it.

At first sight – my children – my God, they looked like scarecrows. Their skin was chapped and they had no shoes on. My huts had collapsed. My in-laws were still there and they labelled me a witch, a murderer. God, I did not know what to do. To add more injury, I was shown the grave of the child who had died. They said I had eaten the baby. I had nothing on me, no money. I had travelled using a warrant. I started mourning the death of my husband. They showed me where they had put him to rest. I sat and thought about how I was going to look for the children's clothes and food.

Domestic issues – Maureen

I stayed with two relatives for a week and then they went back. I had no blanket, no pot. I only had one clay pot to use for all my cooking. My children could not go to school. I had no school fees. I thought what could I do? I started joining others in co-operative farming. I cut grass to thatch my huts.

Life at my husband's home is still unbearable. At times we exchange morning greetings but at times we can spend a month in silence without speaking one word. Sometimes I can sleep without a meal. When I find something to eat, it is well. I wish I could get money to obtain a passport so I can go to South Africa like the other women. I can even go to Mozambique.

Some of my children still want to go to school. I still look after them. The elder girl is married. I cannot look up to my son-in-law to look after my family. He chips in when he can. I got nothing from my husband's pension because he died after quitting his job. As for the girlfriend, well, she was one of those only interested in spending his money. She packed her bags and left.

I would like to urge people to be slow to anger. I even thought of axing my husband to death. I thought if I killed him, what about his mother who influenced him to get my money so they could drink beer? My intention was to have them all dead in the hut. It really pained me that I worked hard for two years only to benefit other people. You can imagine what the cotton plant does to your skin. It pained me to work for other people.

Now I pray to God that my children will not get such satanic thoughts. I do not want them to go to jail. Better to suffer out of jail, than commit an offence and languish in prison. If we suffer now, I know God will show us some light on our way. In jail, you serve one sentence during the day and one during the night. If you receive a letter, you quickly shed tears thinking about what your children are thinking about you. It is worse especially when a relative visits you. You suffer inwardly. All the time I was in jail, my husband never visited me. Our relations had been cut. I was a witch in his eyes. Not even a relative from his side visited me.

Really, life in prison is hard. If I am to see someone dropping a bag full of money, I will tell the person that he has dropped it and should pick it. It will be up to the person to give me some as a thank you or not.

13

Jane

interviewed by Keresia Chateuka

I am Jane. I was born in 1953 in Chigodora. We were ten in our family, six girls and four boys. One girl passed away. We farmed and our mother used to sell the produce in town. Both our parents are late: they passed away when we were young.

We did not get enough education but I reached Standard 6. My other brothers and sisters have no permanent jobs. They buy and sell goods. I got married in 1972 and gave birth to my first born in the same year in August. My husband was James. He worked for a company in Mutare. My husband did not make it to the birth of the second born; he left me when I was still pregnant.

The comrades took him in the middle of the night. We heard a knock on the door. We had just returned from a meeting at the base. They instructed us to open the door saying, 'We are your children.' My husband opened it. They asked where I was. My husband woke me up. They told me they were taking my husband. He was told to get his national identity card and documents from work. I knew right then that they were going to kill him. I started crying. They told me if I did not stop he would die in my presence. I quickly stopped.

Well, I asked the comrades if we could pass through his parents' place to inform them. They did not want to kill him near or at the base. They agreed. I put my child on my back and went to his parents. My husband was already their prisoner, carrying the goods that had been taken from people's shops. I knocked and woke the parents, and told them I had come with the comrades. They told my husband to bid them farewell saying 'I am going to war, I do not know if we shall ever see each other again.' He said so. My mother-in-law started crying. She volunteered to die instead of her son for he had many responsibilities. They told her they do not reverse their decision.

They did not tell us why they wanted to kill him but there were people who saw him with the old Z\$20 notes at the bottle store. They said he was showing off money he had been given by the soldiers. They labelled him a sell-out. His friends had reported him to the comrades. The comrades pointed their firearms at his mother. They debated whether or not to kill her. Some said she would sell them out. (It was typical of them to debate every time they wanted to kill a person.) In the end it was resolved they would stick to their culprit. They took him and other boys. Hey, this was the fate of my first husband. I never saw him again. His body was found near the border. It had already decomposed.

The following morning the soldiers came asking for the comrades' whereabouts. We showed them the way they had used. The soldiers then beat us and burnt our houses. We were exposed. We had nothing to hold on to any more. The headman intervened and summoned the village. He instructed the people to cut grass and thatch our huts. Everybody helped and soon we had our huts roofed.

Then I gave birth to my second born. I was now staying on my own. I feared the comrades would return so I packed my bags and left. I returned to my parents. I stayed there. I could not make ends meet. It was at the time when cattle were being stolen from the farms. I joined the people who killed the cattle. We shared the meat that we sold in the villages and sometimes in town. We got orders from many people. The residents looked for customers for us. Life was now bearable.

Then, I fell in love with a man who was also involved in stock theft – a business woman in love with a business man. In such cases, pregnancy is inevitable. Love was floating in the air. We had a child together. He started helping me carry some of my meat that we packed in cardboard boxes.

We fell in love when the liberation struggle was at its peak. He decided to look for a butchery to rent. We got the meat to sell from the farms. He did not marry me: we just stayed together. My relatives came after me and told him I was somebody else's wife. I told him to give a deaf ear to them. I am not the one who killed my husband.

So we had our butchery and we continued selling the meat. I then got caught – by then my husband had stopped the stock theft. I was caught red-handed so there was no way I could deny it. Well … I tried saying the meat was not mine. It belonged to the boys. Then the CID tried looking for the boys after taking the meat. They told me I was clean but had to tell them where the boys were. They did not know I was pulling a leg. They beat me with a sjambok under my feet. I then told them I did not know where the boys were since we used to meet in the farms.

Of all the people involved I am the only one who was arrested. I suffered alone for I never sold my husband out. The officials from the CID beat me up but I never told them anything.

I was arrested in Chimanimani. They took me to the police station. I stayed in the cell for two days. Then I was taken to court. A sentence was passed. I went into prison in 1985 and was released in 1988.

Three years was the 'overall' [statutory] term for stock theft: some months were suspended as this was my first offence. However they moved me from Chipinge to Mutare, where I spent a week. Then I was taken to Chikurubi since my term was quite long. I served my sentence at Chikurubi.

When I went to prison, I had never realised that life there was hard. I did not understand what the magistrate said in court for he spoke in English. I thought I was going home after the court session. So when I tried to talk to the audience [plead in mitigation] I was prevented – I was already under guard. I asked myself, 'Why had I talked badly?' Then I was told that I had agreed to serve my sentence with hard labour.

They asked how I carried the meat with my asthma. They concluded my disease [could have been] caused by [wetness from] carrying the meat.

My husband did not come to court but his sisters did. When I asked if I could talk to them they told me it was not allowed. They were told that they could visit me once a month in prison. I was taken to prison and upon my arrival the police said, 'We have come with more offenders and this one is a hard-core thief.' I could not answer back. They told me I was now a prisoner. I went to sign the date of my admission. They gave me a small sack and I was ordered to take off my clothes. I was given a uniform. I wanted to go to the toilet to remove the clothes but I was told I had to change right there. I had to take off my pants I felt naked. I put on the uniform. Then they offered me sadza but I declined it. I spent two days without eating anything. On the third day they told me it was an offence not to eat and I pretended to eat.

By then my baby was three years old. Prison is not good especially for females. Maybe if you do not have children it is better. Sometimes I failed to write a letter to my children because I soaked the writing sheets with tears. We wrote letters once a month. At times after you wrote your letter you were called and asked if you were being ill-treated because you might have said something in your letter. Then you would be beaten with a hosepipe. Your blood would change to black.

Staying in prison is very hard especially if you are female. In the morning we woke up at 6 a.m. and went for roll call. Afterwards we went to bath. By seven we were having our tea. The tea is prepared overnight. It will be black and at times you will find flies inside. The flies in the kitchen are just too much. So you remove the flies from your cup. Sometimes we got sadza with stale chicken but we liked it. With pork it came with all its furs. You debated on whether to eat the meat or not. We removed the fur and ate it. If you do not eat you will die from hunger.

We squatted. My legs started swelling. I could not squat. You lifted your hand and they would ask, 'What does this thief want?' (They called us by our crimes.) I asked if I could kneel but the female jail guard said, 'If you do not want to squat then why did you commit an offence?' I told her to beat me for I could not take it any more. Other guards told you not to walk with a watering can but to run with it. But sometimes you found generous guards who were understanding.

The bell rang at 4 p.m. Every day before we were locked inside we undressed for inspection. Nobody laughed at anyone. We passed through the female guards and opened our legs for them to inspect. We wore our uniforms at the door. We had no pants even during our periods. We had to use old rags, those red ones. Life is hard.

The jail guards beat prisoners — maybe for wrong-doing, or what they said was wrong-doing. I repeat prison life is not for women. If you are caught sitting alone, they ask you what is on your mind. You are ordered to take a watering can and water the garden alone. They say you have nothing to do.

I never liked prison at all. I will never commit crime again. When I was near the end of my sentence they took me to Mutare, and when there was only one week left, they took me to Chipinge. I was released there. You are released at the station from which you got arrested.

My husband came once in a while to visit me. Finances restrained him. He once fell ill when I was in prison. I prayed for him. We put ourselves in a hard situation. I do not know if we will ever be back to normal.

I found him waiting for me. It is hard when you get out of jail as everyone – your family and relations – turns their back on you. It is quite hard for you to go to church. Only those who do not know your story will be your friends. My family is always scolding my children, and always reminding them that I went to prison.

I urge women never to do anything bad that can land them in jail, especially those with children. All your plans come to a standstill. Your life is no longer good. Two things were unbearable in my life, my first husband who was killed by the comrades and staying in prison. I thought God had turned his back on me.

Right now I need to get a job to buy food and clothing for my children. Their stepfather does not look after them well. Bad words are exchanged, like, 'F... off, I do not look after children who are not mine.' It really pains me.

I urge people, especially women, not to do anything that leads them to prison. It is better to borrow money and pay it with interest, *chimbadzo*, and buy goods for resale. It is better that way.

Section: 3

Domestic issues and
fear of witchcraft

14

Rhoda

interviewed by Chiedza Musengezi

My name is Rhoda.* I was born in 1941 in Masvingo. We are four in my family and I am the eldest. My father was a village head. He was not employed but he managed to send me to school. He was a farmer and he sold some crops and livestock to send his children to school. I went to a mission school where I met the man who later became my husband. I married him in 1964 in the Dutch Reformed Church. I lived with my mother-in-law, a pleasant, kind woman. She treated me like her daughter. In the morning I would wake up to do housework: sweeping, cooking, and warming water for my husband and mother-in-law to bath. My husband got a job at a sugar estate, cutting sugar-cane. I used to visit him for short periods after harvesting our crops because my mother-in-law wanted me nearby most of the time. She loved me very much. She was also old and dependent on me. Whenever I stayed at the sugar estate longer than she could bear, she would send someone after me and I would go back to her.

I had my first child, Claudius, in 1964. I had him at hospital. It was an easy birth, no problems at all. When I went back home with my baby everybody was happy. They slaughtered a goat for me and bought me three dresses. In 1966 I had a second child, a daughter called Auxilia, and then another daughter, Chipo, then Lilian, Simbarashe, Vimbai and Takudzwa. Claudius died at school: he was a boarder; he came back in a coffin. His teachers brought him home. When his body arrived, it was still warm and he was bleeding from the nose. We buried him two days later as we had to wait for other relatives to arrive.

---

* Rhoda was interviewed in prison.

In our village there lived a poor woman called Mai N.... Sometimes I used to help her out with food and other things. One afternoon, about three days after the funeral, Mai N... walked into my yard. She was naked and had a machete in her hand – you know the one used for cutting sugar-cane in Chiredzi. I wrestled the machete out of her hand. She said she had my deceased son's body parts. She used his penis as a whistle to blow, calling her friends in the night to go out to bewitch people. I demanded my son's body parts back but she refused. She said that if I [were to] have them back I would die.

I took her machete and followed her to her home. When I went inside I saw her husband, her brother-in-law and her nephew. We fought again but this time I was mad with anger. We knocked over a pot sitting on the fire and it put out the fire. I had closed the door and it was dark inside. I swung the machete in any direction with the intention of hurting whoever was in my way. Two people died – the six-year-old nephew and his father. The others had deep cuts. It was such a violent fight that I was left only with my petticoat and a torn skirt. My blouse was ripped off my body. I wanted to avenge the death of my son. Nobody came to stop the fight. People were frightened. When I realised what I had done, I passed out. My relatives bathed me and gave me clean clothes. I stayed at home that night. I was numb with shock; I did not talk. The police came the next morning. They asked for the machete I had used and I gave it to them. They asked if I had committed [the offense] by myself and I told them nobody else was involved.

In the meantime, the family of the man and child I had killed demanded compensation. My husband paid 24 head of cattle and two goats. He also bought the coffins.

The police took me to their station where I gave a statement. I was transferred to Masvingo where I was in remand prison for eight months. When they took me into the cell I became really frightened. It was dark except for a little light that came in through a tiny window. For two weeks I was isolated in this cell. They let me out to wash. I wished I were dead. They told me that my case was too serious for the magistrate's court. I was going to be tried at the High Court in Harare. Relatives used to visit, encouraging me to be brave because all I wished for was death.

In February 1984 I was in the High Court. They asked me if I knew about my crime. I pleaded guilty and they sentenced me for life [imprisonment]. I have been here in Chikurubi for eighteen years now. I have made a lot of friends. We talk, knit, sing, do Bible study and pray. On Sundays somebody comes in to take us for service. There are a few women who are in here for murder.

I miss my family a lot. Some of my children died while I was here. It is painful. I have now learnt to control my anger. Anger is a bad thing. I have also learnt how to get along with others.

15

Ellen

interviewed by Paidamoyo Magaya

My name is Ellen. I was born in 1952 in Mutare. We are eight in our family and I am the second-born. My parents are late. My father was Obert. My father did piece work in the rural areas. My mother made clay pots. We managed to get education and I managed to attain Standard 6, which I passed, but I could not go further due to financial constraints. This was in 1964. Afterwards I got a job as a housemaid for a certain nurse in Bulawayo. I worked for her for two years. I stayed well with her.

After I left work I came home and started helping my parents and then later, in 1973, I got married. We had a wedding at the magistrates' court. My husband paid the bride-price. It was a lot of money in those days. I am the fourth woman to be married by my husband. The other women left him with their children. The first one had one child when she left. The second one was pregnant and already had another child, the last one was a Suthu, and she had a little girl. His relatives had cast an evil spell on him and that is why they left.

My in-laws received me well. Now I have seven children, five girls and two boys. They are all alive. Their father is a pensioner. Three girls are married, one has a child without a husband, and the other one did not do well. One boy completed his O-level while the last-born, a girl, is in Form 4.

Money is hard to come by. The children were sent home sometimes for not having the school fees. I cannot borrow the money for I will not be able to pay it back. The father's pension is not adequate to cater for all the family's needs. Many a day we sleep without eating any food.

I went to jail because I fought with my aunt, my father-in-law's sister. We fought because she broke my window and stole my knickers[*] when I had gone to Mutare to sell mangoes.

When I came home, I found my bed unmade, though before I had left I had made the bed. I could not find my key: it was not in its usual place. I called my uncle, a senior in the CID, to witness my misfortune. I was scared to get inside the house for I had a baby on my back. He came with another uncle. We went inside the house where I found my wardrobe doors open. We quickly concluded that someone had been looking for money. We waited for three months without taking any action.

My husband then came back from work and I told him the whole story. He asked why I did not contact the police but I told him nothing was missing. We put the incident aside.

At the time, I was still having my periods. After three months I started experiencing severe period pains or I skipped them like a person on some contraceptive method. I then went to the Apostolic Faith Church where the Holy Spirit would communicate with an individual. I sought counsel. The Holy Spirit told me that my house was broken into and my father-in-law's sister had taken my undergarments. I had noticed that they were missing, but I thought my underwear had been lost at the river or I had misplaced them. I started asking around. I went to an elder.

I realised that I was getting seriously ill. I was haemorrhaging. I told the aunt, my father-in-law's sister, that I knew she had taken my clothes and I wanted them back. She closed her door in my face. We tried six times to settle the matter but to no avail. I went to the Chief who told me he had to call ZINATHA.[†]

---

[*] It is believed that before anyone can put a spell, or have a spell put on another person, they must have an intimate garment belonging to the prospective victim.

[†] Zimbabwe National Traditional Healer's Association.

You know how it is with people from the same family. I went to the village committee, who said we had to consult the *n'angas*. We settled for September. Before the due date, the aunt went to the police to report she was being accused of stealing clothes. They asked her who had laid these allegations on her. 'It was Tofa, the member of the village committee,' she told them. He was called and he expressed shock when he saw the aunt at the police station. He asked her why she was there when everyone was waiting for September. The police told them to sort things out first. My aunt wanted to disrupt the flow of the whole procedure because she feared being caught as the culprit.

Then my father-in-law went to plead with the village committee to close the case but it was too late. Instead, Chief Z. took it to Chief M., who gave them his sub-chief and a diviner to work with. We went to a spirit medium, who instructed us not to say anything at all, but she allowed us to ask questions if we had any. The aunt was there too. She was ordered to prepare porridge for me to recover. She was asked why she took my clothes because I was now unwell. 'If she dies what will you say,' the spirit medium asked her. She told me that when we returned I had to go to the aunt's place and have my porridge prepared. We reached home late so the ritual could not be carried out till the following morning. My husband, the aunt, the aunt's brother and me were present.

The aunt prepared the porridge, saying that next time I had to consult her instead of exposing the family's name. I kept quiet. She ate the porridge first and gave me my share. I washed the plate and placed it aside. I then asked for my clothes but the aunt's brother told me to first wait for the effects of the porridge. It is alleged that the underwear had been tied on a reed at a waterfall. I queried if that did not mean more trouble but they told me to be patient. We went back to Chief Z. and explained what had transpired. I asked what would happen if I fell sick again since the aunt had refused to give me back my belongings. He told me to consult the prophets and we were told to quickly leave that place and never come back. (You know these days if you do not have money, you are the criminal as the rich always go scot-free.) The aunt went unpunished.

My husband realised his relatives were wrong. My husband was on my side. It pained me to see him troubled over my sickness. I thought he was going to leave me after seeing all my blood – it used to gush out, I used all the material I could get hold of to stop it. I washed the used clothes at the river at night to save trouble.

Once I fainted because of this. I really feared for our relationship for you know that a woman's blood should not ever be seen. My relatives were not happy but they did not want him to get married again, for they feared he would stop looking after them.

Two weeks later the problem resumed. I went to the aunt with my husband to get my clothes but she told me not to bother her. 'Go to the chief if you have any problems,' she told me. I replied telling her it was useless to go there because I knew who the culprit was. I went back home. Around 10 a.m., while in the garden, I started bleeding. My husband was at work. The blood flowed down my legs. It was uncontrollable.

I headed for the bus stop where she was and told her that I needed my underclothes. She kept on saying I should leave her in peace and she started trying to choke me. I got angry. I started beating her. Her nephew tried to beat me as well but I overpowered them. I took a log from a garden and beat her with it. She could not walk any more. The nephew reported the matter to his uncle. I had left the place of scene. My hands were paining because of the vigorous action I had carried out.

I had beaten her on her legs, her mouth, and her hands. I went home. The relatives stopped the policemen who were on their way to Burma Valley. They asked for me. I was by the roadside. The aunt was bleeding profusely in the mouth. I hit her legs too. When I hit her mouth, she fell. Her dress was soiled with blood. The police took me in; it was in September 1996. They left the aunt at hospital. I was put in a jail cell. I heard the following morning that she had passed away.

I was taken to the high police officials, where I narrated the events as they had taken place. They asked me if I suspected something else could have led to her death. I confessed she died because of the beatings. They took a statement from me. She was buried and I was sentenced to five years of which three were suspended. My crime was culpable homicide. I served my sentence in Shurugwi because Chikurubi was full. There had been a strike and some food riots, so they said we had to relocate to Shurugwi.

The life in prison is not admirable. You have no freedom to do what you want. You lose your dignity. In prison we crocheted doilies or went to the garden. Generally they kept us well. We ate what was available. At times, we had sadza with spinach. We also ate pork. While at Chikurubi I never got a supplement for the pork, which I did not eat. Shurugwi was better for they gave us beef from the Cold Storage Commission. I actually gained weight. I served my sentence hassle free and got out on 24th February 1999. The guards advised me to go home and look after my children.

If you abide by the rules in prison you will be OK. If you misbehave the life will be hard for you. They teach people not to be hard-hearted so they do not commit crimes again. It is hard especially for some of us who have to leave our families behind. Right now I have high blood pressure because I used to think a lot. During the rainy season you wish you were home ploughing in the fields.

After I got out, I went to my home, but my husband's family was angry. Some wished me dead. After my release my relatives decided we had to appease the dead aunt's spirit as per our culture. We went to the Chief who gave us his sub-chief to do the consultations. The spirit demanded Z$10,000, two buckets of millet and a female white goat. The aunt's children were present. The uncle's son asked if that was all and indeed, that was it. We were instructed not to add or reduce the goods. When we were asked if we were all satisfied, we all said yes. We reported our findings to the Chief who told us to go and gather the goods and bring them all one time. My brothers did so. We went back to the chief where we called members of my husband's family. They came and they refused to accept the goods. They were few, they said. Some said the money was not worthy to replace the aunt, it was only enough to buy groceries. We were amazed at their sudden change of behaviour. We left the goods and went home. When we got home, we saw their sub-chiefs coming to our house where they abandoned the goods. My brothers had already left so I had to run to call them back. I gave them the money. I told them what had happened. The goods stayed for some time with us before they were taken to my parents' home. We reported the latest incident to the chief.

Then came Y., a known trouble-maker in the village, a self-proclaimed chief. He said that what we had been told was wrong, we had to go elsewhere. He forced us to go to a diviner whom he had already consulted earlier. His policeman let the cat out of the bag when he told us the diviner already knew our story. We then confronted him but he later denied knowing anything. What this diviner told us left us in a state of shock. She claimed the dead aunt wanted six cattle because we had killed her. My husband was to offer a cow to be slaughtered during the beer brewing, but he was not to eat it. I asked why since he was absent at the time of the offence. We told them we were not satisfied. My brothers refused to pay the cattle. They suggested the matter be taken to another level.

My husband's family started being a nuisance until September when they sent a messenger to tell us to come for a hearing. I was fortunate not to go or they would have killed me there and then. They decided to come to our place. It was on Sunday morning when I saw X. and another man from the neighbourhood coming to our home. They asked if members of my husband's family had come and I said no. They had decided to have a conference at our home without our consent. They went to my in-laws' home where they called M. (They opened my gate as if there was a car coming in.) X. asked the family members what they wanted. The elder one, said he wanted me to go back to my parents and come with the cattle and money as charged. My husband asked 'does this woman', meaning me, 'not have a husband?' because they wanted to chase me away from the home, he was ignored.

Then M. told the boys to do their work. They were armed with hosepipes, sjamboks and J., the teacher, had some handcuffs. He tried to strangle my husband when he asked what they were all doing at his house. There were more than fifty people who had come. This meeting had been arranged at Y.'s place. I was ordered to get into the house and pack my bags. They beat my husband so badly our child started crying. The policeman tried to make 'order' but he was one of them. They tied my husband to the gate. They then dragged him out of the yard. Some blocked me so I could not see what was taking place. All the time they wanted my husband to agree that I had to go. He pleaded with them to let him go. They surrounded the home. When he finally said, 'let the wife go,' I was rooted to the place where I was standing. Then they started beating me. M. was the commander ordering people around.

Now I am disabled, my father-in-law's young brother, the aunt's husband and two uncles beat me. A. and B. were among the men beating me. I sat down, covered my head to shield it from the beatings. My hands got broken. I could not pack my bags. My child dressed me. My clothes were soiled. I went to the hospital like that. I managed to pack one dress and I left. They ululated shouting, 'We have won, she is going.'

97

Women from my husband's family were there. They told me if I wanted to visit my children I had to come with a policeman. Also, if I wanted to collect my remaining 'garbage' I had to come with a policeman. They ululated again. They told me we had to pass through the scene of my crime. I was ordered to clap hands telling the aunt I was going with her to my parents. The policeman was given Z$300 for a job well done. All the way to the clinic we exchanged words with him. He told us to proceed with the journey alone. He also told my brother to pass through Chivhu to say we had taken the child but we refused. We met policemen who knew the story. They told us to get *combis* and go to hospital, their truck was full. We did so. They called the hospital telling them that a patient in a critical condition was coming. I was admitted.

My husband left with the policemen to arrest the culprits. Only one was arrested the rest got summons. They continued saying rubbish and threatening me with death. I had to go to the theatre for my arm was out of shape; it was in a plaster for one and a half months. Now I am disabled. I could not even hold a spoon. My son fed me. My little girl bathed me. Right now I need to see a doctor.

After I was discharged from hospital, we went to the police and asked where we had to go. They told us to go home. I got a peace order in September last year. It is expiring this month. I wanted to go back to the police because I am not happy at all. When I was released from jail all my assets, plates, goats had been stolen.

16

Tabeth

interviewed by Keresia Chateuka

I am Tabeth. I was born in 1945 at Marimira in Shurugwi. We are four in our family, three boys and a girl. Unfortunately all the boys passed away at very tender ages, prompting my father to move away from the rest of his family circle to resettle at Copper Queen in 1977. He suspected that his relatives had bewitched his children. I was an only child. My father had money to send me to school. However, I did not go further than Standard 4 due to poor health. I suffered severe headaches; they were so severe sometimes they left me mentally unstable. I received treatment and I got better. I then joined the Apostolic Church where I met and fell in love with George, the man who is my husband now. My parents are both alive. I have three children, the fourth one passed away in 1997. My first born, a girl, is now married. She and her husband are both employed. The second born is doing Form 4, the third born, Kudzai, is late and the last child is doing Form 2. My husband works in Chakari at a mine. I live in Sanyathi.

Kudzai passed away when she was in Grade 3. She was the reason why I went to prison. I loved her very much as I did, and still do, my other children. Word reached me that she was saying bad words about me at school. Kudzai used to sleep in class and this troubled her teachers. When asked why, she told her friends that she and I did not sleep at night. Instead we spent the night walking from one place to the next looking for people to bewitch. The teachers never discussed Kudzai's situation with me. I heard about it through gossip. I confronted Kudzai and she admitted that it was true. I lost my temper and beat her with a sjambok, then with a cooking stick. She pleaded with me to stop and cried out that I was killing her. I carried on until she was silent. I was very angry I could not control myself. Kudzai lay motionless. I thought she had temporarily passed out and would soon recover.

I went to the shops to buy bread. I made myself some tea, took a bath and still she had not woken up. I realised then that she was dead and I quickly left for Chakari to inform my husband what had happened. I did not know what I was doing I felt as if I had had a black-out. All this happened in the presence of my son, Tawanda. He had run away and hid in the cattle kraal. It did not cross my mind to inform my neighbours. I reached the mine in tears and narrated the event to my husband. He was not convinced. He did not believe my story; he could not believe I could do such a terrible thing. He said we had to go back to our home. Before we left my husband got a telephone call from the police informing him about the death of Kudzai. The police thought I had run away. When I left Regis, my other son, noticed I had boarded a bus while Kudzai was still locked in the house. He informed our neighbours who reported the incident to the village head, who immediately reported the matter to the police. So when the telephone call came, my husband told them I had not run away and we were on our way back. We arrived at the same time with the police.

Our homestead was full of people, mostly our neighbours. That is when I fully realised that I had killed my own daughter. The pain in my heart has not eased. I still think that one day I shall see her again. The police carried the body and took my husband and me to their station. I remained behind while my husband returned home. I gave a statement. They asked me to give the statement a few more times. They examined me and found me to be in a sound state of mind. They took me to Kadoma. The day I appeared in court my husband came to see me. He told me our daughter had been laid to rest. I wailed: I was in pain, such deep grief. When they told me I was going to prison I did not care. I was thinking about my daughter the whole time. Also my husband handled the matter in a manner that I did not expect and this troubled me. He is a quiet man. He did not blame me. I expected him to beat me up and shout at me. It bothered me that he remained controlled throughout. The court sentenced me to five years; two of which were suspended. I served the remaining three years.

They took me to Chikurubi Prison where other female prisoners were. At Chikurubi I registered my name, surrendered my personal things and got a uniform. I was told to adjust to the new life. The prison guards took me to where other inmates were, most of whom had crimes similar to mine. These included those who had murdered their husbands or children. We were not many in our group as most crimes committed by women were stealing and baby-dumping. Since our group was not allowed to work outside, we did nothing but sit most of the time. Others worked in the garden, cut firewood, cooked meals and swept. We woke up in the morning, bathed, and went for roll call and then for tea. We were counted twice, in the morning and evening. We had sadza and vegetables or beans for lunch. Beef was scarce, maybe once per week. There was a clinic and a nurse to attend to those who were sick.

Life in jail is hard. Your mind gets restless, especially in my case, as I dreaded the inevitable, seeing my daughter's grave. I lost my appetite at times. I found it difficult to eat. Fellow inmates tried to comfort me, urging me to forgive myself. I did not have problems with the prison guards. Obedience is the key if you want to avoid trouble with the guards. Sometimes they could be quite insulting, addressing me as murderer. Again my inmates consoled me. We slept in a big building with bunk beds. Everyone had two blankets each.

My husband came every month, my children came sometimes but other relatives did not. I was released in August 2000. The day before my release my mind was in turmoil. I asked myself many questions for which I had no answers. How was I going to face my daughter's grave? Was I going to be allowed to live in the village with my family? The prison guards gave me my clothes to wash. On the day of release I went to Kadoma in a prison vehicle. They gave me a warrant and I left for my husband's workplace. I stayed there for two weeks before I went to the village.

When I arrived home I found out that people's attitude towards me had changed. My friends never wanted to speak to me. They told their children to run away from me because I was a murderer. I felt like I had started to serve another sentence. I left for the homestead. I was deeply hurt especially when I saw my daughter's grave. I threw a small stone on her grave, according to our culture and mourned her till it hurt. I asked her to forgive me. Even now I always make time to go and talk to her asking for forgiveness. This is the time I finally accepted that my child was no more.

I got a warm reception from my children. I learnt that that my parents came to bury their granddaughter. They also came to check on the family when I was in prison. When I returned from prison, I went to stay with them for a while. During the first days they did not want me to be alone, they feared that I would hurt myself, commit suicide perhaps. Whenever I went to a funeral, people kept a safe distance away from me. It was clear in their eyes that they regarded me as a danger. I was now an outcast. My husband and I went to the village head with a hen to ask for pardon. He accepted our hen, as a token of our apology. I am now a Christian, and am always praying to God for forgiveness. I want people to know that it is wise to be slow to anger. If you are provoked, wait till you calm down then you can take action. We are now settled in the village though my spirit is still tormented. Telling the story is a painful experience for me and I do not think I will repeat it. I do not know what evil had possessed me to do such a thing.

Section 4:

Fraud

17

Mercy

interviewed by Tawona Mtshiya

I will begin with my background. Firstly, I'm 26 years old. I was born in 1975 in Bulawayo. We are a family of six, three boys and three girls, me being the fourth. We moved to Harare where I did my education. I went as far as the university. I acquired a BBS, Honours, and I started working for a division of the United Nations. I was an assistant project researcher, and then I moved on to Citrus Estates, where I worked as the sales and marketing administrator for about three years.

Unfortunately, when I was still at university, my parents divorced due to some problems which I've never understood. Life became very tough for us, so I had to start being very responsible at an early age, and taking care of my mother. After my parents divorced, my father sold the house and that left us homeless. So my money was needed urgently for us to be able to acquire accommodation, as my elder sisters were married. (You know when you get married in the African society; you cannot keep coming back home.)

My eldest brother was a student pilot; he couldn't get any money to look after us. Life was very tough even though I was working because I was responsible for my young brothers as well.

Unfortunately, and maybe because I didn't know God then, I tried all means to make the ends meet – I would do this and do that, scrounge, work overtime, work other jobs in order to get money for a living. In a way it was a blessing because I learnt a lot of things: how to cook, hold functions, how to withstand pressure, especially during weekend jobs.

My mother appreciated my hard work but I would not disclose anything to her especially about where I would have got the money. But, frankly, when I was at Citrus Estate, I think I got into bad company. Unfortunately, I made friends with someone and I thought we could make quick money. We had a very poor accounting system and I was in charge. Anything could go leaking or missing and hardly anybody will find out.

During discussions, my friend advised me that we could get one or two things without the company noticing. I didn't put much thought into it, all I thought was money. We defrauded Citrus Estate of 30 tons of maize and 30 tons of soya beans and split the money.

By that time I was married, so it was tough because my mother and my husband wanted me to explain where this excess money was coming from. They knew I came home sometimes with an extra Z$3,000 to Z$5,000, but not Z$75,000 at one time. With so much money, the only things you can buy are things like furniture or property, but it is difficult to spend it because everybody wants to know where you got the money. I realised that this was a bad move. I had a guilty conscience. My friend said, 'Let's go for another bite. Let's do it again. Let's enjoy the money again.' But I felt guilty. I was a Christian by then and I was feeling guilty every time I looked at my boss and saw how he really cared for me, how he put all his trust in me. I resigned and everyone was excited. I was expecting a baby so I used this as an excuse saying, 'I am not feeling well, but once I am fine I will get a job.' People accepted it but my husband smelt a rat because I would still spend money, buy fancy clothes for him, and spoil him. Fortunately, or unfortunately, the auditors came and our little game was discovered, and even though I had resigned they traced me. This happened in 1999.

I was at home with my husband, I hadn't given birth, there was about a month to go. By then, my friend had been arrested and she was in remand; it was difficult to take her to court without me. And like anybody else, she was pushing the blame on to me because I wasn't there to answer for myself. She was trying to clear her name. Then it so happened that about three days before my delivery, I went to town to see my gynaecologist, and to sort out a few medical bills. (I still had a bit of money.) As I was coming out of the bank, this CID dressed in a suit looked at me. I didn't know he was a CID. I just saw this guy nodding. Then before I could walk any further, two guys are following me. I think who are these people? My heart beats fast. I think, 'It's them, the police.' I tried to walk faster but I was in the city centre, you can't run, you can't do anything. And this CID was so big and round, and he just walks very fast as well and he comes up to me and says, 'Excuse me, are you Mercy?' I said, 'No, I'm not.'

'Look at the photo,' he says. 'I know you are Mercy, the former Sales Administrator for Citrus Estates.' The other guy said, 'Look I know you. I came to Citrus Estates dealing with another fraud case and I met you. You are now caught. Look at this picture. I'm taking it to the *Herald* today. Tomorrow, or the day after, you are going to appear in the paper. You are running away?'

I said, 'Yes I am.' He looks at me and says, 'But why? You are expecting a baby. Why are you doing this? Speak to me.' He is not making noise – he is not attracting a crowd, people hardly know there is a problem. People are just passing by doing their normal business. So I said to him, 'Please can we talk?' Then he said, 'What do you want?' I said, 'Look, even today I could go into labour. Please can I give you any amount you want and let me give birth to my baby. Then you can come and get me afterwards.' The guy said, 'I cannot do this because I'm not allowed. I'm with someone.' But he looked attracted to the idea of money. He said, 'How much can you give me?' I said about Z$20,000. He said, 'No.' I said, 'About Z$40,000. I'm not worried about how much I spend but I just want to be with my baby.' I'm thinking 'Prison and baby, they cannot go hand in hand.' Then he said, 'I would like to help you but unfortunately, I'm with somebody else. I'm stuck. I've got no choice.'

So they took me to the police station to the fraud squad. They spoke to their superiors. 'Here is this prisoner we have been looking for. We need to go with her to Bindura.' I still haven't phoned or communicated with anyone. The first person I think of phoning is my brother-in-law, my sister's husband, because we have been very close. So I phoned him. He says, 'I have to come and get you, but did you phone your husband?' I said, 'I can't. How do I tell him this.' He said, 'At the end of the day you have to be honest. You have to tell him this, but anyway I'm coming over there.' He speaks to those CIDs. He is a prominent man, and he tries to use his influence. The CID says, 'No, I cannot let her go, she should have told me she is your relative right in the beginning. I've already brought her to my superiors.' So my brother-in-law says, 'Okay I'm going to send somebody to take you to Bindura in a car, to drive you to Bindura.'

I go to sleep in the cell. Finally, around midnight, my brother-in-law and family have decided to approach my husband. He is very short tempered and cannot understand some of these things, but he had no choice, he just had to come down to prison. I think they came around around 1 a.m. They were not allowed to see me, they had to wait until 6 a.m.

Even then, I couldn't open up. I couldn't be honest about what had happened. Instead, I said, 'I'm being framed.' But my husband said, 'I know you are not being honest. This explains the life we have been living.' I told my brother-in-law the truth. I went to court the same day I was given bail of Z$10,000. As I got home at evening, I went into labour and I gave birth to a baby girl. My mother decided to call her, Bongani.

But, unfortunately there is a sad story to that too. Now I had two children to look after on remand. My son Sipho, who is five, and his baby sister Bongani. It wasn't working. Problems started erupting between my husband and me. He is telling me that he doesn't trust me any more. (Now my husband is being supportive, though he goes on complaining.)

You know, when you are on remand, you have to be in court every two weeks – back and forth, back and forth. I had to report to a police station every Monday and I had to go to court in Bindura every month. So it was a problem for the little baby but my remand wasn't for very long. Then I went on trial. By that time my baby was five months old.

You know with a trial, they want you today; they want you tomorrow. They don't care whether you are coming from Harare or Masvingo, whether you have transport problems or whether you have got a little baby. They don't care. You can't argue with the magistrate. It was tiresome for me because within one week maybe I would have to go to Bindura three times. I got sentenced in April 2000. I remember it well. I was given six years in prison one year of which was suspended for good behaviour, two years suspended if I pay back the Z$351,000 to Citrus Estates and two years for me to serve. If I don't pay the money back, I will serve four years.

I went to prison. I took my baby with me. She was still very young. You know the conditions in prison especially when you are new and not on good social terms with officers. So you can't say, 'Can I have warm water – or this and that – for my baby, please?' When you ask, you are sometimes told, 'This is not home. You knew that you wanted to look after your baby very well. So why did you commit a crime?' You keep getting reminded that you are a prisoner.

I remember my first visit, the day after my sentence, in April. I spoke to my mother. I was in tears. She came with my brother, my sisters, everybody came. I said, 'I can't look after Bongani in here. It's cold, she didn't bath last night, and she didn't bath this morning. I can't get milk for her.' My mother said, 'Look, we will see what we can do, maybe we will take her.' Like every other parent they were trying to prepare an appeal for me. My father says, 'You are coming home, I will do everything to bring you back home.' I have this hope that I'm going home any time. They gave me extra uniform and I said, 'No, I'm going home,' because at that time I believed my family had the power to do anything. Little did I know that once you are in prison, that is it.

After two weeks my baby started to show deteriorating health, she couldn't eat anything. She cried most of the time. I asked to see a doctor. You know how it is with the inmates, you ask them and they said, 'You should push, you can see a doctor.' I tried and I was told they couldn't do that; they couldn't let Bongani see a doctor. So when my family came I asked them to take her. They took her home. Then I was transferred from Bindura Prison to Chikurubi Female Prison. After about a month I was in Chikurubi my baby passed away. That was the most painful part.

Then I realised I wasn't going to go home until I'd served my sentence and I had problems with my in-laws. They came and humiliated me in prison and they blamed me for their son's downfall, for the loss of their granddaughter. Everybody could make a story out of it. It was so tough for me that I started getting sick, mainly from stress. I remember very well at one time some prisoners even said that I had AIDS.

During that tough time I met a friend, an old lady. Older than me. She was a devoted Christian. She was always there for me. She would come and share and talk and I could get the wound off. She told me that I must receive Jesus Christ as my saviour. She said, 'Mercy, when you are with God you are not going to be sick, believe me.' It was tough. It was very difficult because I thought that to survive I must live on tablets, Stopayne.

Anyway Jubilant and me got very close and I have changed. I'm very glad. I'm very glad for her and I want God to bless her, for she saved my soul. I just changed. I try to look back. I don't know where but I know I changed. I realised the power from God. I realised all my errors and where I was going wrong. I realised where I was cheating myself and cheating God and I turned my life to Jesus. I'm happy to say from then on I have peace of mind and my health has changed. I accepted prison; there is a time for it. I will go home one day.

Jubilant said to me, 'Mercy, I want you to pray. I want us to pray. I want to spend the whole week praying. We want your mother-in-law to come back and apologise for what she did to you, the embarrassment and humiliation she caused you.' I said, 'That is impossible, we can pray for something else.' She said, 'You know you are being unfair to God. You are trying to say your mother-in-law has power over God.'

During that time when I was praying I could see visions. I remember once I was sleeping. There was a lady who was sick. She was a friend of mine. I saw white, just white and I heard a voice coming down, saying to me, 'You must pray for Zodwa' and I was scared. When I woke up the following morning, I told Jubilant. She was happy. She said, 'Mercy, you have got the Holy Spirit in you. I can feel it sometimes when I pray with you. I feel the power.' I was so happy I wanted to spread the news to my family.

So when my mother came the first time afterwards, I said to her, 'I dreamt last night you would come to see me wearing these green clothes.' My mother laughed, and she was happy. Every time I write my sister a letter, I say, 'I've dreamt this and that.' She asked, 'how did you know?' And I tell her that I'm getting close to God and all those problems are going far away from me.

I'm glad to say God does work, because my mother-in-law pitched up. It was a month after we had made a prayer. I had forgotten because to be very frank I wasn't really expecting her. However, she just pitched up and when I was called to the gate I thought it was my mother or sister or my usual family or my friends. I went to the gate and I saw my mother-in-law. The thing that I can't believe is that she is dropping tears for me after all the pain she has taken me through. She told me how much she cares for me and she apologised. She asked me to pray, and I said 'I am praying.' I was so happy for that. I wanted to share the joy, because I could feel I was getting back into track. I was becoming a human being again.

110

You know you have day-to-day problems in prison. You know how it is. People quarrel, fight; get jealous over petty things. You know how it is with females: they don't like each other for certain reasons such as, 'Oh! She thinks she is so educated.' 'Oh! She thinks she is so superior.' Things like that. But now I could withstand it. At some point somebody will come and say, 'Did you know so and so said this?' And I answer, 'No problem.' Maybe they expect you to ignore that person. You know how women are. 'I will ignore you because you said this.' But I would talk and laugh as if I had heard absolutely nothing, and just give them love you know.

People would say things like, 'Oh! She just wants to share everything she has. She likes to give things away.' Not that I'm rich but I thought the little I have I should share with someone who doesn't have. What's the use of keeping three pairs of something when somebody has got absolutely nothing. Now I know God is a giving God. When you give you will receive and that is true. I'm here to testify to that. So many times I gave away what was mine, what I still wanted but I just said, 'God says just give to one who doesn't have.' Friends have brought me little things – soap, all sorts of petty things – and I realise that you give and you receive. I couldn't go to bed without talking to God.

That place was a very tough place. You wake up today, the rules have changed. Whichever officer decides: today you don't use this pathway, you use that pathway. Oh! My God, they don't care. They just change the rules whenever they like. Somebody can just make up a story because they don't like you. They tell the officers and you are in big trouble. Nobody wants to testify in your favour.

I would watch people die – Zodwa, for example – or speak of dying and I said God please help me. I know you are going to take me one day and God I want to be with my family. The most important thing I wanted to share with them is the inner me, the new part of me. I wanted them to experience it with me. I just wanted to show whoever is near me that I'm no longer that old Mercy. I wanted to be able to help where I knew my family was going wrong. I wanted to be able to join hands with them and stand in the middle and I was able to do that.

The treatment in prison, honestly speaking, depends on who you are. If you are somebody from a well-off family, when you get sick, you see a doctor. The prison doctor comes or you say, 'Listen, my family can bring my doctor.' And, by the end of the day, you will have seen a doctor. If you are just a normal person having nobody coming to see them, you are bound to suffer. You get sick, there is no doctor. Who cares? You are told so many stories, 'You are a prisoner, these are not your privileges,' and the like. But you also meet born-again officers who remind you that you have got a future; that it's not the end of the world being in prison. It is not everybody who is bad. Unfortunately, they don't have much authority to help you but at least they remind you that there is God. It's a comfort.

We were only two graduates in the whole prison of roughly 450 prisoners. There is not much education on the female side. Instead, if you want school, want education, you hear, 'Who do you think you are? You think you are so educated. You don't want to garden, you don't want to work because you want to read.' Such things will bring you down. There is a typing school and if I had to do something, it might have been computers but I realised I would be wasting my time. There was sewing club that was very helpful. I learnt how to sew, do patchwork, embroidery and candlewick work. I learnt how to draw free hand on cushions and so on for embroidery purposes. I really enjoyed it. Sewing is the skill that I mainly acquired – of course if you see someone doing such a thing, you can say, 'Please, can you teach me to do that.' We taught ourselves. We were even teaching the officers. There was also a dressmaking and tailoring officer. She is very good. She taught us on the machine, but as far as handwork is concerned we were teaching them instead.

In prison, you are classified according to your sentence. If you are serving a short period – two months, six months, eight months – you are bound to go to the garden, but if you are serving two or more years, you go to sewing, or knitting or typing. When you have maybe three months left, then you can expect to go to the garden. If you are in sewing and doing good even if you have two months left, you still remain in sewing because you are needed. You sew uniforms and clothes for the prison officers: we were doing a lot of things for them so they will rather have you in sewing.

When we wake up in the morning, we first clean our rooms and have a bath, make sure our uniforms are washed and clean and have breakfast. In our cell we were ten. It wasn't a big cell. It was free. It was not that bad. It was fine. You were comfortable. We were not so squashed. There were times when you were squashed for two, three days, but then they were bound to move people out to other free cells. I was fine in my cell though some people complained.

We had a mat. You know the normal mat like a carpet and you have your own blankets, everybody will have six blankets. If you have a special case like maybe chest problems, operations, asthma, you could get up to as many as ten blankets. So you do your bed, make sure your place is clean, neat, because they came for inspection every day after you have finished cleaning.

After that we would go and work: gardening, sewing, typing and the like. At 12:00 p.m., we break for lunch, queue up for food, have our lunch. The advantage was that you just leave the dishes: the ladies from the kitchen will do the dishes. You rest for about thirty minutes and then you go back to work. At three we break, 3.30 you come for supper. From 3.30 to around 4.30 p.m. you are expected to do your washing, relax and so on. At around 4.30 in the evening you are locked in your cell until the following morning: between 5.30 and 6.00.

It is a long time in the cell, but you can't read. You know we come from different social backgrounds. In that cell if you read, maybe there are three or four people who think, 'Who the hell does she think she is? She wants to read.' They will sing, and make noise just to distract you. You will come to a point when you think, 'No! This person is obviously stressed and she is just taking out her stress on me.' So you just get in your blankets and cover your head. You start thinking of home. You get stressed again because somebody is trying to stress you, because if you had been reading you wouldn't be thinking of home or searching yourself. The problems come when you are thinking all that time until the following morning.

You also get bullies. They will just shout, 'I will fight you. I will hit you. I will do this.' They will swear, and be rude regardless of older women. It is bad. We are not separated. You look at someone old and you think what if she was my mother, but you hear someone my age saying, 'I will hit you, I will kick you. What are you doing in prison, when females of your age are looking after grandchildren?' It is painful because she will come back and say, 'What are you doing in prison when girls of your age are at work?' Sometimes, you meet even older people who want to fight. Oh! Yes, they would fight. 'You stole my this ...' and they will shout at each other: 'You are in prison for rape ... You were stealing ... You are penniless.' All sorts of things. You know it's a small place. So rumours are spread. You can't really keep a secret. That is how tough the situation can be during that time when you are locked in from 4:30 p.m. till the following morning.

Everybody is supposed to get two visits a month, one every fortnight, but there are some people who don't get any visits at all. Then there are the fortunate ones, who get visits once a week, though sometimes they say, 'No she had a visit last week, you can't see her.' I have a very supportive family. They were always there for me. If my parents couldn't come, my sisters, my brothers will send someone instead. All my friends were very supportive. I must be honest. There was never a time when I miss anyone. I always had somebody coming to see me.

Visits are fine but you can't talk much. I can't start telling them what I'm telling you now. There is an officer there and you are not supposed to tell anyone from outside what is happening inside. I will give an example. There was a girl, an escapee, but unfortunately, she didn't win. She got caught. But during the time when she was nowhere to be found, the male officers beat us all. But in prison you have no friends. There is no one you can trust. You are on your own unless that friend and you are both true in Christ. Anyway this girl escaped. They searched for her, but they couldn't find her. It was terrible because so many people were really hurt. At the end of it, a doctor had to come in. Everybody was beaten. I think some people are still now carrying scars and wounds.

These are some of the things you want to share with your family, but you cannot. I remember one lady did tell her sister and she got in deep trouble after her relatives had left. But she was clever enough to say, 'Listen if you give me problems for telling the truth, I will give you more problems.' I think the warders realised that this could mean trouble. So though they promised her punishments and beatings, nothing happened. I think they came to their senses.

With visits you have no secrets. If there is a problem at home, and your family tell you this and that, the whole prison will know because the officer sitting next to you will tell a prisoner and that prisoner will rejoice in your downfall or in your problems. She will spread the rumours. By the time you go to bed everybody will know about your problems. You can't trust the officer sitting next to you unless she is your friend, and then she will sympathise and keep quiet.

I served two years. My family paid the Z$351,050, so my restitution was paid. And I came out in April this year. My family accepted me with a lot of compassion and sympathy. My brother said that it is a load off his shoulders, to have me back at home. Everybody told me to relax. Enjoy your freedom. We laugh about the experiences, even my sister's children will say, 'Auntie, remember that girl . . .' or whatever. There is no mistrust because they can feel that it is no longer me, but Christ. So they are telling me to take my time and this is a big relief to me.

Firstly, this feeling comes from God; secondly, we should give credit to our families. If your parents stand firm behind you, everybody else will. People may talk behind your back, but once they are within your vicinity they will try and respect you. My relatives, those that my parents were open and straight with, showed me sympathy. I don't want to see things that will hurt me. I don't have to say it out that I'm changed. They will see it. I don't have to tell them. I want them to see it on their own.

My best friend is Jesus. He is setting the agenda for me. Many people in the community don't know that I was in prison for two years. Maybe they thought I was somewhere abroad. Even though I was quite naughty I wasn't so naughty that people could think I would end up in prison. The few that do know just show me a humble attitude. 'Oh! We are happy you are back home.' People are not saying things like, 'Don't do it again.' No, and I am happy for that.

You know your release date in advance. So the last month drags. I was counting the days. Every time somebody came to see me, I would say, 'Don't forget I'm coming home on the 16th'. I was so excited. The last week I couldn't sleep. The day I went home I was so happy.

It was raining and this old lady who had been sentenced for life came to me and said, 'Mercy, do you believe in God?' I said, 'Yes I do.' She said, 'What does rain mean? God loves water you know. It means your life is already washed clean.' And she just gave me a hug. Before that I was asking myself, 'Why does it have to rain when I'm about to go home!'

All my family came at around 8 o'clock in the morning. My sisters, my brothers, my mother, my cousins, my friends and the funny part was my husband came as well. He hadn't been supportive, you know. He would come just when he felt like it and I had already heard that he was living in with some other female. So, you know how it is with families, they all had like cast him out. Let him be happy with whoever. Anyway, he just pitched up, but I was not aggressive. I was very good. I told him, I'm happy I'm out. With my family, it was hugs and tears because when I was in prison I lost my brother-in-law. The one I had confided in. He was very supportive. Two months later I lost a sister, so I had lost two people in two years.

Before we went home I said, 'We are going to pray.' My sister said, 'You can't be serious,' and I said, 'Yes I am.' We prayed just outside the prison fence. And then we drove home.

We were happy. It was on the 16th and the 18th was Independence Day. They said we are going to have a party to welcome you home. My son had grown so big and he was asking, 'Mummy were you at work? Are you going back to work?' I said, No I'm not because I hated seeing you over the gate. I always wanted you to come in so that we could play together.'

That night I slept with my mother and my son. My mother gave a very powerful prayer. I liked it because when she finished she said, 'Sipho, pray,' and he prayed even though he was mumbling. I said, 'God bless him' and I was happy because they had raised my child in a way that I wouldn't have difficulties in getting him under control. That was my first day out.

So I am not with my husband any more. I made my decision that I will look after my child and I will communicate with him but I will not live with him. Right now I'm in the family business though I'm not yet established. My sister and my brothers go to Britain, and they buy clothes and we sell them here; and we sell stationery to Citrus Estates, Stock Exchange, the Metropolitan Bank and so on. I source orders, mainly in clothing because stationery orders are very time-consuming. It's not very easy. But I can really talk. I can talk them into buying; I use my sales and marketing skills well.

Finally I would say that prison was a very tough place, but it's up to you to make something of it. You should think someone has lived in prison for ten years, even for 22 years in there, and has managed. It will be the worst place if you are not a principled person and if you don't humble yourself. I really don't know how to phrase it but in Shona they say, '*Wauya panzvimbo pevanhu*'* . Let them rule, let them take control. If they say today you are doing this, let it be, because God is with you. That day can be tough but there is always tomorrow. Whoever said, 'Problems are here to stay,' was lying. Problems are here to pass.

If the warder says, 'Run,' run: it does not matter if you were driving a Benz at home. We used to say look at whoever is telling you, 'Clean my shoes'. You know we judge ourselves on our financial status: where do I live? Do I have a satellite

---

* You have come to a place that does not belong to you.

dish? And so on. And when we look at that person, we realise it does not matter if she is only earning so much, she is happy, she has got freedom and she has got her children. So do what she wants you to do, the day will pass anyway. You will not be shining her shoes from morning to sunset. It is not going to cost a bit. You even live better because, at the end of the day, you won't have problems with them. She will not say you are stubborn. If you are stubborn, it is the one who is up there who will bring you up. At the end of the day they will respect you for not boasting and they will lift you up. This is what I discovered about prison. Don't try and fight the authority, not at all.

My advice to women is that it's good to be honest and it pays. You need a straightforward life and you will see the fruits you will bear. Be open and know what you want. I have been in prison; it is not a place to be. There could have been a purpose for me because it has awakened me and I'm seeing the real world. I was blinded before. But I am not saying go to prison and learn those things. For me God had a purpose but for you his purpose might not be in prison. So it all starts with honesty. As long as it is the truth, people will accept it, even if it hurts. You will hurt me more if you lie to me. If you don't want to end up in prison, you must be honest and be hardworking.

You know there is a lady, a vendor, at our church who is happy with a profit of maybe four or five dollars. She is living. She pays tithes. She is happy because she is hardworking. She is honest with her God. She is not going to pinch things to sell. Whatever you are selling as long as it is blessed you won't have to beg. Somehow God will provide. It all comes when you are honest and hardworking and you give yourself to God. I want to tell women never ever to want quick money. Be careful of who you socialise with. You can't blame someone if you accepted whatever they said. Do not admire things in a friend that are worthless in life. Right now most of my friends have gone to Britain so what I do is to play the radio that has become my friend.

The friend I had at Citrus Estates served time in prison as well but as she had gotten arrested two months earlier than me so she was released two months earlier. We were good friends – buddies – when we were outside but in prison there were times when we did not talk to each other, or see each other at all.

Jubilant asked me why. People laughed and said these are the co-accused, they are suppose to be friends but look at them they are enemies. But I am glad she was born again as well. So we could stand for each other mainly as far as the heart was concerned. We were there for each other because she lost her husband when we were in prison, even though they were divorced, he was the father of her children. She lost her sister as well. So she went through a very tight time. She also got sick and suffered from stress but she caught up and I am very happy. I talk to her sometimes on the phone. She is about ten years older than me and she says to me I hope you are not being naughty and I say I hope you are not either. She says, 'You know me I am an adult. I think straight now.'

She did not have O-levels, but she had a job and she was enjoying her money. So she never thought of going back to school. When she was in prison she wrote her O-levels in English, Commerce and Bible Knowledge. She only passed two, but I was happy because she used that time wisely. I help her but sometimes I lose patience and I walk out. Then eventually we smile at each other and we get together again. I am glad because she gave me the credit on her last Sunday at the prisoners' church.

On her last Sunday she stood up to say farewell to everybody. She said, 'You know prisoners? I want to tell you when Mercy got arrested there was a time when we were enemies, but I want to tell you that God came between us and we are friends in Christ now. I owe her because I have got a certificate to carry home. She was patient enough to help me with my O-levels. She taught me for free.'

It is nice when prisoners are going home. You see 15 to 20 people standing up and saying that this was a good person, and you feel good. In the world, who has time to say you are a good person or realise the good in you? Nobody.

Sometimes I meet some of these prison officers and we talk, I do not run away and I do not feel ashamed because I was not a problem when I was inside. One warder has been home to visit me, and this makes me realise that my time inside is really over.

18

Fortunate

interviewed by Keresia Chateuka

My name is Fortunate. I was born in 1960 in Rusape. When I was five years old, my parents separated. My father died in 1986. He was a caring and loving father and he was the one who raised me with the assistance of his second wife. We were seven children in the family but three died and now only four of us remain: one boy and three girls. My father sent me to school – I went up to Form 4 at a secondary school in Chipinge. My father used to work with horses in Harare. When my parents separated, my mother went back to her people in Makoni in Rusape, and this is where she still lives with another child whom she had after she left my father.

When I completed Form 4, I did not manage to get any training because it was during the war and we lived in a 'keep'.* As a young woman my movements were restricted and many young women had a lot of problems. However, in the keep I met the man who was to become my husband. He was born in Chipinge but grew up in Mutare. He worked in the road department, repairing roads. We married in 1978 and his family was good to me: we got on well. We had five children, Mazvita, a daughter who is now married, Esnath who is now also married, then Kudzai, Rudo and Tendai. Two are in the UK and one is in South Africa.

---

* A 'keep' the colloquial name for what the Rhodesian forces called 'protected villages' but which were often viewed more as prisons, as both movement in and out was subject to surveillance, in order to 'protect' villagers from the enemy: the freedom fighters.

I went to prison and this is how I landed there. I was working at a secondary school in Penhalonga after doing a secretarial course at a college in Mutare. As you know, sometimes when a wife works, the husband stops providing for the family: that was exactly what happened between my husband and me, so I failed to meet the day-to-day living expenses.

At the school, it was my duty to collect fees from the pupils and I started to steal the money. Then I used to lend the money to other people, especially teachers, at a high interest. It was stupid of me to do that but I did not stop. I went on doing this for a long time until someone reported me to the school authorities. Then my luck ran out. One day the headmaster asked me to hand over all the accounts books for checking. I immediately fell sick and did not report for work for a week. That made the headmaster more suspicious. On the day I went back to work I told the headmaster that I had lent some money to somebody who wanted to buy a car and that the person had not returned the money. I lied. I handed over the accounts books and whatever little money I had. He never asked me a question; he immediately reported the matter to the police who came to pick me up. It did not occur to me that I could ask to pay back the money. I could have borrowed from relatives. It was about Z$40,000, and that, in those days, was a lot of money. In fact by this time I did not have a clear idea of who owed me what and how much because I had used the money for personal things. I did not recover any of it; people took advantage of the fact that I had been arrested. Although my husband did not have the details of what I was doing he was aware that I was handling a lot of money. He even borrowed from me sometimes. However, after my release from prison, I was shocked to hear him say that he never knew about what I was doing with the school funds, and that I took the money to give my relatives.

I was taken to Penhalonga Police Station on a Friday. I stayed there for four days. It was in June and I cannot remember feeling that cold ever before. I asked the police to let my husband bring me blankets from home. They understood and they let him bring me blankets. I cannot describe the police cells because I cannot find the words to describe them. The walls, for example, were covered in human dung. I was the only woman in the cells, the rest were men. Fortunately, I was in my own cell. At lunchtime I asked for a few minutes to wash myself with cold water.

Men did not bother to wash. In any case the police were reluctant to give us time for such things. They only allowed us to collect food brought from home by family. Other than that, the police did not harass me. They asked for the usual, a statement from me. I never changed my statement: this was that I had indeed stolen money from the school. In court they asked me if I had stolen money and I told them, 'Yes I stole.' They sent me home on free bail. After two weeks I went back to court for sentencing. Before passing judgment they asked me if I had anything I wanted them to consider. I told them that I had a family to look after. I was sentenced for three years or I was to repay all the money and then do community service for two months. I chose to do community service at the police camp.

I went to my relatives to borrow money but no one could help me. I thought it was better to sell the fridge at home to raise money so I did that. I raised about Z$10,000 and I went to Mutare where I had to pay it at the Charge Office. As soon as I arrived in town I got into more trouble. After I got off the bus, as I walked towards the Charge Office I came across some young men who said they had a bale of second-hand clothes for sale. I do not know what got into me but I told them I wanted to buy them. I thought I would be able to raise more money and pay off the money I had stolen, all at once. I gave them all the money I had. The boys walked me towards Girls High School. Just after crossing a little bridge we came to a treed spot. They told me to wait there while they went to look for the rest of the group. That was when I realised that they were thieves. I was left standing all by myself.

I walked back to the Charge Office. I went to the Clerk of Court to pick up my file and went to court. After calling out my name the court official asked me to pay the money. I told him that my money had been stolen but he did not believe me. He asked why I had not reported the theft to the police. That is how I went to jail for a year and six months. My husband came and promised to sell our car to raise the money but he failed in the end. When I heard that I was going to Chikurubi Prison, I could not believe it. I worried about what my husband thought about me. His behaviour had changed since my arrest. He did not believe that the money was stolen. I had not managed to explain fully to him what had happened to the money I intended to pay for restitution. I sat in a group waiting to be transported to prison.

As soon as I arrived at Mutare Prison I was issued with a uniform and blankets. I felt like a small child, quite helpless and only waited for instructions. Wearing shoes or even slippers was forbidden at Mutare Prison. One walked barefoot all the time unless you had a medical excuse. I found out that the relationship between women prisoners and prison guards was not good. It is an area that could do with improvement. I think prison guards need thorough training on how to look after prisoners. They never had a good word about us. Their language was vulgar. They shouted obscenities that I cannot repeat. People did not observe good manners. You came out of prison worse off than you were before. It is impossible to come out with an improved character and I hope that other prisons in the world are better than ours. From the books I read and the films I watch, I see that other prisons in other countries are different. They care about the mental or spiritual rehabilitation of a prisoner. In Zimbabwe prisons are only concerned with inflicting physical pain. The real person, the inner person, is left untouched and unchanged. That is why people go back to prison so often because the prison system does not make an effort to influence you to behave better. I think prisons should separate inmates according to the crime they committed and not to put all criminals together: petty thieves, those who sold *mbanje* and murderers are thrown in together. This is what happened in Mutare Prison. The inmates learnt from each other. That was what I noted. There was nothing to do. We were locked in at four o'clock in the afternoon and the doors remained locked until the following day. What else could people do behind the locked doors except talk about criminal activities? We did role-plays sometimes. One person would pretend to be a judge, and the other would be a prosecutor and so on. We carried out our own trials, advised each other on what to say. This is why in remand prison people change their statements when they go back to court, and sometimes the advice works in their favour.

The sleeping arrangements at Mutare Prison were bad. To start with, the toilet is inside the cell. Now, using a toilet is a private matter, you need to use it alone without anybody watching you. The toilet could not be flushed from inside so at night all the inmates had to force themselves not to use a toilet. If one of us had to use the toilet at night it meant that all of us inside would suffer the bad smell until the following morning. Even though sometimes the person who used the toilet covered it with a blanket, it really did not work. I stayed at Mutare Prison for three months. At first my husband used to come but with time he stopped.

You know how it is in our culture. I was not fit to be a wife because I was in prison. People encouraged him to leave me because they thought I had stolen money and gave it to my relatives. So my husband stopped his visits. My own relatives did not come. I did not know whether they knew what had happened to me. Or if they knew, then they did not know what day and time to come. Communication was a problem. I am confident that they would have come.

After three months I went to Chikurubi Prison. This time I had arrived at a real prison. As soon as I set my foot in the prison I was issued with blankets and a uniform. The inmates had already had their sadza but they gave me some left-over food. I went to the reception room where the new prisoners got told the rules and regulations. I knew to a large extent what to expect because of my stay in Mutare Prison. I found the interrogation by fellow inmates quite intense. They wanted to know details of my crime: what it was, how I committed it and the sentence. The relationship between the prison guards and inmates did not encourage reform. What was lacking in prisons was counselling. Churches did their best to help prisoners become better people, but what was required was professional counselling.

We used to work. I arrived at Chikurubi during the rainy season and we used to go out to cut grass in the rain. Cutting grass with grass-slashers is usually a man's job but we did it all the same. We used to get soaked in the rain and we did not always have change clothes. Prisoners with babies and those who were pregnant shared the same cell. My husband did not visit at Chikurubi; he only came just before the end of the sentence. However, my relatives in Harare used to come especially on public holidays. I appreciated it very much. It was a demonstration of their love for me. I was afraid of rejection. I do not think that it is wise of the people not to visit their relatives in prison because you never know; tomorrow it could be them behind bars. It is important to visit people in jail and to bring them good food, and soap, although sometimes the prison guards discourage relatives and friends from bringing scented toilet soap.

The cell I was in did not have a toilet. It had a bucket. Inmates were encouraged not to use the bucket throughout the night. I learnt not to use it and for the year I slept in this cell I did not use it. However some people used it in the night. Inmates took turns to empty it. However you could pay someone to empty the bucket for you if you could afford some form of payment. For instance, you could pay with a slice of bread. Those who were well off could pay with Vaseline, body lotion, soap, socks, underpants or pen and paper. It was possible to have a servant to work for you if you had any of the items I mentioned to give someone who would then empty the bucket, sweep the cell or book the shower for you. We all ran for the showers in the morning because only a few showerheads worked. We had to shower fast in order to line up for roll-call in time. If you were late for roll-call you were punished. We could only shower after making our beds and we did make them in style. In fact, we did not have beds but foam rubber mattresses. We folded up our blankets in three different ways, the TV, radio and flower styles. First we folded the mattress and then the blankets that we put on top of the mattress. We used to have competitions to see which cell had inmates who folded their bedding the neatest. If you were really good at it you would teach your inmates and you would become what was called 'cell staff'. I became a cell staff. However it did not matter how clean and neat the cell was, it crawled with lice. Because we lived so close together it was easy for lice to spread. Also we did not iron our clothes because there were no irons in prison. We were not allowed to have needles, razors, mirrors or anything the prison officials thought prisoners could harm themselves with.

At meal times we had sadza and pork. Those who did not eat pork because their churches forbade them had to overlook their church rules. I personally did not see any sense in regarding eating pork as sinful. However the food was not well prepared. They dished it and left individual plates in the open and uncovered and attracting flies while we arranged ourselves into a single file.

The prison took good care of you if you were sick. There was a clinic and a nurse. Drugs were usually available. If your condition required specialist attention, then you were taken to Parirenyatwa Hospital. Those who were not well were excused from manual work. They did light work indoors. I have heard people say that prisoners go to school. I would like to tell you now that this is not true. I noted that prison guards look for teachers amongst the inmates. These then taught others. I did not see any serious learning and teaching. It was possible for one to learn computers: there was a white woman who came in to take people for computers but entry into her class was controlled. For instance, they only wanted people who had long sentences and with a certain level of education. Sewing classes were for those who could sew already because they made the prison guards' uniforms.

Towards the end of my sentence the prison officials reminded me that I was close to going home. They gave me my personal clothes a day before my release so that I could wash them. I felt like a little girl who had been given a chocolate bar. I jumped up and down with excitement. I failed to sleep. In fact the inmates of my cell were excited as if they were the ones about to go home. We had become very close. However, on the actual day of release, I became extremely anxious. I was not sure if anybody would come to meet me. I was afraid that my family might not want me back home. Fortunately my sister who lived in Milton Park in Harare came to meet me. She took me to her home where I stayed for two days. When I came out I looked terrible. I had gone quite dark in complexion and I had lost weight. The clothes I came in were now too large. After staying in Harare with my sister for two days I went home to my own family.

When I got home I could see that a lot of things had happened. Fortunately I was now a person who prayed so I prayed for strength to accept the situation. I was happy to see my children and my husband. I could not tell what my husband thought of me. He was quiet at first. Some village women told me that he used to say bad things about me when I was in prison. I chose not to get upset even though I saw evidence in the home that he was up to no good. There were condoms and women's underwear in the bedroom. The children were badly affected by my absence at home. My first-born was supposed to go to college. They did not look like they were well cared for. Their class performance deteriorated. My second born who was in Form 4 failed the examinations. He could not take any training courses and now he is in South Africa. Many people in the village used to come up to me to ask, 'You were in prison, how come you are still with your husband?' I replied that if my husband were the one who was arrested I would not leave him. I reminded people that in life all sorts of unexpected things happen. We needed to learn to accept and forgive even murderers. Also some people committed crimes but they did not end up in jail. At least I had paid for my bad ways. I was a free person in the world. Some people also asked my husband why he had let me back into his home.

People are not yet ready to accept a woman, a wife and mother that can go to prison and come out to continue to be a mother and a wife. Our traditions do not accept such things and yet it happens. After I got home I asked my husband to give me a little money so that I could start something to make me earn a living. He did not give me any. As I am talking now he has married a second wife. However, my children are supportive. They help me now and again with money. Now my husband always tells me that I am not fit to be his wife because I went to prison. However, I told him that I could not stand the sight of his second wife walking through the gate into my house. He built her a home elsewhere far away from me. My children, especially the ones in the UK, send me money. I'm fully aware of my situation so I spend it wisely.

I find my husband's attitude quite worrying. Even though he married a second wife, he leaps at every opportunity to embarrass me especially before visitors who do not know that I once went to prison. 'You see this woman here, she looks like a decent woman but she stole money and went to prison.' This is now my husband's standard introduction to people who do not know me. It is his slogan; it readily comes to his lips when he talks about me. I made a single mistake and now I am branded and everybody must know about my black mark. He is unforgiving.

To end my story, I would like to point out that going to jail does not benefit the prisoner and this is why we have repeat offenders. What prisoners need are effective rehabilitation centres that offer counselling so that one can appreciate the value of hard work, honesty and of sharing personal problems with family and friends. Going to prison does not also benefit the people who have been wronged. Take my case for instance, the school lost its money, it will never get it back because I went to prison. I could have been allowed another chance to repay the money I stole. It would have benefited the school. Finally, going to jail does not mean you have ruined your life forever. Life goes on. You need the resolve not to commit crime and faith in your efforts to build a better future for yourself.

19

Sandra

interviewed by Chiedza Musengezi

My father is late. He had two wives. My mother is the junior wife. She says that he was so much older than her: he could easily have been her father. She and his senior wife's daughter were about the same age. My mother has ten children. I am the third born; I was born in 1977. My father's senior wife has seven children, so altogether we are seventeen. My mother was not happy in her marriage. She felt she was regarded as a servant, taking care of everybody including my stepbrothers and stepsisters. When the rains fell and it was time to work in the fields, my father's senior wife claimed she had asthma and refused to go to the fields. My mother and us, her children, did most of the work.

My father lived in Harare most of the time, he was a builder, and worked in the city while we lived in Chiweshe. I did not like my father very much when I was young because he was always angry. He seemed to direct his anger at my mother and us, the children. Soon after arriving home from Harare, he would go straight to the fields to inspect them, an exercise that never failed to trigger his bad temper. He would come back and shout at us. 'Why are the fields full of weeds? You sleep and eat, sleep and eat all day. You are lazy!' He would order us to go to the fields immediately. It did not matter whether we were in the middle of preparing a meal; we would leave everything, scramble for our hoes and rush to the fields. I have a clear recollection of his foul moods. He did not smile at us or joke with us. When I look back now I think that maybe my father regretted marrying my mother and having many children. He seemed to get on well with his senior wife. She was a lucky woman: he loved her. My mother did not mind being a co-wife because she had run away from the poverty in her family. At home, there was always enough food. My father understood good farming. He provided fertilisers and oxen to pull the plough. He had many cattle. We children provided labour. The boys ploughed and we girls weeded. My mother hoped that their relationship would improve with time.

All children went to school but most only managed to complete primary school. I was the first girl and the only one in the family to obtain O-levels. I was good in class and with time my father became proud of me. However, my stepsisters who were already married were jealous of me and were discouraging. I went to school in Chiweshe for my primary education. My performance improved when I was in Grade 6. I liked school very much. I had ambitions to be a nurse or a teacher. In Grade 7, I was promoted to the A-class. I passed with good grades at the end of Grade 7. My father was pleasantly shocked and was proud that he had an intelligent daughter. I took my results slip and went to a nearby secondary school to look for a place to do Form 1. I went by myself because my father was in Harare and did not know enough about school to assist me. In 1991, I started secondary school. English and Agriculture were my favourite subjects. I had good teachers. My class teacher appointed me garden master even though I was the youngest in class. I carried out my duties without any difficulty: we were all friendly to each other in my class. However, I did not do well at ZJC.

In Form 3 the school introduced new subjects, Bible studies and Literature in English. We had a good English teacher. I enjoyed literature very much. I read *Animal Farm* by George Orwell, *Harvest of Thorns* by Shimmer Chinodya and the *Trial of Dedan Kimathi*. I worked hard and after writing my O-level examinations I said to my mother, 'Look Mama, I have passed these subjects.' I showed her a piece of paper where I had listed the subjects I knew I had passed. My mother was not convinced: she used to come into my room at night to blow out the candle because I would have fallen asleep with a book in my hands. When the results came out I was proved right. I had B grade in Agriculture and literature and I had C grade in Shona, Bible Knowledge and English language. I told my mother I could have got better grades had it not been for the long distance I walked to school every day. The school was about seven kilometers away and I used to wake up at about four o'clock in the morning. I would be very tired at the end of the day and there was work to do at home. However, I had school holidays to catch up with some of the schoolwork.

My father, by then, had retired because of ill health so I looked for a job as a temporary teacher. To my surprise he was not supportive. He said he did not have money to buy clothes and blankets. He refused me permission to go. I started to pick cotton at a nearby commercial farm in Glendale. It was hard work. A lorry used to pick us up at four o'clock in the morning. We carried some sadza and *mahewu* to drink. We arrived at the farm before sunrise. We would pick cotton, grade it and have it weighed. Grade A cotton fetched good money. I was not good at picking cotton. My cotton was not clean, it was usually B or C grade. I did this job for three months, May to July. I used to make Z$30 to Z$40 a day depending on how much cotton I picked.

My brother-in-law, my stepsister's husband, found me a job, selling in Mr Nhingi's shop at Rosa. My father allowed me to go this time. Maybe because he had retired, there was not enough money at home. He had no pension. I stayed at Rosa for three months. I did not have problems with my job. Sometimes the shop owner would make me do housework and sometimes I would be in the shop selling. Mai N..., the shop owner's wife, taught me how to operate a till. I did not find her a nice woman. Sometimes she would get into the bedroom and search my bag. We were three young women being trained to operate the till, Constance, Viola and myself. We all shared a bedroom and Mai N... searched our bags at random. She suspected that we stole money. I later learnt that a young woman who was there before us had stolen from the shop. After completing the training, Viola and I were sent to a Growth Point. The shop at the Growth Point was the biggest in Chiweshe. It was a wholesale shop. It stocked nearly everything: sugar, furniture, building materials and many other things. This is where I started to steal.

One of the girls I worked with said, 'Look here my friend, do you know that we do not take stock here?' She told me that I could help myself to anything and the shop owners would never know unless somebody told them. That is when I decided not to let my mother suffer. After all I earned Z$300 per month even though the minimum wage for my kind of work was about Z$700-Z$800 per month. We used to make an average of Z$75,000 per day when we added the takings from all the shops. The shop owner came every evening to collect money for the day. It was hard work at the wholesale. There was hardly a moment to rest.

The customers were always calling for help. I had to serve them all, writing out receipts for the goods they bought. The first thing I stole was a big towel, the kind we use for carrying babies on our backs. I wanted it for my mother. I stole that and some nappies because my mother had a baby and she had no baby clothes. I gave them to my mother when I went home on my off days. I also took some money from the till. Oh, I was so young and foolish. I took the money and hid it in my tennis shoes. I took about Z$2,000.

Sometimes I would roll up Z$100 notes tightly and stuff them into a bottle of Camphor Cream. This was when the Z$100 note was introduced. It was now easy to steal a large amount of money at once. I would remove all the cream, put the tight roll of notes inside and put back the cream on the top. I would take the bottle to the selling point and pay for it. I would take the bottle to my mother and say, 'Here is a bottle of Camphor Cream, please keep the money in a safe place.' My mother did not like it at all. She scolded me but I told her that everybody did it at the shop. She still refused to accept my money. She was not happy. She refused to talk to me for some time. I had to lie that I had bought the towel and nappies else she would not have accepted them.

I brought home more stolen goods and towards the end she didn't mind and went along with it. I stole a lot of money, about Z$10,500. I also stole about 30 bags of fertilizer. I used to write receipts for all the goods and gave them to my relatives to take out of the shop. Nobody knew who my relatives were so I had an advantage. One day I had my eyes on the kitchen unit. Again, I wanted it for my mother. I wrote out a receipt for it without having paid anything as usual. I waited for a relative to come. My stepsister, my father's senior wife's daughter came to the shop. She was married in the area. I thought since she was family she would not betray me. I gave her the kitchen unit to take to her home. I was going to pick it up later to take to my mother.

My father also came and I told him, 'Father, come and get some fertilizer, this is how we are going to do it.' I described everything and he agreed. He went home and came back with an ox-drawn cart and we loaded 30 bags of fertiliser onto it. I told him that I would not be arrested unless he told the shop owners or the police. I also gave him bags of cement, groceries and roofing sheets, the twelve-foot long ones. I wanted him to roof my mother's house. Satan was working on me. I told my brother to come and get some more building materials. There was really nothing to fear because everybody at work was doing the same. It seemed so easy. A relative would come and I would pretend I did not know him or her and serve them like I would any customer. I would give them ten-kilogram bags of sugar, tins of powdered milk and other foods. My stepbrothers' wives would come and they would leave the shop with whatever they asked for: soap, groceries and towels for carrying their babies.

However, my stepsister, the one I had given my kitchen unit to keep began to complain. She threatened to have me arrested. I did not take her seriously. When she next came to the shop, I did as usual. I gave her a lot of groceries. I also gave her some to take to my mother. I gave her tennis shoes that she immediately put on her feet. I did not realise that a young man who worked in the shop and was related to the shop owner had seen us. Unknown to me, he took my stepsister aside and inspected the goods and the receipts, unknown to me. She revealed everything and on top of that she demanded to be given a job. They took her to the shop owner's at Rosa, in a truck. I do not know why he decided to act like that because he also used to steal. He had even built himself a home in Harare. Meanwhile my aunt, my mother's twin sister arrived. She wanted white material for her church uniform. I gave her six metres of cloth and a receipt even though she had not paid for it. The same young man who had driven my stepsister to Rosa followed my aunt, picked her up and took her to Rosa for questioning.

The shop owner came to fetch me. He slapped me on the face so hard that I had a nose-bleed. I collapsed. The clinic wrote a report about it. I was then taken to Chombira Police Station in Chiweshe. A docket was opened. The police had a lot of information from my stepsister. They already had a list of the things I had stolen and I never knew I had stolen so much in less than a year. They questioned my father about the fertiliser and roofing materials but my father denied everything. The shop owner and the police went to our home and found a kitchen unit only. The fertiliser had already been used and my father had harvested an excellent crop of maize. The asbestos sheets were already on the roof of my mother's new house.

I was given free bail. At Chombira I was not put in the cells. There was only one cell and it was full of men who had stolen cattle. I slept in the charge office where people came to report. When I got home I asked my father about his daughter who had reported me to the shop owner and the police. I wanted to know why she had done it even though I had given her a lot of things including the money to do a course with the Red Cross. My father put it down to jealousy. She was jealous and evil. When I was on free bail the police carried out further investigations. When I was working at the wholesale shop I had met a young man Mathew at church. Even though I stole I went to church, something which caused me some anguish. I suffered a lot of guilt. When I was on free bail he came to our home to pay *lobola*. My father received the *lobola* but he did not tell Mathew that I had a problem. It was my mother who had to tell him. Fortunately he did not change his mind. He brought five head of cattle as part of the *lobola*.

When I left home to start a life with my husband, I left behind everything I had stolen. I said to my father, 'Look here, you keep all the money it is your start-up cash. It will help you stand on your feet. Do not spend it on things unimportant, buy fertiliser, work the fields and have enough food for the family. You have some start capital now.' I told my mother the same because she too had money I had given her in the Camphor bottles.

Mathew worked in Mutare at Funeral Services. He was a carpenter. He made coffins. I spent eight months with my husband but I knew that I had to go to court in September. When the date was close I left Mutare for Chiweshe. I went to stay with my mother-in-law. I was there when the police came to pick me up in a Santana Land-rover. I was working in the fields with my mother-in-law when they arrived. The village people knew about my case and they talked. I went to Chombira Police Station where they instructed me to go to Bindura. In court, my stepsister who had testified against me denied that I had stolen anything. The police then charged her for giving false information. She was sentenced to three months in jail, all of which was suspended. She was free to go home. She was overjoyed; she ululated and confessed that she was under pressure from relatives, to say I did not steal.

In March I was in court and the magistrate said, 'Sandra, tell the court exactly how you stole.' I did not beat about the bush. I told the court that I stole in an effort to survive. My father had refused me permission to go and work in Mt Darwin. I asked for forgiveness. I admitted my crime. I did not want to be in remand prison anymore. I asked them to pass judgment quickly; I wanted this over and done with. When the court asked me if there was anything else I wanted considered before the sentence was passed, I told them that I was pregnant and that was all.

They sentenced me to 36 months. Somehow in my ears I heard 36 years! I passed out. *Ambuya gadhi* who was with me did her best to comfort me. She said, 'Sandra get up, it is 36 months not years and some of the months would be suspended.' That is when I sat up. I did not hear how many months were cut from my sentence because my mind was not all there. *Ambuya gadhi* took me to Bindura prison. She persuaded me to eat my sadza at lunchtime. I was crying when she explained to me that I was only going to serve eighteen months.

I was back in the cell at Bindura. I did not like the cell at all. The toilet was inside, and we were many: those in remand prison and those convicted were all put in the same cell. Sometimes we were as many as fifteen. The number was never the same from one day to the next. Some would pay a fine and leave and some would be brought in. Sometimes we were few, about seven or eight. One day *ambuya gadhi* said, 'Sandra, pack your things and climb into the truck. You are going to serve your sentence at Chikurubi in Harare.' I did not expect to be moved because I was now big and heavy with pregnancy. They took me to Harare Central Police Station first, then to Chikurubi. *Ambuya gadhi* who had travelled with me from Bindura introduced me to the people at Chikurubi. I was taken aback by the warmth of their reception. The prisoners who had come from Bindura were especially friendly to me. They asked after some of their friends whom they had shared a cell with. I knew some of them. From then on I never cried. I had found friends of all ages. Some were the ages of my mother and grandmother. I was not alone: there were so many of us. However the problem I faced at Chikurubi was food.

I was pregnant and needed to eat well. We had our supper very early, around 3 p.m. or 4 p.m. In addition we were given a tiny amount of sadza. It was not enough for me. By the next morning I would be famished and without strength. I would bravely drag myself around until breakfast time. Sometimes I did not like the food at all. I devised a little plan. I went to the kitchen and asked women who cooked not to throw away any leftovers. They understood my problem and kept leftover sadza for me in a safe place. I went to see the nurse and asked if I could have a small tin with a lid to keep the sadza in. She gave me one. A woman from Kenya, who was also in prison, gave me another small tin can where I kept milk. I kept my tins of food and ate whenever I felt hungry. Sometimes I would eat in the cell and other times outside the cell. I was in the cell reserved for pregnant and nursing mothers. We got on well because we understood each other's difficulties. When one of the pregnant ones went into labour we would call for the nurse through the window. I made friends in the cell. We read books. I was not fond of knitting and crocheting. After serving five months, I was called to the office. I was told that the magistrate had come to let me know that my appeal had been successful. I had lodged an appeal that the sentence was too long. I was pregnant and not well. I had listed a few other difficulties I had. I was given transport to Bindura. The court told me that if I paid restitution, Z$8,000, I would be able to go home. If I did not have the money then I would have to serve a further four months.

I did not have the money and there was no way I could get in touch with my mother or my husband. In fact, my mother had spent a fair amount of the money I had given her on bus fares when she visited me in prison. She also used to buy food for me. My husband visited me every month. Each month end his employer, the owner of Funeral Services, used to give him a lift from Mutare. He used to drop him off at Chikurubi. My husband used to bring me a lot of food especially during public holidays. My mother-in-law too used to visit me. She brought me chicken. My brother also came offering to pay the Z$8,000 but I told him to spend the money on something more useful to the family: buy a cow, or pay the children's school fees. After all, I had only a few months to serve. I asked them to pray for me. That was all I wanted from them. I stayed in Chikurubi and had my baby there. When I felt pain I was not aware that I was in labour. The nurse had not told me about what to look out for even though it was my first pregnancy. She used to take us to Parirenyatwa to be weighed and examined. I went to hospital in handcuffs. It was embarrassing and humiliating. I never enjoyed my pregnancy. The doctor examined me in the presence of the *ambuya gadhi*.

The day I went into labour, a friend, Nyasha, came along with me to hospital. She too was pregnant and was about to give birth. I do not know what went wrong but she and the baby died. I lost a close friend. I feared for my life too. I never thought I would get out of hospital with my baby. To my great joy, in March 1997 I had a healthy baby girl. The hospital telephoned my husband to tell him the good news. He came immediately. We named the baby, Nyasha, after my [late] friend. The baby brought me great joy and comfort for the rest of my stay in prison. I was released in July. My baby melted away my sadness: however, my problem was food. It was too little. I also fell ill and Tracey, another prisoner, was a great help. She used to carry my baby to the vehicle that took me to hospital. I would climb into the vehicle and she would put the baby in my lap. Because I had a baby I was not in handcuffs. *Ambuya gadhi* was not nice to me. She shouted at me, 'Get up!' She did not appreciate that I was sick and I could not walk. *Vanambuya gadhi* could be mean to pregnant inmates. They would say things like, 'Don't bother me, I didn't make you pregnant.' However, the prison nurse was pleasant and helpful. She sent me to Chikurubi Maximum Prison clinic for a TB test. The tests showed that my chest was clear. The nurse put me on a course of tablets and my cough was cleared. The time I was ill was my worst time in prison. I missed my family. I wanted them close by. *Vanambuya gadhi* could be cruel. There is a day I do not forget when *Ambuya gadhi* N... slapped me so hard on my face I fell to the ground. She said I had taken too long to come after she had called me. I had got her message but could not go immediately because the door to our cell was locked. The junior *ambuya gadhi* responsible had not unlocked the doors yet. These were the hardships I had to endure at Chikurubi. One *ambuya gadhi* told you one thing and the other would tell you the opposite. It was like a war and I was caught in the middle.

The days just before my release were the happiest. My inmates sang and prayed for me. They gave me good advice. They did not want me to come back to prison. I had to get along with others at home and had to submit myself to my husband because he had been especially good to me. Some of the married inmates had been divorced. Some husbands turned up with girlfriends to tell their wives that the marriage was over. Or sometimes their husbands' relatives would come especially to scold them for disgracing their family. My inmates praised my husband for supporting me throughout the time I was in prison. Some promised to come home and thank him personally after their release. My fellow inmates were happy for me: it was encouraging. I looked forward to leaving prison. I so much wanted my baby to be free. She was growing and was healthy. She had good food from her father and relatives: Cerelac and peanut butter to add to her mealie-meal porridge. *Ambuya gadhi* gave me back my clothes. I washed them and I got out in July. This was the happiest day of my life. It felt unreal. It was like a dream.

On that day, who turned up to take me home? Not my husband or my mother but my own father. I was touched. He came with a cousin who worked near the

Chikurubi Maximum Prison for men. He and my father gave me good counsel. I promised not to break the law again. I went to my parents' home and stayed with them. My mother-in-law came to see me. She brought a live chicken and maize meal. We had a special meal of chicken and sadza. After the meal she told my family that what I did was wrong and I had embarrassed her. She was also upset that when my husband came to pay *lobola* my father had behaved as if all were normal. Nonetheless she was prepared to put everything behind her. She had come to take me and my baby home to live with my husband's family. When we got home in August my mother-in-law was protective. I was the one who told neighbours that I had been in prison because I wanted them to know. I did not want people to talk behind my back. Only one of my sisters-in-law shamed me now and again about my prison experience. Everybody else was supportive: my mother-in-law was particularly supportive.

What I found most difficult in prison was absence of family. I missed my family. I was lucky that I had my child with me. Other inmates had left their children behind. The strain of being away from their children was unbearable for them. Other times I learnt that a relative had fallen sick or had died. Such news caused me a great deal of pain. I could not visit my sick relatives or attend a funeral and grieve with others when someone in our family circle died. An accumulation of this kind of emotional pain can make you physically ill. Sometimes inmates fell ill and died and losing them was as painful as losing a close relative. During the period that I was in prison six or seven inmates died. Sometimes we spent the night with a dead body in a cell. I found it sad and frightening to see a dead inmate. Once an inmate had difficulty with breathing. It was at night. We called for help through the window but nobody came. Towards morning the inmate stopped breathing, she died. *Vanambuya gadhi* removed the body in the morning. This is what used to happen in prison. I felt insecure and at risk of infections like TB. Some of the inmates had TB. Some went for treatment but some did not even though they were treated for free.

When I came out of prison I went to ZACRO headed by Mr Myambo. I did a course in dressmaking, including cutting and designing. I passed all the subjects and I have a certificate, which I can use to apply for a job. I'm living with my husband now. We have two children: Nyasha and Liberty. Nyasha is the one I had in prison and sometimes relatives joke about it, calling her 'jail girl'. We built a home in Chiweshe. We have a two-bedroomed house with an asbestos roof and a round kitchen with thatch. When the rains come I plough the fields and plant crops with the help of my mother-in-law. Recently my brother-in-law married and his wife has joined us in working the fields. One more person makes the work lighter. We get enough food to eat from the fields.

My husband now works in Harare. The company he worked for in Mutare transferred him. I love him and have a deep respect for him because he is an extraordinary man. He stood by me from the time I got arrested up to now. He saved money and bought cattle when I was in prison. When he gets his wages he hands over the entire pay packet for me to manage. He is an unbelievably good husband. God bless him.

20

Sheila

interviewed by Virginia Phiri

I am Sheila.* I was born in Harare. I am the first-born child, and we are five children in our family, four girls and one boy. My family was poor: we lived in a single rented room. At night we, children, went to sleep at our uncle's house in the same township, where there was some space. I attended primary school, Grades 1 to 4, in Mhondoro where I stayed with my maternal grandmother. From Grade 5 to 7, I went to a primary school in Highfields. I was now staying with my parents. My parents loved us. They managed to send all of us to school. I went to high school and passed five O-level subjects; English, Accounts, Shona, Fashion and Fabrics and Commerce. I got married soon after finishing school because I got pregnant by a young man in the neighbourhood. I had to get married to save my parents the embarrassment. At first we married traditionally and in August 1986 we had a church wedding. I was happy and so were my parents, I had not disgraced them. When I got married I then discovered that the man whom I thought was my father was my stepfather. I was disturbed but my good relationship with him did not change.

I had a baby girl in September 1986. I was happy because it was an easy birth; the baby was healthy. My husband was happy and so were his family. We named our baby Viola after my husband's eldest sister. When I got married I changed to the Anglican Church, the one to which my husband's family went. Before I got married I went to the Salvation Army. I did not attend church frequently after my marriage,

---

* Sheila was interviewed in prison.

as I did when I went to Salvation Army. My husband and his family were not regular worshippers, so I also followed their way of life. I tried to find a job as a temporary teacher. My husband did not like it. He did not want me to leave him in Harare while I taught at a rural school. His family influenced him to behave this way towards me. After my second child, a boy, who was born in May 1989, I did a secretarial course for a year. I achieved intermediate level in typing, bookkeeping, accounts and office practice. My husband paid the college fees. I then fell pregnant again. My third child, a boy, was born in May 1991. All my boys are May babies.

When the baby was six months old, I got a job as a data capture operator. I worked for this company from November 1991 to January 1995. I then got a job with PTC as a clerk in the human resources department. I started at B1-grade, which is the lowest entry point in PTC. In 1997, there was a vacancy in the stores department and I applied for the job and got it. I then moved to grade B2-grade, when fell pregnant again. A baby boy was born in August 1997. At the stores department there were mostly male employees and I wanted to move to the banking section, where there were mostly female employees. I eventually found someone to swap departments with. In 1998, I was employed in the Post Office Savings Bank. At that time I was studying with the Institute of Bankers Zimbabwe in the evenings. I did most of the work at home during weekends. I managed to write examinations in Financial Accounting 1 and Management 1, that is the first level. In 2000 I stopped studying because my son, the one born in 1991, had been seriously injured in a car accident. An oncoming car hit him when he was walking back from school. I was still a bank teller. My son was in hospital for eight months from May 2000 to January 2001. He suffered severe head injuries and needed to be assisted all the time. When I was at work a nursemaid from St Giles Rehabilitation Centre, whom I had to pay, looked after him. My husband and I loved our son, we paid his medical expenses. Moral support also came from his and my families. Financially, my parents were poor and none of my sisters were able to help them especially now that they were married. As the eldest child in my family I had to help my parents who had struggled to educate us. I seriously believed it was my duty to help them and to look after my own family too, including my injured son. I got my salary through my own Post Office savings account and used my salary as I saw fit, that included looking after my parents.

In 2001, my husband and I decided to open a joint bank account where we had individual signing powers. My husband did not allow me to give money to my parents after we had opened a joint bank account. Unfortunately that was the time they needed help more than before. Life had become unbearably expensive in town and they had moved to Mhondoro, our rural home, and needed help to build a house. I was under tremendous pressure to help them. I borrowed money from unregistered money-lenders at an interest rate of 35 per cent. They collected the money on paydays. It was now difficult for me to access the money from the Metropolitan Bank because it was a joint account. I then decided to sign withdrawal slips for my Post Office savings account. I knew very well there was not much money in the account since my salary was now going through another bank.

I continued to write and sign withdrawal slips and got cash until my account was Z$62,000 overdrawn. This was over a period of nine months – from March 2001 to December 2001. I used the money to build a house for my parents in Mhondoro and to meet other expenses for my injured son. The overdraft was found out in December 2001. I had planned to clear the unauthorised overdraft in late December 2001 the time when we would receive our back pay which PTC owed us. Overdrafts with POSB were not allowed but due to a technical fault in the computer system, money deposited by clients took some time to reflect on the computer. Clients only had to show proof of deposits and then they would have access to cash. I took advantage of the computer technical problem.

I tendered my resignation when the irregularities were found and the personnel from the fraud section of POSB decided that the Z$62,000, which I had overdrawn, would be deducted from the back pay late December 2001. However, the POSB accountant of the fraud section decided to take me to the police station. A statement was taken and I was asked to go home and return to the police station the following day, when they took my fingerprints and asked me again to return on the 20th December 2001.

Meanwhile I had not informed my husband about the problem at work. I lied to him. I told him that a conman had swindled me of Z$62,000 at the POSB and I had to pay back the failed loan, failing which I would be dismissed from work.

POSB had promised to withdraw the case once the Z$62,000 had been deducted from my back pay, on the 20th of December. On the morning of 20th December

I went to the Harare Police Station where I was expected. They told me to come back in the afternoon since the POSB fraud section had not turned up. In the afternoon, the POSB fraud squad had still not arrived at the station. The police then asked me to go to the POSB fraud squad offices to find out what was happening. The accountant told me that they would notify me about the withdrawal of the case by telephone. I did not hear from them until after Christmas. I telephoned them and they told me that they were looking into the matter.

On a Monday, after New Year's Day, the police station telephoned to advise me that I should go to court in January 2002. I went to the POSB fraud squad offices to check. The boss was not in, he was the one who had authority to withdraw the case. There was nothing else for me to do except go to court. Since my husband now knew of the overdraft and the police, I suggested he hired a lawyer to defend me. He did not think it was necessary since I had paid back the Z$62,000. We went to court: my husband, my father, sister, my husband's brother and myself. I agreed that I had taken the money without permission, hoping that they would let me go. To my surprise and shock they demanded Z$6,000 bail. My husband paid the bail and I was asked to return to court on 16th January 2002. I made sure my children went back to boarding school. They both attended a secondary school in Bromley. Evans who was thirteen was in Form 1 and Viola who was sixteen was in Form 4. On the 16th of January the court passed a judgment. I was sentenced to 33 months; eight of which were suspended. I cried. I thought I would die. I felt that my life had come to an end. I did not believe that the court could send me to prison. I came to Chikurubi on the same day. My husband promised to appeal the case. I applied for an appeal in February that was not responded to; I applied again in May and I am now told that it is being typed. I miss my husband and children. I had hoped for amnesty in April but fraud cases were not considered.

In prison, I associate with women of my choice, especially the older ones. They often comfort me when I break down. I cry a lot. My husband visited me regularly at the beginning. Then one day he told me that he would not visit me anymore. He did not tell me why and I did not know what had got into him. He resumed the visits after some time. I did not question him. I was happy that he was coming to see me again. He still loves me. My mother, sisters, father and my husband's relatives visit me. When I finish my sentence I will go back to my marital home.

My husband will take me back, but I do not know if he has forgiven me for what I did. I miss my children a lot, especially the one who is not well. I hope he is being looked after properly. I am told that he is being looked after well but I cannot be sure about that. I am not there to see for myself.

In Chikurubi Prison we are treated well. They try to heal our pain. The atmosphere is different. It is not a place one would like to be. We have food and medical attention. We are sick.* When I get out of this place, I hope to get a job. But you know how it is when one has been in prison for fraud.

---

* The contradictions contained in these few sentences are indicative of the anxiety felt by prisoners, interviewed in prison, should they want to say anything negative about their situation.

21

Lilian

interviewed by Keresia Chateuka

My name is Lilian. I was born in October 1970. We are four in our family and I'm the third born. Our mother brought us up because she separated from my father and returned to her family. My oldest brother helped to pay for my education. I was very fortunate. I went to primary school, and then to high school. I lived with my mother who worked as a housemaid in the suburbs. After completing secondary school, I first became a temporary teacher and then I started to train as a teacher in 1993. I was posted to a rural town for teaching practice and then I went back to college to complete the course.

In 1997, I got married. It was unfortunate that soon afterwards, when my baby was only six months old, I had serious disagreements with my husband. You see, he was the oldest and he was responsible for the rest of his family because his father had died. As soon as he started working, he quickly secured a loan to buy a home because he worked for a bank. The house became a family home. When I married him, his family thought I might force them out. They felt insecure. I did not do such a thing. Nonetheless our marriage broke down completely because of too many demands from relatives from both my side of the family and my husband's.

My oldest brother, whom we regarded as head of the family, died leaving five children. I had to assist them financially. On the face of it, we should not have had problems because my husband and I were working. However, as you know, teachers get their monthly salaries earlier than most people, this meant that most of my money would be spent before he got his own. In the end, I did not have money to

143

give to my mother and to pay rent for the family of my older brother. With both my husband and I giving money to our families, there was never enough money between the two of us. That is when we started to have disagreements that eventually badly affected our marriage. In fact, he moved out of the house and I stayed on looking after his sisters, brothers and, sometimes, his mother. He came back and his family tried to bring us back together but they were unsuccessful. That is when I packed my things and left. After all, it was not my house; he was still paying back the money that he had borrowed from the bank. We had not married in court or church. We had no marriage certificate.

I went to prison for fraud. Government teachers earn little. My salary was not enough to pay for the groceries for all the relatives who lived with us, plus rent for my brother's house and groceries too. I also needed to look after myself. I could not pay for all this. I needed more money. I started to order and sell house-cleaning materials. Because school finished at 1.00 p.m., I would have the rest of the afternoon to sell them. In addition, the school holidays provided me with a lot of time to do business. I sold the materials to a certain company in town. The accountant wrote out a cheque worth more that the value of the goods. For instance, instead of the company paying me Z$48,000 the accountant would discuss with me and write out a cheque for Z$68,000. I would then give him back the difference Z$20,000. This is what used to happen. I did not always conduct my business this way – most of the time it was clean business. I was not arrested the first time I did it. The third time there was a difference of Z$30,000 that we shared. That is when our deal was uncovered and I was arrested. We used to work well together but on this particular day the accountant was on leave when the cheque arrived from the bank. They examined it against the goods I had sold and they found out that I had been over-paid. They re-examined the other two cheques and found out that the same thing had happened. When the company officials asked me about it, I told them the truth. The accountant and I were both arrested in the middle of December 2000. I was doing my Christmas shopping in town to take groceries to my sister in Mutare.

The police took me to Mbare. They told me that they were only interested in how I was going to pay back the money. The policeman who took me to the station just left me there. I never saw him again. I was at Mbare Police Station for four days. The policemen on duty did not seem to know anything about my case. In the meantime I feared for the safety of my child who I had left in the care of a housemaid. They said that it was possible for them to accompany me to go and fetch my child but my case was in the hands of a senior police officer. They could not act without instruction from their senior. I spent Christmas day there and the days of the 26th and 27th December. At home, nobody knew what had happened to me. My landlord tried to find out what had happened. She even went on radio. They only found out when I was already in Chikurubi Prison.

I went to remand on the 27th December. The police informed me that they were putting my papers in order because the law did not allow them to keep me for long without any charges. They quickly prepared my papers and sent me back to the Central Police Station. The court put me on remand until 2nd January 2001. I went to Chikurubi remand prison. The accountant was also in the cells at Harare Remand Prison but we never met.

In court it all seemed like a dream. It was my first time. The man I had committed the crime with was also on the docket. The statement I had given at the police station was read out. The magistrate asked if I was guilty or not. I pleaded guilty at the beginning of the trial. There was nothing the accountant could do but tell the truth. Before the magistrate sentenced us he asked if I had anything to say. I asked for leniency because I was the breadwinner in the family and my daughter was asthmatic. He assured me that my daughter would receive adequate medical care in prison. I was sentenced to 24 months imprisonment: six months were suspended because I was a first offender. Of the remaining eighteen months, six months were suspended if I did not commit a crime in the near future. Out of the remaining twelve months I was asked to go to prison for six months provided I paid the money back to the company. I hoped to raise the money but I failed. I was quiet for most of the time in court, only when I set my foot in Chikurubi, did I cry.

When I arrived, the prison guards on duty were all out to humiliate me. 'Here come the teachers who earn a lot of money. They have turned into wheelers and dealers.' Another one said. 'Is she the one with beautiful long hair? She'll have to cut it right away.' Sometimes one would talk to me kindly, asking what happened, then another would shout, 'Give her one of those yellow dresses full of lice! And a blanket to match! Teachers must learn that prisons have lice. Prisons are not classrooms.' I felt totally humiliated and out of place. The first day was the most difficult. I cried all night. I regretted what I had done.

Since my arrest I worried about my child. The housemaid had left and my child was in the care of my landlord. He then brought my child to Chikurubi. There was no one to look after my child at home. My mother was not well: her health had been poor for a long time. My child was a problem for the prison officials. Children are allowed in prison when they are two years and below and mine had turned two in January 2001. The officer-in-charge wanted my relatives to come and collect my daughter so I gave her my uncle's phone number. He contacted my sister in Mutare. My sister's husband came to prison immediately. However, prisons have strict rules. Those from outside do not know what days and times they can visit. When he arrived to collect the child, the prison guards had already locked the gates. They refused him entry. He pleaded with them; he told them he had taken a day off work and needed to go back to Mutare. They still refused him. He was deeply disappointed. I learnt about it the following morning. When the prison officers phoned him again, he did not turn up. My child therefore stayed with me for all the time I was in prison, a whole year.

Children do not get prison uniform. Clothes have to be brought from home. Fortunately there are organisations that help: for example, Prison Fellowship together with Greystone Women's Fellowship used to bring clothes for children. They visited monthly. They would bring clothes and peanut butter for children. The children would have porridge with peanut butter and sometimes they would get fruit. These were the two most helpful organisations. I was most active in children's division because I had a child who was older than the rest. I was made responsible for children's food. Every day I would write out a list of children. I did it every day because some children would arrive in the night with their mothers. Roughly we had an average of 30 children per day. Let us say my list had sixteen children, I would then inform the ration office of the number of children present. The ration office would measure out a quantity of sugar, meat, salt, etc., enough for sixteen children. Each child was given a share. The food would be measured every day. Prison only gave maize meal and meat, they got everything else from donors who gave cereals: Cerevita and Cerelac. They also got beans and vegetables and cooking oil and peanut butter. Not all the donated food would go to the children. Some of the prison guards would take the peanut butter to spread on their bread. They would also take cooking oil and they would do the same with sugar. Even though it was my responsibility to oversee children's food, I was a prisoner. I could not tell the prison officer not to take children's food. The officers would tell you that the food belonged to prison: it was theirs. 'Is this why you came to prison to eat the donor's food?' they would say if you expressed disapproval. Sometimes, therefore, the children had porridge without peanut butter and that was not good for their health. It all depended on the officer on duty. Some were honest and kind and some were not. Children's food was prepared separately. Mothers did not really see what happened to the food. I was fortunate enough to be involved, otherwise I would have never known.

When I was in prison, I met people from Prison Fellowship. Their aim was to help you come to terms with your situation. As I said before, when you set your foot in prison you feel out of place. Negative, unpleasant, thoughts crowd your head. Some people were so troubled by these thoughts that they fell ill. Parents and relatives would have been disappointed and disgraced. They did not follow you up: sometimes no one visited. In the meantime you needed Vaseline, soap and sanitary pads. Where could you get these things if your family did not visit you? Many wished they were dead. That was when Prison Fellowship really helped. They would tell you, 'It does not matter what crime you committed; you are a child of God. Keep praying.' They urged you to turn to God, to change your bad ways and make a new start. That was their teaching. They encouraged us to meet on Fridays as former prisoners to pray and talk about our experiences. If you learnt skills like sewing, they assisted you with job placement. Sometimes prison officials phoned Mr Peter Mandiyanike, the director of Prison Fellowship to come to prison to assist with difficult prisoners. If you had a project you wanted to do, Prison Fellowship could assist you with a loan. They put you in touch with organisations like Zambuko. That is what Prison Fellowship did. They helped to prevent you from going back to prison.

In prison, we did many activities and they varied according to what class you belonged to. A-class prisoners were given errands to do by *vanambuya gadhi*. C-class prisoners had longer sentences. They were separated from the rest. Their space was walled. D-class prisoners were not allowed to go beyond the fence. They were only allowed to get out of their cells. They did not work. They have long sentences, ten years or more. Their crimes included murder, armed robbery, drug trafficking and so forth. I was in the B-class. Some of us did gardening and some attended typing classes. Typing was donor-funded. A certain white woman used to take us for typing lessons. She was given a small wooden room. That is where she kept her machines, paper, books, and so forth. Some went for sewing while others cooked food. Some also helped out at the clinic. The elderly prisoners looked after our children. We would get up in the morning, wash, get counted and then go to our respective places to do our work. That was when our children would be taken away from us to be looked after while we worked

When the morning bell rang, we got up. Then *vanambuya gadhi* would check to see if we were all there by counting us. Afterwards we washed. When the bell rang for tea, we would all have our tea. Afterwards, we grouped ourselves into those who sewed, worked in the garden or the kitchen. The elderly took care of inmates' children. We attended to our duties up to 12:30 p.m. After lunch we went back to our duties. I did typing. After doing gardening for a day, I sat an entrance test for typing and I passed. It was an English test because the books that we used were in English so you had to read and write in English.

It was worrying to leave our children with the elderly prisoners. They were criminals, and we did not know if they liked children at all. Some of them did not like them but some did not mind. They would look after a child of any age, some only three months old. It didn't matter if your child was sick, you would give him over to the older prisoners to look after while you do your duties. If the child cried, the mother wouldn't be allowed to go back to breastfeed. If the baby cried most of the time, then the old woman carried the baby on her back. The old women used to feed the babies. The babies would have their food before us, at 12 noon. It was painful to have your baby looked after by somebody else. The older women who look after the babies were not guarded. Usually they sat in a small room they called the crèche or they sat in the open, but inside a fence, while the children played. Some of the old women were alert, and would not let the children out of their sight. Some were not so attentive and the children would wander about and get hurt. Prison life is tough especially if you have a child. Your child would be exposed to bad language. The child picks up vulgar words. When we came back, tired from working in the garden some talked as they pleased without any consideration for the children. Some were reckless with their use of language. It harmed the children

Nobody visited me from January to July. I would like to thank Prison Fellowship because they were the only visitors I had. The donors came once a month to give me a bar of soap that lasted a month only because my baby did not use nappies.

The small 150 ml bottle of Vaseline also lasted a month. I needed more soap and Vaseline. A cousin who had been transferred to work in Harare was the first family member to visit. I could not blame my family for not visiting because they were poor. They could not raise the bus fare. All things considered, I was fine as long as I could write to them and they could reply to my letters. You lived with the simple hope that tomorrow you would wake up again. I did not think much about the future but thanked God for having gone through the day. If you tried to think too deeply about things then you would be stressed.

The stories you hear about prisoners' ill-treatment are true. They can beat you up even though the laws are against it. They do not beat you up for nothing, of course. Sometimes you would have done something wrong. But usually it is not something that warrants a beating. For instance, the bell can ring while you are bathing and you delay slightly to line up with the rest of your group, because you have to wear your dress. It does not matter how old you are, even old women with white hair are beaten up with a big stick. Sometimes a prison guard can ask you to take a certain item, food or whatever, to put it in her basket. If the officer-in-charge finds you with this item, then the guard who sent you would deny any knowledge of what you are doing. If you were brave enough to tell the truth then the guard who sent you would wait for an opportunity to give you a good kick. They are very good at kicking with their boots. Sometimes they ask you to wash their uniforms. If they find stains on their clothes then they would think you did not want to do as they instructed. That is one of the reasons for which you would be beaten.

Sometimes things went missing. We prisoners knew that *Ambuya gadhi* N... took them. When the officer-in-charge found out, the officer involved would blame it on the prisoners. She would rally the other prison guards to support her. Six or seven of them would come and beat you very hard. They would order you not to say a word about the missing items. That was the life inside prison. Even when you were not feeling well, they would accuse you of pretending. You are stripped of your rights in prison.

I heard stories about women who slept with other women but throughout my time in prison, I did not see it until the arrival of a certain girl. It was her third time to come to prison. Her name was S ... . She was more of a man than a woman. She had a deep hoarse voice. She was strong and could cut logs into small pieces to put in the fire. She did everything like a man. A story circulated about her. Some said when she was in remand she was in love with a certain woman. They were beaten very hard until they confessed that it was true that they slept together. Some said that S … did not wear dresses outside prison. She wore men's clothes and she had small breasts. Those who had seen her undressed said she had no male organs. That is the only case I heard.

Those who fell sick went to the clinic for treatment. I was unfortunate in that I had a child. Those who had babies shared a cell with those who were pregnant. When one of the pregnant prisoners went into labour one would shout through the window for help. The guard on duty would phone the nurse to come. Sometimes the nurse came, took one look and declared that the person was not sick. She did not bother to check her properly. The pregnant prisoners suffered the most. We would again shout for help through the window when they went into labour. The nurse would shout back to tell us if it was a first pregnancy then she would be fine. We feared a lot for the pregnant prisoners. The nurse took long to take them to the hospital. They would humiliate them. 'Why did you bring us a pregnancy?' The nurse would shout back through the window. Some would give birth in the cells. Others would assist with the delivery. Most of us knew nothing about being midwives but we had to help out.

People died when I was in prison. One girl died in the remand cells. She had had an abortion. Two more died in bed in the sick bay and another older woman in the D-class also died. Two children died during the same period. Two more girls died. I think they were as many as ten. Those who lost children in prison were not given the chance to bury them. Again it all depended on the officer on duty. One woman whose baby died while I was there spent a month without burying the child. The officers explained that it took long for their head office to give them instructions about what to do. A kind officer would suggest that the dead body be removed from the cell if the baby died in the night. She could be over-ruled by others who did not care. Children suffered the most. They did not get good medical care in time. If you asked for help for your child they would tell you hurtful things like, 'Prison has no free medicine, our husbands pay taxes.'

When I was in prison, I communicated with my family. I wrote letters to them and they wrote back. I received three letters. Every month we got paper to write our letters. The letters were read before they were put in the post. They censored our letters. When we received letters they were also read. This process caused delay. It used to take one and a half months to get a reply. Sometimes there would be one prison guard to read all the letters. They gave excuses like shortage of officers.

The worst thing for me was that my child was older than the rest. She had some understanding of what was happening. Children do not forget. She shocks me now and again with her prison memories. She cannot forget. For instance, sometimes when I am bathing and I take long, she will stand at the bathroom door and shout, 'Mama if you are late *ambuya gadhi* will beat you up.' When you were close to the end of your stay in prison, you needed to be careful. You could commit a crime or a guard would send you to do something that she knew was against prison rules. When you got caught, the guard would deny it and her friends would support her. That's why you had to be careful. You would be grateful for each day you went through without a problem. You counted each day until you got to the last one.

Upon your release you went to collect all the things that you brought. You checked if everything was there. You then signed some forms. There was a small amount of money that you got when you were in prison. One did not get it in the first four months but from the fifth month onwards you would get Z$2 per month. That is the money you would use for your bus fare. If you did not have any money then they gave you a warrant. They made a good effort to make it possible for you to get to where you were going. My sister visited me on the Sunday before the Monday I was released. She came back the following day. She was at the gate waiting for me. We caught a lift with one of the combis. The next day I caught a bus to go and see my mother. She had been seriously ill since August. She had been informed that I would be home soon. She always used to say that she would not die until I got out of prison. Sure enough, she died two weeks after my release.

I went to Mutare with my child. When I took a seat in the combi, I felt that I did not belong. My sister who came to pick me up received me warmly. Her husband had been to prison too, so maybe she knew what to do. Everybody else in the family followed her example. She also hinted to other family members that she did not want anybody to insult or humiliate me. When I got to the city everybody was friendly. My youngest sister who was working brought me underpants and clothes for my child. My child sang to my mother, the song she had learnt in prison. She amused the relatives. I was touched that relatives warmed up to my child.

I started applying for jobs. I studied computers in prison. My sister scraped a little money together to send me to college to add on to what I had done in prison. Jobs are hard to get. Sometimes I teach for free just so I would keep young adults out of trouble. I will keep doing that until I get a job.

For the first offenders like me, imprisonment can drive you mad. Sometimes you may not get on with prison guards and your cell inmates, who may be long-timers, like to relieve their boredom on newcomers. They can be unpleasant. Sometimes people at home forget about you. Such things may worsen the situation. In the end you can fall ill or even die. The most important thing is for the people at home to visit prisoners regardless of how serious the crime the relative committed. When you are in prison you dread the day of your release because you are too embarrassed to face the people at home, especially your parents.

And another thing, when people visit you in prison they should try not to scold and lecture you. I noted some visitors, who as soon as they arrived at the gates shouted at and blamed their relative for getting into trouble. *Vanambuya gadhi* relish this kind of situation, they simply love it. They join in, rubbing it in. Such prisoners usually find themselves with nowhere to go upon their release and in no time they would be back in prison or become commercial sex workers. One needs strong family support in prison. People outside should not forget those in prison because one day they will get out and join you.

Some visitors tell you news that really disturbs you. They tell you far too much; how life is getting harder, the children are not well. It is hard to cope with such situations. Such news rings in your ears all the time. You worry about it a lot. If you are a mother, for example, you may be told that your children are not going to school because fees have not been paid. Or, worse still, if you have a small child you learn that she is sick because nobody is taking good care of her. Some people say that long back the small children of women prisoners used to be put in a children's home. Today there are no places. Relatives and those who are not in prison should try by all means to support prisoners. In my case I lost a lot of things. There was nobody to take care of my things. So much was lost. I so much desired to be part of my family and society. I am so grateful to my cousin who visited often and never brought me news that caused me worry. A lot had happened when I was in prison but she knew when and what to tell me. Most of the things she told me after my release from prison. I also told my family what happened but they did not demand that I tell them. I told them because I was ready to talk about it. At the moment, I live with my aunt in the high densities. She said it was fine for me to stay while I look for a job. I am fortunate: I have a place to stay. My concern is my own family. My mother is late; my sister who has two children of her own is also looking after my one child. She looks up to me for help since I am the one who went to school, who has an education. My brother died. His wife went to London and left the children behind. My hope is that I get a job and help out my family. I have a lot of moral support from my family. I find it encouraging. I so much want my life to be normal again, be able to pay rent, and so forth. Marriage is at the bottom of my priority list. The situation at home is desperate. My sister is supportive; she does not want me to slide back into crime. I love her for that. Prisoners need this kind of encouragement.

Prison is supposed to reform you, put you on the straight road, but there was no rehabilitation at all: if anything, prison worsens the situation because the very people who are supposed to assist you are the most unhelpful. They destroy you psychologically. Prison officers need refresher courses to make them better at their work. This does not mean that all of them are bad. A few individual officers try their best. Sometimes a hungry child may cry for food before the prison kitchen food is ready, and the officer may offer food from her own lunch box to stop the child from crying. Sometimes when a child has hardly any clothes, a kind officer may bring a few of her own babies' nappies from home to the mother.

Being in a marriage can worsen your time in prison. Some married women are rejected or divorced by their husbands at the prison gates. A word would spread that so and so was divorced by her husband yesterday. Sometimes the husband hires a lorry to bring all your property. The wife would be in a cell while the husband offloads her property at the prison gate. In such cases, the prison officers phone the director of Prison Fellowship. He will take the property for safe-keeping until the woman completes her sentence or he would look for a willing relative who can keep the property in store until the woman completes her sentence. Organisations such as Prison Fellowship help former prisoners a lot. Sometimes they offer material help but, more importantly, they help you to understand why you are in the situation. They also emphasise that even if your family rejects you, it is not the end of the world. There is life after prison.

To end my story I would like to emphasise the importance of accepting a former prisoner back into the family and society and not to treat her like an outcast. The people whom you call habitual criminals say that they have nowhere to go. They cannot come back and knock at the prison gates to be let in. The prison system does not work like that. They have to commit a crime in order to be let in. That is what happens. I regard life as still worth living. I strive hard to get back to normal. I am grateful to Prison Fellowship for their help.

Section 5:

Commercial sex workers

22

Viola

interviewed by Audrey Chihota

My name is Viola. I was born in 1969. We were ten in our family but only four of us remain. I am the eighth-born. I had four brothers and three sisters but I did not grow up with my brothers. When my father left work to come and live in a village, I stayed in Kwekwe with *sisi*: she brought me up. She was married with nine children. (She passed away last year.)

I went to school in Kwekwe but I didn't finish my education. I only went up to Grade 7 – that was in 1984. *Sisi* told me she could no longer afford to pay my fees, even though her children continued with school. They all went up to Form 4. It hurt me. I felt she was treating me like a maid, but that's how I survived, as a maid in her house. She also worked as a maid – somewhere in the suburbs.

Kwekwe is the place where I met my husband. He used to work at a mine and he married me in 1986. I had my first child in 1988 and the second in 1995. In 1996 my husband died.

I left Kwekwe in 1997 to come to my rural home because I could not afford the lifestyle in the city since I had no husband any more. His relatives are in the rural area. It was a difficult situation since we are not exactly in good books with his family as his death was suicide. He killed himself by drinking poison. He was not in agreement with his father's notion of inheriting his late brother's wife. His father wanted him to marry the woman but my husband refused. The brother had died and they all said it was TB. So my husband was always fighting with his father, but since he was on the quiet side, he just drank poison and died.

My in-laws took away my children. I communicate with them about the children who go to school there. Their uncles are responsible, so I'm not worried about them because they are comfortable. I last saw them in August. So I stayed at our rural home, but staying there with no husband and trying to get along with sisters-in-law is a problem.

I only started having affairs after my husband died. While I was married I never had any. I never even entertained the thought. I used to go to the Roman Catholic Church and I still do. At first, I tried buying and selling clothes in the rural areas to earn a living, but I decided to drop this after my friend introduced me to beerhall life in Kwekwe.

So, eventually, I came here to the growth point to keep my uncle's house in the township. I then got used to life here and also to visiting the beerhall. I go there to 'catch' to enable me to earn a living. We are scared of the [AIDS] virus, so we protect ourselves using condoms. We use them all the time. There are those clients who do not want to use condoms, but because we want to preserve our lives, we just say, 'Get out of my house and never come back.' Sometimes we get money. These days it's better even though the money today doesn't buy much. It's about a thousand dollars per client all night and using a condom.

I learnt to move around with a knife from my friend. She always carried a knife, and she said, 'Viola, whenever we go to the beerhalls, we must carry knives,' so I got used to it. The knife that I carried was not in a cover [sheath]. It is a six-gear *okapi* knife that opens at the push of a button. I came to own the knife because we had affairs with soldiers. However, the soldiers often abused us, and beat us up. [On one occasion], when they were beating us, one of them dropped his knife, and I quickly picked it up. I did not buy it.

I once stabbed a guy who works in Kwekwe. I stabbed him in the stomach. I had had an affair with this guy, but he always avoided me when he did not have money. One day, his payday, I met him at a musical show at a night-club. He asked me to partner him. When he got overly drunk, I took his pay and ran away. I went to the growth point for about a week. I then returned to Kwekwe and met him in a hotel. He started harassing me, so I brought out my knife and stabbed him. He was carried off to the hospital and I was taken to the police. But the manner in which they reviewed the issue was that he was the one who had attacked me first; I was just reacting in self-defence. That's why I stabbed him to the ground. However I paid a fine. It was still very cheap those days. I paid Z$500, now it's about Z$1,000.

One night, in 1999, I left my house at around 8 p.m. It was raining. I was in the company of three uncles and this man approached me. He was continually after me, but I always rejected him. Anyway, he said, 'Hey you, why do you refuse to take my money? Do you see it as currency that is out of circulation?' So I said, 'You can't force a person to fall in love with you.' Then he started hitting me. This is what made me stab him. My uncles – my grandmother's brother's children, moved away. One of them is a policeman at Morris Depot. When I started fighting he quickly moved away, he probably did not want to be a witness.

At that time, I used to walk around with a knife. (I have since stopped. I do not feel safe with a knife any more.) So I brought out my knife and started stabbing him in the back. He was not conscious of it, or maybe he was numb, I don't know. I shoved the knife into him, and pulled it across through the ribs. I gave him two deep cuts. The third one is the one that brought him down. I stabbed him right here, near the right eye, and pushed out two of his teeth on the upper jaw. He just fell down and I thought he had died.

When they saw it, the elderly people ran over, one of them held the man. Others ran to the police to report [the incident]. He was taken in a Defender to the clinic. He had gone stone quiet – it's said he passed out on the way there. At the clinic they were told that his condition was beyond them, and he needed to be rushed to Harare. So he spent one week on the oxygen machine, unable to breathe properly.

This guy used to work in a night-club. He used to force himself onto me whenever he saw me. I could not even enjoy a beer. Every time he saw me, he'd wrestle with me and say he wanted to go with me. He did not want anything serious. He just wanted to have me then, as he saw me. I also never liked him for his personality. I often saw him harass other girls and hit them. If he took a woman to bed, he would claim his money back, and hit the woman. So I really hated him for doing things like that. I said it was better to have none of his money at all.

On the day I committed the crime I wept. I wept for the *ngozi* I had invited into our family for no reason. I actually thought the man had died. At the time that I stabbed him, I had such a nerve, I actually wanted to kill him. But an hour later, I started crying, thinking, 'Oh, no, I have brought *ngozi* into my family and my lineage.' I was more worried about the *ngozi* than the police, since we are told that Chewas have a terrible kind of *ngozi* and that guy is Chewa.*

I did not sleep that night. I truly failed. So as dawn was breaking, I went to my friend's house. I said, 'Anna, I killed a person at the beerhall last night.' She wanted to know the details, and she asked if I thought he'd survive and I said, 'No ways.' Thereafter that friend did not leave me; she thought I might be suicidal since I thought I had killed someone. The police found me at her house. I never thought of running away because I knew the crime was mine. The police asked if I knew my crime. I said, 'Yes, I stabbed a man last night.' They asked if I knew how many times and I said, 'It must have been three times.' They ordered me to go with them and I did. I asked if I could wear proper shoes, since I was in slippers but they told me that I was in their custody and it was not possible for me to fetch my shoes.

At the charge office, I gave my statement and all other details. They took my fingerprints and told me I could not leave their custody until I had been tried. I consented. So I just slept on the bench in the charge office.

The following morning I went to court. From there I was remanded in custody and I was taken to jail while awaiting trial. When the date arrived we were all put into a big truck, males and females. One thing that really hurt me was that we were treated the same, there was no respect of how men and women sat. We would all be packed together – but the authorities say that the jail truck is never full or overloaded.

Eventually my sentencing date arrived. I was convicted on the 14th August. I had suffered a lot, not being allowed to see my relatives. They were all told that since I had not been sentenced, I could not be seen. Sometimes I would long for them to bring me soap, since there was a soap problem in the prison, but the officials refused.

---

* Ethnic group from Malawi.

I was convicted and sentenced to fifteen months in jail but when I left the courtroom, I had eight months left to serve, and when I got to jail they further suspended the sentence. Effectively I served hard labour for four months in Chikurubi.

Life in the remand prison was tough. You are woken up at 6 o'clock. Everyone rushes to the showers to bath. If you have not been sentenced you go right back in to be locked up and wait for tea at 8 a.m. The cell in Marondera was very small, too small for seventeen people, we could sleep but we could not turn over. If you take three doors and put them together lengthwise the width would be two metres. Imagine seventeen people in that space! We were separated from the men by three fences: men on one side and women on the other.

In terms of cleanliness, Marondera is excellent. But you could only go to the toilet whenever the officers came to open for us and the toilet was far from the cells, so you had to hold your bowels and your bladder. That is what caused us to use the buckets (made from the cooking oil empties) we kept for urine, if you really had to. You would then take your blanket and cover the excretion. If you did this, you would be punished for fourteen days – 'making everyone else's bed' they called it. You would have to clean the toilets and the cells and wash the blankets from the duty room.

Once I was sentenced, I felt a lot more at ease as I was now able to walk with the others inside the fence. When I went to Chikurubi, my docket was written D-class. This meant I was not anywhere near release and I would be enclosed. If I had visitors I would be given leg irons. But when I got to Chikurubi, the officer-in-charge said 'If she can live with others harmoniously in the yard, we can let her stay in the yard. But if she's ever involved in a fight, since her crime is grievous bodily harm, we will take her to D-class and lock her up.'

In D-class you do not come out at all – even with laundry you have to ask someone that might be passing by to please hang out your dress, and you might be lucky to get the next person to take it off the line for you. If it's stolen, tough – you will still be lucky to have at least one dress though you may not have a change. (Each person gets two dresses.)

Eventually I was put in the B-class. I never went to D-class. In B-class people go to work, leaving the yard and going into the garden. When I was there a new rule was introduced: all those with stabbing crimes or murder cases could not leave the prison yard, but had to tidy it up. So it was our job to clean up, seeing to the beauty of the lawn, the flowers, weeding and picking. We saw to all that. If there were visitors from the Prison Fellowship, we used to clean the shed they used, putting Cobra polish to make sure it looked smart. That was our job.

We used to go to Prison Fellowship meetings, presenting our problems there. If you had children you wished to be visited, they would go and see them for you and return with feedback. Everyone could go to Prison Fellowship meetings. Even those in C-class who are normally locked up would be released just for that experience. (C-class is for baby-dumpers, infanticides – depending on how you would have killed your baby – and those that stab others and burn people inside their houses.) The reason they were fairly lenient with me is that they checked my records for the time that I was on remand in Marondera. They saw that I did not have a problem staying with people. I never quarrelled or fought with anybody. So they could see that change in me and they attributed it to my being sorry about the crime I had committed. They thought I had learnt my lesson and reformed.

They used to unlock the doors at six and do a roll call. We would be counted over and over again. I was in Cell 2 and they always started with us. After the counting they would let us go and bath. There were about eleven cells. They are lovely cells because they are big. They are like classrooms. One sleeps freely. There would be about 40 of us in the cell; sometimes others would be moved to emptier cells. Each cell has a capacity of 52, and you sleep comfortably.

After bathing, the bell would ring again and we would go and be counted in the shed. After that we would have tea and a slice of bread and then go to work, we all knew which groups we belonged to, according to our work. We, the yard cleaners always stuck together. Our work schedule was not timed. They just wanted us to organise ourselves. The *ambuyas* would be there, but they did not push us around. We just worked as we felt like. If we chose to concentrate on the lawn and flowers, that is exactly what we did. We also picked up papers from the yard because it was never to be found dirty, we would also sweep the whole prison yard and pick up all the leaves so that it really looked lovely.

My best experience was on Independence Day. We were happy. Relatives came to see us bringing us good food from outside – even sadza was allowed. Relatives brought so much on that day. My sister's husband visited me. He brought me food.

I just saw him for a short while because there were a lot of visitors on that day, so we have to give others a chance. If the visitor had brought food that was prepared at home, the bringer of the food had to taste it immediately; but if the food came from shops, it did not matter.

My worst experience, the saddest day of my life at Chikurubi, was when I was coming from the toilet. I wanted to sit down and there is a room called the Condemn where all torn and tattered linen and clothes are kept, and I wanted to go and sit there. I did not know that people had been chased away from there by *ambuya mugadhijere*. So when I tried to sit down this *ambuya* appeared and held me by the dress. I started wrestling with her and in the process knocked off her hat.

I was then called to the office and severely beaten. I was beaten several times on my backside. It took me quite a while to be able to sit down again. It was the same *ambuya* that I had wrestled with who beat me up. She had not warned me because as she held me, I also held her by the collar. It was in self-defence.

She claimed I was the one who had run away from her earlier, but it was not me. I had only just got to that room. She insisted that the person she had seen was me. So when she tried to hit me I said to myself, 'No ways! I cannot be beaten for someone else's crimes. I am already serving a prison sentence for God's sake! How could she want to further punish me?' So I just grabbed her and we wrestled until her hat fell from her head.

Ha, I get really angry at times. It is when I am provoked that I react, as I find fit at that moment.

I did not do a single course in prison. What used to happen was that one would be asked what one was good at. I was good at crotcheting – doilies especially. So I was just given wool to keep me busy and I made doilies for the prison guards. We just worked for nothing because we were constantly reminded that we were 'prisoners'. There were courses, but my education was the hindrance. They wanted five O-levels. Also courses depended on your sentence. If you are serving a short sentence you cannot go to school. Only those serving twelve months go to school. They often leave prison with certificates. I could not go to school because I was in there for four months. Even the money that one gets upon leaving jail – the Z$2 per month, we never got, because we had served a short period.

What I really missed in prison was having beer. I was a person used to drinking beer and moving around and sleeping with different men, so it really bothered me. I would also occasionally feel like having a man, but it would just be a fleeting thought, it didn't affect me too badly. What I truly missed was beer. I started drinking beer when my husband was still alive, even before we got married. We both used to go clubbing until we had our two children.

When I first got to Chikurubi, there was a certain girl who was a real problem. If you saw her walk you would think she is a man. She did not have breasts but she had a beard, yet she was female. She was quite old – maybe in her forties, because she was quite old. On arrival in prison we would be warned to keep away from her because she would actually fondle other women. If she lusted after you while you were dressing, she would come over and fondle you.

When I first got to Chikurubi there were beds. They were then removed to ensure that each person slept alone because others would sneak in and share beds. That girl would creep into the blankets of whichever woman she would be lusting after, and fondle her: the next day the woman would be given a payment of bread and a piece of meat.

She was the only one I saw harassing others with lesbianism and I never wanted to be anywhere near her since I had been warned. If you were seen with her you would be punished. The *ambuyas* knew her and her ways. She would really behave masculine even though she was a woman. She is the one who mended the prison officers' shoes, fixed the umbrellas and sorted out the firewood. Her crime was alleged to have been murder, but I only met her when she was getting ready to leave, so by then she had been put in B-class.

What I despised in prison was the food. Sometimes we had to use pumpkin as relish for sadza because there were no vegetables. At times we would pick sweet-potato leaves to be eaten as vegetables. Sometimes the sadza was cooked out of rotting mealie-meal – you would actually remove the worms as you were eating. Sometimes we only ate sadza once a day – because there would be no vegetables to go with it. We ate twice at 12 o'clock and 3 p.m. then at about 4 p.m. we would be locked up. Breakfast was at about 7 a.m. with one slice of bread, sometimes with margarine at other times jam and occasionally with nothing.

The problem we encountered as women was that of menstruation. Sometimes we would not be given pads even though they were there. Women would say spend the day with one pad. Sometimes we would end up using tissues, something that would hurt our uteruses, because we had no choice. Among us there were prisoners who worked in the D-clinic. They were not from D-class but they helped the nurses in administering treatments and other things, they are the ones who went to the sick-bay and gave patients their medication. Most of them were in for fraud. So they knew that there were stocks of pads for our use.

I do not think prison is the best way of discipline or punishment, because prisoners exchange notes on how they commit crimes and sometimes get away. Someone might even say, 'Oh, I had a boyfriend and I went and burned him and his wife in their house and I have served ten years. I am getting ready to get out.' You then realise how minor your crime is compared to other women who are real criminals. I guess it just depends on your perspective: do you feel hurt by the prison sentence you are serving or do you want to try what other prisoners might have shared with you.

My greatest desire was for the day that I would leave prison. I wished for my father to send me a lot of money so that I could drink beer. When I was arrested I wrote a letter to my parents and all my relatives to say please do not come to see me or write to me, even in the event of a death or sickness. I did not want to know, because it would only make me cry, and if you cry a lot in prison you will be beaten up by the officers, even if you are grieving for the death of a relative. It's really better only to hear about everything when you are released.

I did not even think of my children – I just pushed them out of my mind. And a certain preacher – Mr Hlongwane – used to say, 'Do not think too much about the children, because you cause them illness through thinking too much.' And even you wouldn't be OK in jail because your mind would be disturbed, if you think too much. When I thought, 'What will my children say when they hear that I am in prison,' I cried.

Once my husband's young brother, who was looking after the children, came to see me. I explained the whole story to him. Having had a fight with him while his brother, my husband, was still alive, he was not too shocked at my case. He spoke immediately, right in front of the prison guards, and said, 'Amaiguru, I once told you to control your anger. Now look now where it has landed you. Murder! If that man dies, our children will suffer because of the *ngozi*. Living in your homestead will be a nightmare, because of the *ngozi*.'

However, I later learnt that that man [the victim] had not died. He actually came to see me in Marondera when I was in remand. He asked if I knew how many times I had stabbed him. I said I did not remember and he said, 'Three times'. Then he took off his shirt just to show me the wounds in the presence of the jail guard. That worried me even after he was gone. But I think he has forgiven me. I asked for forgiveness when he came to Marondera. It was then that he said, 'Let's live together as husband and wife,' but he is married. Even with his wife, he still came to see me and kept harassing me.

He also came to visit me in Chikurubi. He was proposing to wait for me on the day I was released but I refused. He wanted me to go and live with him after that, though we had never been intimate. To this day he still bothers me. Surely it can't be love. I really don't know what it can be but I am afraid because I do not know what he is planning. Now he has left this growth point, but he comes here often. We don't talk. We haven't ever got close at all. He has since divorced his wife. She comes with us to the beerhalls now. But he took away their child.

When I came out of prison, I decided that I would not ever want to go back, so I was thinking of starting my own business. I started cooking fish and knuckles and potatoes and meat, and selling them at the beerhall. I stopped when the people renting the shop near my stand said they did not want cooked food being sold in that place, so I stopped.

Now I sometimes cook sadza by the braai stands and sell it. I still find men for business but these days I have kind of slowed down because I have got a boyfriend who is looking after me. We are not exactly living together but he is looking after me. He gives me money for food and pays rent and sometimes buys clothes for me. So I have kept away from other men. I am afraid of being caught out because my boyfriend can come any time he feels like it.

The sadza has been keeping us busy until the shortage of maize, a bucket now[†] costs about Z$800, and it is increasingly difficult to buy. If you cook one pot of five litres of sadza with one kg meat and vegetables, you can get about Z$1,300 or Z$1,400, so its not too bad. The other thing that brings me money are these vendors that go to Jo'burg, we sometimes crotchet doilies for them and they give us money, or some of the stuff they bring back in exchange. What else can I honestly do for myself at this age? What I am doing with myself feels adequate.

---

† October, 2002.

I saw my children last year in August. They were very happy. The older one, the boy, cried when he saw me. He said, 'Mum, please do not ever stab people again.' The younger one did not understand and she asked where I had been, so I told her, 'I went to jail my child.' My wish is that my brother-in-law remains kindhearted and continues to send my children to school.

My daughter once saw me hit somebody with a bottle – here at the growth point. The child saw it all. This man had forcefully opened my door while I was staying at my uncle's. So I just took a bottle and hit him. I had once had an affair with him but on that particular night, the time that he had chosen to come was not right. It was about 2 a.m. and he was stone-drunk. I was alone with my children who were sleeping. He said he wanted to join us and he said he would pay but because of his drunkenness, I just said, 'Leave me alone.' I was afraid that my child might be raped – the young one – if I allowed a man to sleep over when I was also drunk, but he insisted on coming in, so since I was also drunk, I just took the bottle and stabbed him.

I kind of grew up very violent. I do not know I can explain it. When a person first provokes me, I keep quiet but when they go on and on, I lose control. Like the boy that I beat up on Friday. He came up to me and said, 'Hello *hure!*' For me to be called a *hure* by somebody who has never slept with me is very insulting. So I started hitting him. He jumped behind the counter of the bottle store and I followed. The owners evicted us from the store, but the man was already bleeding. He couldn't hit back because when he fell, I kept kicking him with my shoes. If he had ever had an affair with me, I would not have minded him calling me *hure* because we would know each other. So, yes, I still fight but I do not use a knife, neither do I use bottles: now I use my bare hands.

My anger must have started when I was young. We used to sell bananas and were always on the look out for the police. Whenever I was beaten by someone, even if he was older than me, my sister would say, 'Fight back you should never be beaten.' Once while I was selling bananas, a certain boy, Clemence, came and fondled my breast. His girlfriend saw him. I asked Clemence why he was doing this to me? His girlfriend, Chipo, answered saying that I had always wanted her boyfriend. I asked her, 'How can this be, when he is so much older and so are you?' Then Chipo started hitting me.

When *sisi* came home and found me crying she wanted to know why. I told her and she said, 'Go and fight with her!' I told her I couldn't because Chipo was too old and she said, 'Go fight with her till you beat her!' So every time I was beaten up *sisi* would beat me to invoke my anger. So that's when I really got easily angered and thereafter I did not care whether one was male or female, young or old, I would just fight.

A lot of girls do not dare come near me. They are afraid. Even if they see me with their boyfriends they just keep quiet. I would say that these two friends of mine and I are the champions of fighting here at the growth point. I do not have room for negotiation. Only when I am sober, I am a bit shy, but not when I am drunk.

To this day, I fear no one. I am always ready to protect myself. The man that I am seeing now says he wants to marry me, but because of his age – he was born in 1982 – I do not think its possible. He says it doesn't bother him that I am older than he because his parents have died. I really love him but I am afraid to get pregnant because I might have problems in the future. My heart says no. It won't be nice if we have had a baby and then we separate or divorce, and I am left with the child. Ah, ah, I do not want to have a child. I want to be married to him but I am afraid. I feel I must see his relatives first and he says this is no problem. His relatives might have a problem with the age difference.

He got a farm during this resettlement, though he's standing in for his uncle, and he's got a house that his father left for him in Marlborough. We've actually been there. He sometimes, tries to force me not to use condoms but I do not want this. I have never been tested, we have spoken about it, and he has agreed that we shall go for the tests.

I don't know what the future holds for me but I would like to lead a good life.

23

Martha

interviewed by Keresia Chateuka

My name is Martha. My father is Malawian and my mother is Zimbabwean. She comes from a village in Goromonzi. I was born in 1968, I am thirty four years old. My father is a gardener in Mt Pleasant. He lives at his work place. My parents separated when I was young. Until recently I had no clear memory of my father. If I were to come across him, I would have walked past him without recognising him – something that drove me to find him. I found him, with the assistance of my older sister's neighbour, who knew him because they used to drink together in the beerhalls in Tafara. She took me to meet him. At first he was reluctant to see me, but after a week he eventually met me and we talked. It turned out that he was my real father. He has another wife but no other children besides my brother and me. My mother remarried and has another child with her second husband.

Our grandfather – my mother's father, took good care of us. He loved us. The trouble started when he died. We could not go to school any more. We had no decent clothes. Food was short. My aunts, my mother's sisters, often beat us for no good reason. They complained about my father, how he never sent money for our food or school fees. They wanted our mother to live with us. They made my brother and me sleep in an open bathing shelter – a rough circular wall of thatch grass, which was a distance away from the houses. That is where we kept our clothes. Our mother did not come to get us. She only sent us clothes that we never wore. My aunts took and wore them instead. My mother did not know about it.

I decided to run away and live at a growth point with some girls who knew about the way I lived. It was hard leaving my little brother behind. The girls invited me to join them in what they were doing. Most of what they did was bad but I had to survive. They were much older than me – unmarried, but with children. They went to the beerhalls and brought men home. They slept with these men for money. I used to follow them everywhere, so I got to know what they did. Sometimes they used to bring a man to me but they received money on my behalf because they gave me food, a place to sleep and blankets. This is how I learnt about how I could make money in the beerhalls.

One day I met a man in the beerhall, Stanley. He rented a room for me. Soon after I went back to my aunt's and brought my brother to live with me at the growth point. I made a little money that I used to pay his school fees and buy him clothes. He went to school and I cooked for him. After school he would be hired by some women at the growth point to sell eggs or freezits. He earned a little money from this. He went as far as Grade 7 and could not go further because he had no birth certificate. I sent messages to my mother about the problem but she did not come to see us. She sent back a message that it was pointless for her to come because she would not be able to register our births. She did not have my father's identity papers. Up to now I do not have an identity card because I do not have a birth certificate. I have tried to register our births but it is impossible without grown people who were there when we were born to be witnesses at the district offices. I approached some important people in the district but it did not work. I tried filling in forms but nothing has come out of it. I was told nothing would happen until I found grown people who witnessed our birth.

Recently I asked my mother to come with me to the district offices. She brought some witnesses. We filled in the forms again and they also took our fingerprints. This was in February 2003 but up to now the birth certificates are not yet out. Whenever I phoned the district office, officials said the identity card and birth certificate would both be out at the same time. I worry about this problem a lot because my own children are growing and without the identity papers they cannot go beyond Grade 7. They will be like me, poor and without any education. In my desperation, I went to the police for help but they told me to go back with witnesses to the district offices, where the registration office is. Without money, a father, and a husband, it is hard to get these papers. It is a chain of events – one thing leads to the other. My father did not have an identity card. I do not have one and my children cannot have birth certificates. I am afraid to travel to Harare because of the police roadblocks. What would I tell the police if they were to ask for my identity card? I have no chance of getting employed even as a housemaid without it. Any employer would want my ID.

Stanley and I lived together for six months then he disappeared. I was deeply pained because I thought we were in love and would later marry. However, I found another man, John. He agreed to pay the rent for my room. Our life together was good until I got pregnant and had a baby. Then he spent most of his time away from me: he stopped buying food. It was hard to force him to provide for my child and me because he had not paid anything towards *lobola*. I was not his wife. He had no obligations to me. Nobody in my family made an effort to force him to pay *lobola* and to see that he cared for me. I had no one to protect me from abuse. There was nobody for him to be scared of — nobody else to answer to beside myself: he behaved as he pleased, walking all over me as if I were nothing. Then one day I got angry. I found out that he had another girlfriend. I asked him about it and he beat me up: that is when I decided to have nothing to do with him.

My brother left and found a job with a family at the growth point. He lived with the family. I had approached them for help. He was now a young man and I could not continue to share a room with him. Only a thin cloth I hung across the walls divided the room into two: his sleeping place and mine. It was difficult especially when I brought a man for the night. The family appreciated my situation and agreed that he could live with them. I was relieved because my father had shown no interest in helping out. He told us that we could not live in his employer's yard. The house owners did not allow it. He refused to give us any money. He was simply not interested in us. My mother was not in a position to help and now she is not well. She is in hospital.

After my boyfriend left me, I had a baby with another man. With two children, I thought I would stand a better chance of being looked after in my old age. I think it is better to have two children than one. I took on three more children from my late aunt: one of them is now self-supporting. He is a casual worker at a farm. I also have two more to care for, my late sister's two children, and I still live in a single room at the growth point.

I cannot cope with so many children. I go to the beerhall: that is all I can do to earn money. If I get a little money then I buy food for the day. As long as they have sadza, soap, clothes; then they are all right. Life goes on. One of the children in Grade 3 has been sent away from school because he has no birth certificate. The older one of my children dropped out of school in Grade 6 because I could not raise the school fees. I tell all the children not to worry too much: at least they are not sick. They have health: it's something to be thankful for these days. Even though I go to the beerhall to look for men I am afraid of diseases. Then I think to myself, what disease could be worse than starving my children to death? I protect myself with condoms even though some people say they can burst. I know that they are not always safe. Sometimes I fail to pay my rent but my landlord has a soft heart. He feels for the children. I do not make enough and sometimes the men who have sex with me do not pay. This is what landed me in prison.

I went to the beerhall one evening. My two children were sleeping in the room. There I met a man who asked to come with me to my room. I told him to give me the money before I take him anywhere. I wanted him to pay first because I was in the beerhall to make money and nothing else. He took out his wallet, pulled out a few notes that he waved before my face and promised to pay later after sleeping with me. I asked him if he was telling the truth because I had children to feed. He assured me that he would. I believed him.

We went to my room. My children were asleep and we went to bed. Very early the next day, just as the night darkness was lifting, he tried to run away without paying. First he checked to see if I was awake. I pretended to be asleep. He took his trousers and wore them like somebody who was going outside for a short time to use the toilet. Then he took his shirt and jersey and went outside. That is when I lifted the blanket off my face and asked him what he was up to. He told me that it was morning and he was leaving to go back to his family. I told him that he did not sleep in my room for free he had to pay, and pay quickly, too. I reminded him of the reason why I went to the beerhall: I had children to feed and clothe. Not only did he not pay but he started to fight me. I got very angry with him because I had clearly stated my reasons for bringing him into my home. He made a fool of me, and tried to be too clever for his own good. I was mad. I grabbed a pot by the handle and hit him several times but he hit me back even harder. He was clearly overpowering me so I thought of getting a knife. I shouted to my child to bring me a knife, but he could only cry, as any child would. I got the knife myself and sliced off his ear. It fell on the floor. He was visibly frightened and also embarrassed that people would come to see what had happened to him. He ran away but he did not go to the police station.

I put my baby on my back and went to the police station to report what I had done and that I expected the man to be at the station before me. They wanted to know if I knew where he lived but I did not know much about him. As we were talking about him he arrived. He lived at a nearby commercial farm. He explained that he had run home for a change of clothes, he had bled heavily and his clothes were bloodied. The man was taken to hospital and the nurses sutured his ear back into place. He brought back his hospital papers to the police station. I was in the police cells for two days. When I came out the police took me straight to court. They called my name and asked me to stand in the box reserved for the accused. They read out my charge. 'Cutting off a man's ear because he refused to pay for my sexual services.' I agreed and the court said I would be in prison for a year and four months. I told them I had a three-month old baby. They suspended part of my sentence and I was to be in prison for nine months only at Chikurubi. I felt a deep pain but there was nothing I could do. Tears welled in my eyes. They took me to Chikurubi in a truck. They allowed me to bring my baby along, so for all the time I was in prison, I had my baby.

In prison mothers did not get special accommodation. In the cell we were mixed, those with children and those without. The room had bunk beds and each person had a bed. I shared my bed with my baby. This was in 1989. There was a toilet in the cell but it could not be flushed from outside the cell, something that caused us considerable discomfort especially if somebody had to use the toilet at night. We all tried hard not to use the toilet at night. If you had to then it meant trouble with your inmates because your waste would make the cell stink. Sometimes fights would break out because of it. One would try to contain the stink by putting a blanket over the toilet but some inmates would be irritable with you and beat you up for making them uncomfortable throughout the night. Sometimes you will have eaten food that upset your stomach but still the other inmates chose not to understand your difficult situation. I observed that beans brought about stomach problems.

I had a green uniform but the baby had no uniform. There were some old baby clothes we could use. When we went out to work, elderly inmates looked after the children. The children had porridge with egg sometimes. During my stay in prison I worried a lot about the health of my baby. Sometimes the baby food was not well prepared. So one day I decided to complain because my baby had diarrhoea and on checking the baby food I found out that the porridge was lumpy and no egg had been added as was required. I went up to one of the prison guards and said, 'Look *vana ambuya*, look at the poor quality of food my baby is fed.' As soon as I said that they beat me up – they beat me up at lunchtime. Two of them took turns to beat me with a baton because I had demanded well-prepared food for my baby. They said I was acting proud and important. Oh, they beat me and beat me. I was really upset and I told them that I was going to report them to the magistrates who come to find out from us about our living conditions in prison. They threatened to extend my stay in prison if I reported them. It was too serious a threat. I did not want to stay a day more than necessary. I never said a word against them from that day. I wanted to go back home to my children. However, after this incident their behaviour towards me improved. They were friendly. They offered me Lacto for my baby. During meal times they asked me to feed my baby first. In the end I was taken off the list of people who went out to work in the garden. We got on better than before. Maybe the beatings were a show of their power over me and the other prisoners.

For most of the time I was in prison I worked in the garden; preparing beds, planting vegetables and watering them. I was not in very good health because of an operation I had had before. They stopped me from working in the garden whenever I was in pain. They were quite considerate to everybody who had health problems. Any child who fell sick in prison was treated at the clinic, if the child had a problem too big for the clinic to deal with, then they provided transport to take her to Parirenyatwa Hospital. We mothers were treated in the same way. First we would be attended to at the prison clinic: if we had a serious problem, we would be taken to Parirenyatwa Hospital.

Throughout my stay in prison, nobody came to visit me. Besides my children who were too young to travel to Harare, there was nobody else caring enough in my life. I would have wanted somebody to bring me things to make life bearable. I could have done with some food. I was breast-feeding and I often felt very hungry. Sometimes I would give my share of food to my baby. I could have done with soap too to wash my baby's clothes. Sometimes I exchanged my piece of bread for soap with my inmates. In prison we had sadza with vegetables, beef and sometimes chicken. We had rice too. More effort could have been put into cooking the food properly.

On the day I was released from prison, I went to a high-density suburb in Harare, where my aunt lived. I had money that I had brought with me from home, so I took a bus. I was looking forward to being with my children. My aunt was happy to see me. She did not know that I had been in prison. She was very sympathetic: she gave me clothes and some money for food. When I got home my children were happy to see me and so were my friends. They were surprised at how well I looked. I had gained some weight and my skin was clean and shiny. Even I knew that physically I looked better than I did before. None of my relatives came to see me: none knew about my arrest anyway. The man whose ear I had cut off came to see me. I did not want him anywhere near me. I did not want any trouble so I went back to report him to the police. In addition, I demanded that he pay money he still owed me. The police advised me that prostitution was a crime. I was not entitled to any payment. Instead they could arrest me again. I left them in a hurry.

Prison life is not at all good. I wasted time that I could have used to improve my life. My children suffered, both the one who was in prison with me and the ones I left at home. My baby was a prisoner too even though he had not committed a crime. I found those I left behind worse off. They were unwashed, had no clothes, and no food. They depended on the kindness of friends and neighbours. One of my friends used to regularly check if they were all right. And my next-door neighbour gave them food now and again. That was all the help they got.

Although I know that a life of going to beerhalls in search of men who can pay for sex is bad, I now know from experience that many young girls travel this road because they have no choice. The seed of their problem was sown in their childhood. Take the way I grew up for example: my parents were never there for me throughout my childhood. I had no support system. Sometimes I get angry and wish my grandfather had lived longer. He cared for me, loved me as if I were his own child. He would have given me a better chance in life. I'm sure about that.

24

Chipo

interviewed by Audrey Chihota

My name is Chipo. I was born in a village in Goromonzi. There were eleven of us in my family: seven girls and four boys. I am the sixth-born. All four boys died: now there are only six girls, one also died. My sister, the one I come after, works as a maid in Harare. My little sister, the youngest in the family, and one other both live in a village in Goromonzi with their husbands. One sister lives in Nyabira with her husband and so does another in Marondera.

I went to prison in 1999 after I had been involved in a fight with a certain girl at the beerhall. I hit her with an empty bottle and got arrested. I was sentenced to eight months, which I served before my release.

We were fighting over a man. It all started when this girl saw me with this man. She came up to me, and started dancing in front of us and said, 'This is my boyfriend.' I replied, 'No he is mine!' So we started shouting at each other, then we started wrestling. I took an empty bottle and hit her. We had both been drinking beer. We must have been drunk. The man we were fighting over quickly disappeared.

I left and went home in fear of her friends, that they might attack me. Shortly afterwards the police arrived to collect me. I did not panic. I expected them because I knew I had really hurt that woman. When they asked to see Chipo I answered the door. I knew the police would come for me because when I hit this girl, people started shouting, 'Run to the police, you have been hurt,' and she had done that. The police did not handcuff me. We went to the police camp and I was asked what had happened. I said the fight was over a man, but he had disappeared.

The police took me away. I stayed at the charge office for two or three nights then I was taken to court in Marondera; and to Chikurubi for my prison term. I was convicted for having hit the other person with a bottle. The court said it was wrong to have hurt that person that way. I had really damaged her on the whole left side of the head using the empty bottle. She was hurt enough to spend a few days in hospital. She is all right now: we still drink together. She is my friend. There is no bad blood – but, if she takes my man again, I will fight her again. It is a question of survival. I look for men with money to feed my son and myself. His father – whom I had been with for quite some time, died when the child was one year nine months old. The only other way of earning money is selling vegetables.

I knew I deserved the sentence because I had really hurt this woman. Even when I was arrested, I knew I was not going to be released because I had hurt a person. I am sure that my sentence was okay for my crime.

But prison was difficult. The problem was menstruation. I never saw cotton wool. We had to use tissues. Then we would have nothing to use in the toilet. Each of us was given a bit of toilet paper three times each week. We were not given full rolls. So all we had was tissue. Those with a heavy flow had to ask for pieces of cloth from the officers, to use as pads. But the rest of us with light flows relied on tissue for the few days of the month. I think prisons should have cotton wool because that is what women should use – not this tissue business. Tissue is for the toilet.

And the food: that was the first time I saw black cabbages. I did not know there were black cabbages, and to be eaten with sadza! But we ate them all the same, because if we refused we could be punished. So we ate them. We had to or else we would be beaten up.

In prison they separated us. Those who were there for fighting were in one place. Others with worse crimes were in their own line. Infanticide cases and baby dumpers were in another, and so on. Some are even put in a place where they never see the sun or even know that it is setting. They were considered to be very dangerous and merciless criminals. The prisoners included baby dumpers and murderers. They were denied access to the outer world.

I was in B-class. I served my entire sentence in B-class, until eight months was up. When you go inside, people will always ask, 'What brought you here?' Other prisoners knew my crime. We exchanged stories and we were pretty much scared of each other because you never knew how dangerous the next person might have been.

Different people did different work. B-class is for those serving short sentences and you work from there. We woke up at about six and went to work. At about 12 o'clock, we would go to lunch and then return and work until end of day. At about 4 o'clock, we would have supper, then go to sleep. We would water the garden and cultivate the vegetables. Chikurubi has a vegetable area. My worst experience was when we tilled the whole garden so as to put in vegetables. We worked until the land was as they wanted it. That day I swore I never ever wanted to return to prison. My hands had blisters all over them. Even when I went to sleep, I thought, I would never commit such a crime again.

But generally a day in prison was all right because we worked. It is better than just staying seated. When it's a weekend you just sit: some go to church, and some knit or do likewise, but you will just be seated. You stay in one place. If you try to get some fresh air away from the premises, they take it that you want to run away.

Prison is not a nice place to be, especially for a woman. I could see that I had erred and that's why I was in prison. So I just said to myself, it's best to serve my sentence ungrudgingly until the time comes for me to leave. But it is not a nice place. You are well looked after but just being enclosed, without being able to move freely – haa, it is just not nice. It's really different from being out here where you can move around doing whatever you like.

I did not do any courses in jail. I used to plait the other women's hair. Some used to do schoolwork and self-improvement courses, but I couldn't. My mind was too busy. I kept thinking because I had never done this before. It was a heavy burden on me. So I kept worrying about why I had got myself jailed. I kept to myself, most of the time. I was very quiet, condemning myself for what I had done. During projects, I just used to sit. I did not feel like doing any of them. I didn't have the urge to do anything. I kept thinking and chastising myself.

My relatives came to see me: my brother from Epworth (who has now died) and my brother from Hatcliffe (who has also now died) used to come, and their wives also used to come sometimes. I would get visitors at least twice weekly. They brought me food – Mazoe [crush], bread and sometimes sadza.

The man we were fighting over never came to see me and this troubled me. After all I had known him for three months. I did not know what to do because I asked myself why I had committed such a crime, hurting my girlfriend for a man who never once came to see me toiling in prison. This man, who was the source of my problem, came nowhere near me, yet I was languishing in prison for his sake. Maybe he was already seeing someone else. We did not live together. We had just met at the beer hall. It really took time for me to get this out of my mind.

When you are in prison you have to follow the rules or else you get punished. I never got punished because I was such a coward. From the day I entered, I was warned to be obedient. I was told that if I did not show respect or fear of the guards, they would beat me up until they were satisfied, so I was more than obedient and I was never beaten. Never. When we were in prison we missed the beer. We also missed the menfolk and wondered what to do. But we never abused each other sexually. An elderly prisoner warned me about it. She said if a person showed that she was dull, other prisoners would take advantage of her and make her their husband. I never saw such behaviour in our cell. If you were cheeky, nobody came near you. I never wanted to hear of it, let alone see it. So all we could do was count the number of days before our release.

My best experience, the day that I would say was a good day, was when I was told that I was going home the following day. I even failed to sleep. I kept praying, saying, 'Lord please bless me, I will never commit such a crime again.' When finally I was released, I quickly changed into my clothes. As I was walking out of the prison gates, I kept looking over my shoulder, worrying that I might be called back in. I kept thinking they would say it was a mistake. I kept wishing the ETs would come quickly for me to jump in before these people changed their minds.

I just left Chikurubi and waited for ETs into town. By about 12 o'clock, I had already arrived in Epworth and was now sitting with my brother's wife chatting away. I was telling her that I had had it and that I would never commit a crime to land me in prison again. No, I learnt my lesson. My sister-in-law could not over-emphasise how bad it was and telling me to stay clean from crime. I said, 'Never again.'

When my brother came, he also made his dismay known. He chastised me for having been in prison and asked me why I had committed the crime. I told him such things happen sometimes. But obviously he knew all the details through his wife. I had of course told her. You can't hide such things from a fellow woman. But my brother was complaining that he had spent a lot of his money on me, just coming to see me for my misbehaviour. Could I answer? I was just quiet, but when he would not stop, I quickly bade him farewell. I said that I was going home to see our mother who was looking after my child because it had been a while. I did not even spend the night with them. I quickly boarded a bus that was heading towards Shamva Road at Mbare Musika. I went straight home to my mother and got there at about 7 p.m. My mother was quite surprised to see me. She was very happy. She sat down with me and drummed into me that I was never to commit such a crime again. I assured her that I wouldn't. I told her that I had learnt the hard way and would never do it again.

I have had numerous men, but this man, the one I was fighting over, has now promised to marry me (although I don't quite believe him) and we are living together. So, for the time being, I will be faithful. But if he does not marry me, or provide me with money, I will go with other men. I still go to the pub with my 'husband'. We drink and when we are full, we go home to sleep.

Since my release I haven't committed any other crime, or fought with people because it is not right for a woman to be always in the hands of the police. I do still fight but I do not use dangerous things like bottles to hurt my friends. I learnt the hard way when I did it the last time. I now fear using anything other than my hands for hitting a person. I am now really scared of it. I know fighting is a crime, but often I will be really angry, really mad; I realise that 'Damn, I am pissed off,' but you only regret your actions when the police pick you or when the beer is gone. Then you wish you had not over-reacted.

Only recently, I fought with a certain girl who bit my arm really hard. I still have the scars. We were just sitting and she provoked me. She wanted to take my beer. I told her, 'No, you can't. I just bought this beer from *kwaMuchawa*.*' She refused to understand.

---

* from the Malawian man

Then, a friend of mine, whom I was drinking with, took the beer and spilt it in an effort to quell the whole issue. She asked me to sit down and forget about the girl. But the girl came again, this time shouting at me about my mother, using unprintable words. I then got up and said, 'I cannot have you abuse my mother. She is in the rural areas. Leave her out of it.' We started fighting. I wrestled her to the ground. That is when she bit me — on my arm and on my hand. When I saw I was hurt, I rushed home and wrapped the wounds with bandage. It was unsightly. The following morning, I woke up, got into a car and rushed to the clinic for a tetanus injection.

I have not fought since. I have stopped fighting. I will never ever do it again. My husband was there when we were fighting. He is the one who tried to stop the fight. The girl also bit him on the finger and tore his trousers. If we are drinking, let's just enjoy our beer. I don't want someone shouting at me about my mother who is far from here. Yes, shout at me, say whatever, shit whatever, call me whatever, but *not* my mother. It hurts.

The police can punish you saying, 'We are seeing too much of you here at the charge office. Maybe it is best to punish you.' Sometimes they keep you all day at the charge office, sometimes they throw you a blanket and say, 'Sleep'. It hurts because you know very well that you have a beautiful, comfortable bed at home, but you are spending a whole day, and sometimes a night, at the charge office. Then you say, 'If only I had known,' but that does not help because you will already have committed a crime. It will be too late.

Since I left prison, I have not been in trouble with the police. Even when I recently fought with this girl, I was not involved with them. We did not take each other to the police. We just negotiated our own way through. We had to say to each other, 'Look, we were both wrong. Let this be water under the bridge.' We apologized to each other and took each other to the clinic and that was it. I haven't had to deal with the police to this day. I don't hope to either. Not at all.

I still have one child, the boy. His father died. And I had a little girl by another man two years ago and she died after three days. I used to go to the church, the Madzibaba Church, and we used to pray overnight by the depot. I used to go, thinking I might just conceive again. Haa, I really used to pray a lot … My husband would just go to the beer hall but I used to go to pray, thinking we could perhaps be blessed and conceive a child; but nothing came of it. So we just stopped and agreed to forget about it.

When I was jailed in 1999, I sort of broke up with this man. He still hasn't paid *lobola*. We had just lived together but he has not paid even a cent to my parents. Maybe he will give them something, one day. He is a young man. If you see him, you will not believe it. He's rather young, very youthful. I am kind of older. We just met here, as we were moving around, we spotted each other.

When I was in jail, I do not know if he stayed with anyone else, he moved away from the area, but when he heard that I was back and living with a friend, Loveness, in Goromonzi, then he returned and we are living together again. We spoke, as people that have loved each other before, and we understood each other. We just agreed that such things do happen and he said to me, 'Let's go home.' I agreed and I have been with him ever since. We fight, yes, we shout at each other, but we are always together. Sometimes he is wayward and goes out with other women. Whenever I hear of it, we fight, but he always comes back home.

When I got back from jail I started running a market stall. I would go to the market and buy and sell *chibage*, vegetables, bananas. (I used to sell cabbages before being jailed.) Now I have gone back to the market. The work is overwhelming. We wait for a long time to find *chibage* for sale.

When I was in jail, I wished to be home. I wanted to come and sell at the market, and help my mother look after the family. All my four brothers have died leaving their families behind. The children need looking after. Some stay with their mothers, and others are here with me. So, in jail, it really used to worry me, and I needed to start selling again, so that I could afford a bucket of maize for my mother and the children.

I have three of my brothers' children here. They go to school. One is twelve the other is thirteen, one is in Grade 4, the other Grade 3. The young one is eight, very young. He does not go to school. I stay with him when the others are at school. As we speak, they are at the growth point selling *freezits*, so that they can get money to buy tennis shoes when schools open. My only living brother, the eldest in the family, is the one who pays their school fees.

When I left prison, I swore I would never go back again. I don't even want to be near there. But I have a friend with whom I drink. Just the other day we were so drunk that I couldn't find my way home and I slept right by the rubbish bins. I never quarrelled or fought with anyone.

Whenever I see a woman driving a car, I say, 'Honestly look at this. What kind of background do such people have, where there are no evil spirits? They were born of a good background.' Then I look at myself and see that there is no success story in my entire family — not one. We will all die in poverty; this worries me a lot.

Recently I touched on the subject with Mai Jim. She asked me if I was peddling anything at all, and I told her, 'I am going to stop drinking beer, because its standing in my way as far as making money is concerned. I used to sell very well. My wheelbarrow would always be full of oranges, maize cobs, and I would rise very early to go to the market in Mbare to order my stocks with others but now even just selling at the market is a problem. Simply because of the beer, that's why I want to quit.' And Mai Jim said, 'I'm glad you see it too.' I said, 'Truthfully *ambuya*, I want to quit and get serious about selling.'

With beer drinking you enjoy yourself and you realise too late that you have nothing in the house — no salt, no soap. You wish you had bought bath soap, and you go to your friends asking for a piece of soap, just to scrub your dirty hands. It's disgraceful, especially if you do what I do, betting on my last cent at the beerhall.

Beer is expensive. Right now[†] a pint is Z$550. The scud is also Z$550. Sometimes my friend and I put money together to buy a scud. You want to know how much that is? We usually drink three and that's more than Z$1,500. With Z$1,500 you can still buy something tangible. You can hoard cabbages at that price and make a profit. Imagine the recent holiday! Vendors here made a lot of money. But we also spent money! I told you that we slept in rubbish bins because of drunkenness!

If then, you know medicine for me to quit drinking please help. I have the desire to stop drinking. It's so strong that if I could get someone to put pig's milk in the beer to stop me, I would appreciate it. I want to be like others who look for money. My parents sometimes send my brothers' children to ask for soap, then I wish I had not spent so much money on beer, so that maybe I would have a piece of soap for my mother. The desire to stop is there. Ask my friends what kind of a business woman I am. I used to sell so much that even the beer drinkers would say, 'Chipo come and join us,' then I would say, 'I am busy.'

[†] March 2003

I do not know what got into me. And where in the world is there a place with no beerhall? Everywhere there are beerhalls. Even on the farms you find *chikokiyana* and *kachasu*. Where do you think I should go? Maybe where you come from, there are no pubs? This husband of mine, Alexio, taught me to drink. He always says, 'Don't bother cooking, let's go drinking.' We drink and go home just to sleep.

Women, especially those without husbands, are ready for anything. In the beerhall, life and death are the same thing. A person can just step on your toe, and when you ask why they are doing that, they will pour beer on you or hit you with a bottle. If I am provoked like this, I quickly rise to the occasion and hit you before you can blink. If I do not do this, there is really nothing for me. Can you see my head? All this hair is gone because of fighting, people pulling out my hair extensions. There at Makanda's that's where my hair was pulled out. Plaiting the little that's left is only to cover up the bare head. When you are in a beerhall, you must not be intimidated. For example, when I have a man I insist on using condoms, if he won't use them, we fight. Even if he is stronger than me, I always find ways to outdo them.

I no longer ever want to go to jail. Never. Never. I am only saying that I must defend myself. These days I never use bottles or sticks or anything like that. If I see that you are dangerous, I would rather run and be called a coward, because I will know well that I have protected myself.

Section 6:

'Dangerous drugs'

25

Marina

interviewed by Keresia Chateuka

My name is Marina. I was born in September 1962. I am the third-born in a family of four boys and four girls. My father left us when my mother was pregnant with me. For a long time I did not know where he was. He is alive, I found him recently. He lives in South Africa with another wife. He is a learned man who taught at an American university for many years before retiring to South Africa. He has Ph.D. after his name.

My mother and stepfather come from Malawi. Our education was not smooth as both my mother and stepfather drank beer. At times we spent two weeks at home because there was no money for school fees. We grew up under very difficult conditions with our stepfather. We ended up selling vegetables to raise our school fees. Food was also short. We would go to the Stoddart Community Shops – we lived in Mbare – to ask for leftovers such as stale bread that we would eat with tea. A friend and I decided to go into the streets to beg for money. We used to beg from whites in broken English, 'Madam I want my money.' They were kind enough to give us some money or food.

My stepfather worked for Zimbabwe Electricity Supply Authority: he still works there. My mother was unemployed: she made money through hawking. My sister completed Grade 7. The others did not manage to go to school because there was no money for school fees. I learnt at a primary school right here, in Mbare. I did Form 1 at a college in Highfield. I could not proceed, although I was very bright. My parents only loved the first two. They hated me from when I was still very young. I was called a prostitute when I was in Grade 6 when I knew nothing about men. My sister and mother abused me: they used to beat me without cause until some relatives took me under their care. That was when I was in Grade 6. Life was still hard with them because they overworked me. When I was in Form 1, my mother came for me saying that I was being overworked. But when I went back home things were worse still: they got to a point where they did not give me any food anymore. They wanted me to bring money home like my sister, who slept with men for money. I ate from the bins. My sister was a prostitute and she would bring money home.

When I was in Form 1, I fell in love with a man called Arthur. He had a job in the industries. I thought he could provide me with food and clothes. My sister used to shout at him whenever he came to see me. She told him I was a prostitute. I fell pregnant by him but he denied paternity as my sister told him I was a prostitute. He ran away. At home, life was now even harder than before. My mother told me to take care of myself. Many people thought I was not part of the family. I was never happy. Nobody ever took time to listen to me. I sold cooked mealies in the city to earn a living. Sometimes I had to run away from the police. After nine months God blessed me with a baby girl. That was in 1980. After a while, I started my business of selling goods with my daughter on my back. The father did not support the child at all. He came back when the girl was twenty years old asking me to get back together with him. That, for me, was out of the question.

In 1986, I decided to go back to school. I went to a college to do a tailoring course. I dropped out because I had no money for fees. My stepfather left my mother for another woman. We remained in the house, as it was ours. It was in the name of my real father. He had left it for us. My mother got another boyfriend. I was now drinking beer because of depression. I used to go to night-clubs with my boyfriend. I started looking down on myself. I had, however, started sewing. Our neighbour used to lend me her machine to use. I was going out with a boy named Victor. One day his friends picked me up, they were drunk, and we had a head-on collision with another vehicle. Two people died on the spot, one died on the way to hospital, and the other had a broken neck. I was knocked unconscious. I woke up after a while. When my family heard about the accident, my sister got mad. We went to a witchdoctor who said I was possessed with evil spirits. Nobody liked me.

At home I was beaten and abused. My mother said most women like me were getting married so there was something wrong with me. I drank more. We kept on selling goods with my friends but I did not make much money. I could not send my child to school. She only went as far as Grade 7. Later a woman in Mbare took her to the Honde Valley where she was made to work. In 1995, I met Brian, and we started living together. He had gone as far as Form 6 with his education. He was a junior police officer in Mbare. He did not earn much. Brian did not have a child like me and we had a baby boy together, Lovemore. Brian decided he wanted to further his education, so he left work and enrolled at Mutare Polytechnic to study Personnel Management. Although his father was late, his mother took care of everything. However she did not like me because I was not a Manyika like them.

During the first year, I lived reasonably well with my mother-in-law. Both Brian's mother and his paternal grandmother were widows. We were three women at the homestead. The second year, my mother complained that my husband was using me and she wanted money from me. My husband survived on the allowances he got from college. I asked for a bit of money from him to buy goods for resale. I travelled to Malawi and I got involved in *mbanje*. The business flourished. I got my supply from Malawi. A friend, Koswa, travelled with me. We would go to Blantyre, where we booked rooms at the rest house. From there we went to the locations. There were some boys who showed us where to get the 'weed'. We would then come back. Sometimes we got a bus to Mozambique, where we looked for someone to help us cross the border at night on foot. In the morning, we got buses. We carried the drug in big bags. No one suspected us at first. When we got to Harare we had our buyers ready. They gave us money and we delivered the parcels later. Actually we sold the drug in bulk to people who resold it in lesser quantities. My husband did not know. Not even my in-laws knew. I told my mother-in-law that I was buying and re-selling clothes. All these dealings took place in Harare where my mother lives, even though I stayed in Mutare. On my last trip I told my husband about my business and he cautioned me. He did not trust the people at my home.

On the occasion that I got arrested, I consulted a prophet before I left for the trip. My aim was to see if my trip would be trouble-free. I always did this before I went on these trips. The prophet warned me of an impending arrest. I went to another one who told me he was seeing a person with spectacles looking for me. The prophet told me he could see policemen, so I had to postpone my trip. I told him I needed to go. He gave me some holy water and stones to carry to protect me from trouble. He also advised me that if I did not feel safe I had to avoid boarding the bus. I left the next day. I used to go with my friend but this time I was alone because my friend had made an earlier trip. She is the one who got into trouble. When she heard that I had left she called the police and told them everything about me, my physical appearance, the roads I used, everything. We had fallen out because she preferred to spend her money with a boyfriend. While in Malawi I was feeling weak and tired. I had already bought the *mbanje*.

I consulted a Chewa man. I had had a bad dream. I dreamt I was home with my friends. They asked how I had come back and what type of *mbanje* I had. I opened the bag and found handcuffs inside. The Chewa man told me if I was carrying something bad I had to leave it behind. I could have done that but I had no money with me. I had spent it on buying *mbanje*. He prayed for me. He also told me that if my heart was not settled I did not have to get on the bus. A certain boy told me transport was a problem, so I just had to get into the bus and go.

We arrived at a place full of soldiers. They searched us but they did not find anything. We got to Mozambique. We slept for a while. The man who helped me cross the border was tired. I think the police had set their trap in the forest near the road we used. When I came to the place I saw three men, big strong men. My heart raced. I tried to avoid them at the same time thinking where they had come from. I went to the bush to change my clothes. Everything I did was in their eyes. At 3 a.m. the bus came, I boarded. A car full of what I thought could be detectives passed me. My heart raced again. There were only a few people in the bus so there was no way one could deny responsibility for having the drug. When we were near Mutoko, we arrived at a roadblock. The CID, support unit, policemen and dog sniffers were all there. I froze. The CID searched and found nothing. The dogs came and detected the drug. It came straight to me. I got off the bus and that was the end off their search. They took me to the nearby police station. I had my bags with me. They counted them. I was put in a jail cell. Then the following day they took me to Marondera. I was there from Saturday to Monday. They took me to the Post Office to have my bags of *mbanje* weighed and they were found to be 5.8 kilograms. From there I went to court. When the exhibit came and was opened the magistrate sneezed. He told me that I was dangerous and ordered me out. For mitigation factors I told the court that my husband was not working, I had children to look after. I told the truth. I was told to go outside. After lunch I went back. I was told I was ruining many children with *mbanje*. I was sentenced to four years. I did not pass out. When I slept in the jail cell, that night I thought of committing suicide.

The cell was just a room. At one corner there was a toilet hole. It was flushed from the outside so you could spend the whole night with waste in it. I then thought of my husband who was still in school, and my two-year-old baby. I was alone in the cell. I also thought the ancestors had abandoned me. Two and a half years of the sentence were then suspended. I served one and a half years.

I went to Marondera Prison. There was a female section there. When I got there it was full; I had to go to Mutare. There I was given only one blanket and the floor was filthy. I spent a week there before I was transferred to Chikurubi. I was afraid of going to Chikurubi. We were driven there in a truck. Soon after my arrival I went for an interview. They asked if I could sew and I said 'yes'. They said I was going to join the sewing group under *ambuya gadhi N*. We sewed uniforms for prison guards. They taught us. There was *ambuya A*. She was a prisoner who was very good at sewing. *Ambuya gadhi* taught me to use the overlock machine. *Ambuya A.* did not like it: she started to say bad things about me. Sometimes she lied that I sold some garments to women who had given birth in prison. *Ambuya gadhi* never confirmed that the allegations were true. She just scolded me. I cried, asking God why. She was short-tempered, sometimes she stormed out of the room to gain her composure. Later she would call me to her machine and teach me to sew. She called me to assist her. Really, in the end, she motivated me to do my work perfectly. I then started going to church. I did before but I had not fully converted to Christianity. During sewing, some of *vanambuya gadhi* brought their material for us to sew. We sewed if our supervisor told us to do so. If you refused, you would suffer during the weekends in the garden.

My first days at Chikurubi I slept in a big cell. All new inmates went there. There were some old prisoners too. I had no appetite. I was still thinking deeply about my situation. The other prisoners received me well. They quickly befriended us so that we would give them food. Because the cell was full of people, the toilet would get blocked. If someone used it in the night the cell would be saturated with a bad smell. The blankets were dirty. Some had fleas and lice while others had blood-stains. They were in a terrible state. Later we were screened and placed in different cells. At Chikurubi there was a rumour about lesbianism in the cells. I had been informed about this while in Mutare. I got scared thinking that I was going to be forced into having sex with someone. To my relief nothing like that happened.

In the morning we had a slice of bread. In the afternoon they put sadza on the tables before we were dismissed for the lunch. The big green flies would land on the food. When we went for lunch the sadza would be cold and hard. We had to force ourselves to eat. At times we had sadza with green-leaf vegetables. We had meat on Mondays and during the weekends. Sometimes the meat had vegetables or it was just plain. How it was cooked depended on the officer on duty. When the likes of *Ambuya gadhi S.* was on duty, we had fried meat and the food was well-cooked. Some were terrible. We could tell they were terrible cooks in their own homes. Some cleaned the shed first before food was placed on the tables but others did not care about cleanliness. With regard to our personal cleanliness, they gave us soap once per month but it was not enough. If no one brought you soap from home sometimes you would bath without. Sometimes you sold bread for a cake of soap. A piece of soap could cost as much as ten slices of bread. That meant you went for ten days without bread.

Sometimes we worked in the prison guards' homes, especially in the rainy season. On Thursdays, the officers would choose about eight to ten prisoners to work in their homes. Prisoners dug in the gardens, planted maize, weeded and swept the yards. Personally I once went to work in their houses. I weeded and cultivated their fields. I also trimmed the lawn. If you fell sick you went to the clinic. We got Panadols for *all* ailments. At the clinic the nurse was cheeky. During your periods she gave you half of a pad to use. We ended up tearing the blankets on the fence to use as cotton wool. The material was very rough; it grazed our skin. We would have to use half a pad in the morning and the other half in the evening. Sometimes we got pads for others. Three to four people took pads for others. No record was kept as to who had taken a pad or not. Some of us complained of sharp pains but the complaint fell on deaf ears. They said we were lazy. Sometimes they gave me those tablets, 'maragado' for the mentally disturbed. They made your tongue heavy. You would not talk.

Some prisoners were made to cook for the officers. They took food from the prisoners and cooked it. In the end the officers and the 'staff' shared the food among themselves and we did not have enough. It pained us to see them cook our meat. They stole cooking oil, sugar, anything. The guards ordered the prisoners to get the food for them. Sometimes we knew a guard wanted food because she brought a basket. She would get her filled basket before going home. They were not searched. One prisoner reported the matter to the officer-in-charge and gave the names of the guards who stole our food. The girl got into trouble with the guards. When the magistrates came we could not tell them our grievances because the guards beat us later for speaking out. The magistrate heard the complaints from us and left. In November ghosts visited the cells at night. Those who slept in the cells with the mentally unstable people had things like bricks thrown at them. Nobody knew where the ghosts were coming from. Pastor Hlongwani from prisons was called to exorcise the cell and the ghosts disappeared.

In prison, the officers kept us informed about how long we had before the date of release. Every month we went for what they called a 'warrant check'. They asked for your number and your day of release. If you did not answer correctly they would tell you. Sometimes your sentence could be extended because of mischief. Close to the day of my release they told me I was about to go home. I washed my clothes. I got out in the morning and found my mother and sister waiting for me at the prison gate. They thought I had a lot of money from selling *mbanje* so they told me they wanted bus fare. I told them I had no cent.

When we got home people from the neighbourhood came to see me. Some maybe thought I would be changed or maybe ill. They found me strong, in good health. They were speechless. I stayed home for a week. I wanted to go to Mutare to visit my husband's grave. My husband had died when I was in prison. I looked for my aunt who accompanied me to my mother-in-law's home in Mutare. I had called them earlier telling them about my release and that I was coming. When we got there my mother-in-law was away: we stayed the night. Around midnight we heard some noises. In the dining room were three men and three women. My mother-in-law introduced one man as her boyfriend. The other two women were introduced together with their boyfriends. They were all drunk. I thought I would be taken to the rural areas to see where my husband had been buried, but the next day my mother-in-law told me she was going to Victoria Falls for a holiday. I felt pain in my heart. It was not right to go on my own. When she came back we left for the rural areas.

When we came back to Mutare she made me attend to calls from her other boyfriends while she was entertaining another. I sensed that she wanted me to join her in what she was doing. When my husband died he did he not leave anything for his son. Everything he had was now in the hands of my mother-in-law. She later sold the combi that he had bought. His personal property, I was told, had been taken to the rural areas.

Life was hard. My own relatives did not like me. My brother started insulting me. One day as I walked from the market place, I saw a church. It must have been built when I was in jail. I went inside and started praying. From then on I used to go to the church. From the day I was released to 2000, I was suffering. Church helped me to find peace within myself. Now I stay with my children. The boy is in Grade 2 and the girl is working at a crèche. My mother-in-law passed away last September. I was not told about her death. She lived with my son Lovemore, who was going to school in Mutare. He was being looked after by a brother-in-law without my consent. I went to get my son as I am now at my parents' place. I built myself my own wooden cabin. I want to be on my own. I find no rest in the main house.

I wish prisons had qualified counsellors. Sometimes you commit crime unintentionally. Counselling would help. In the end you will be able to live in harmony with your relatives and you would also know what to expect from them. Prison Fellowship and ZACRO help with training. I went to Prison Fellowship, where they interviewed me about sewing. I passed the interview. The Director then came and told me I could work for his wife. I could not accept that. I asked for a loan of Z$4,000. They told me I was to pay back with a 42 per cent interest. This was not good for I had children to send to school. They told me payment had to start in that same month. They do not give a grace period. In the end I was able to return the money, but with difficulty.

After my release, the first two years were difficult. I then went to South Africa after a certain woman had hired me. I bought my sewing machine there. I went to ZACRO to do a course in sewing for six months. It was free and they gave us everything we needed. This was very good. Now I pray to God that I sew beautiful garments. When I was in prison *Ambuya gadhi* inspired me to take up sewing seriously. She told me her own story that is now my source of inspiration. She is a single parent with three children. She is able to sustain her family through sewing. I said to myself that if she could do it then nothing would stop me from achieving my dream. I very much wanted to go to Speciss College to finish my course. I prayed about it. Now I am doing cutting and designing at the college. I will finish in December. I achieved certificate level. I am now doing a diploma in cutting, designing and tailoring. At the same time I am doing modelling and grooming at Medusa Promotions. I can now look after myself and am learning interpersonal skills. I intend to do a Masters in sewing and interior decor. I am aiming for something big. I do not want to work for a person. I want to open my own company. I wish to help other women prisoners by teaching them to sew clothes.

26

Manswa

interviewed by Mary Olivia Tandon

In this story, I wish to be known as Manswa, which means 'troubles'. I come from a family of eight; four boys and four girls and I am the last-born. My father was from Mozambique. My mother was from South Africa. I was born in South Africa and my parents moved to Zimbabwe (then Southern Rhodesia) when I was two weeks old. My father got a job as a cook in the Rhodesian Military School in Inyanga. My mother was a house girl in the same Military School as my father. Things were difficult but we grew up as a happy family.

I was born in 1953, though my birth certificate shows 1955. This is a mistake but a deliberate one. You see children born in 1953 were not allowed to sit for the final Standard 6 examinations because they were considered too old. So my father changed the year to 1955 so that I could write my examinations. [Chuckles.] I went to St Peter School Kubatana in 1961, and I passed Standard 6, which was the highest grade in that school. I then completed Form 1 and Form 2 at Bonda Mission, but I could not continue with my education because my parents did not have enough money for my school fees. They educated all the older children and they did not have enough money for me to finish my education.

So I stayed at home for three years and helped my brother's wife to look after her twin boys. In the fourth year I got married. This was on 6th Feb. 1976. My husband's name was Winston. It was a love marriage. We wanted to have a nice big wedding but my husband's father was afraid that I might go to Mozambique with my friend to join the War [liberation struggle]. So the marriage was carried out very quickly (chuckles). I was very happy. My husband was then a wonderful man. His father was a pastor and my husband was also preparing to be one. We belonged to the Guta raJehova Faith.

I was very happy in my marriage home. My husband, while studying to be a pastor, was also working as a bus inspector for the Barbara & Cecil Buses. We had our first daughter in November 1976. We named her Ester. Then, that same year, my husband lost his job because a passenger's luggage disappeared from the bus and he was held responsible for the loss. Since then he has never had a job. But we were still very happy and very much in love. We managed to survive. We stayed with my husband's sister. They had bought a place in the rural area, in Inyanga district. I grew vegetables and managed to keep the family together.

1978 and 1979 were the years of the War. It was very dangerous for all young men and boys to stay in the rural areas. So my husband had to leave our rural home in Inyanga. He went to stay with his auntie in Mutare and he tried to look for a job. I remained in Inyanga with the children. The second child, a boy, was born on 20th November 1978. It was difficult to be on my own with children in a war situation. It was not easy to run and seek refuge in the bush with the two children. My mother did not live near me and she worried about me. She kept telling me how unsafe it was for me to remain in Inyanga and insisted that I join my husband. So she sent the children and me to my husband. This was around 1980. My husband was still jobless. Nevertheless we still managed to survive because both of us were under the power of God. We were very supportive of each other. I did not mind that my husband had lost his job. I was happy just to be with him. I did not mind that we did not have anything, so long as the family was together. We were very much in love. It was difficult but we managed to survive by buying and selling vegetables.

On 26th August 1981, we had our third child, another boy. My husband also got admission to a certain school to study for a diploma as a forest ranger. He worked and studied at the same time and he was given a small amount of money, Z$90 a month. This was a lot of money during those days, more than enough to provide groceries for the family. He stayed at the college with the children and myself. His course was for three years, that is, 1981-83.

However, as time passed, the devil got into him. He started to go out with other women. In the beginning I did not believe, it but later I found it was the truth.

Things started to go bad. He still had sexual relations with me but the relationship was not the same as it used to be. There was no love. He left me in 1985 and by that time I had my fourth child, also a boy. This was very painful for me and I cried a lot. He even refused to come and see the baby. It was very difficult, as he did not provide for the children. So, I had the children to look after, to provide their food, rent, school fees and so on. A friend came and consoled me. She told me not to worry about not having money and she got me into deals.

By then, my parents were no longer alive. My father passed away in 1979, and my mother in 1981. None of my brothers and sisters was able to help because they had their own families to look after. So I joined this friend and met her group of friends and got involved in illegal dealings. At that time, I did not think that getting into these deals was bad, because I was getting the money. I started with gold deals. We bought gold from diggers who stole the gold and sold it to us. We, in turn, sold the gold to people who were in that business. This helped me to get money to buy food. Then, we women moved on to bigger deals, the rhino horns. It was very paying. The first deal was a pair of rhino horns, which fetched us almost Z$22,000. At that time one could buy a house for Z$22,000. On this deal we shared the money between the four of us. With this money I bought things for the house. For the first time I had a bed to sleep on instead of the floor, a wardrobe for clothes instead of keeping them in cardboard boxes. I often gazed at the beds and wardrobes in the shop windows and could not believe that I could own them one day. It was a good feeling to be able to have a comfortable bed and warm blankets. My children had new clothes and shoes. Then in March 1987, I was arrested for the rhino horn deals and was sentenced for five years.

We were arrested when we were carrying the horns in a bag. We were working in pairs. Two women carried the horns from the source. In this particular case it was from Mozambique. The horns changed hands in Mutare and were given to my friend and me. We had to deliver them to the buyer. During the delivery we were trapped. We believed that the garden boy of the person who was buying from us reported us to the police.

We stayed in the cell for three days. On the fourth day, an African CID took us to the Court. Before the magistrate came on, the CID told us that if we admitted guilt to the offence and say that we were using the horn for medicinal purposes the sentence will be light – it might only be a fine. If we do not admit guilt, then the sentence could be heavy. We were prepared to pay the fine for we had the money. So we admitted we were guilty to the charge. The court case ended very fast. It did not take even five minutes. We were given a sentence of five years each. The question of fine was not mentioned in the court. We were put in the Mutare Central for the first three days and then transferred to Chikurubi in Harare.

I was shocked to see so many women in the prison. They were shouting and welcoming me to the prison and there I was, crying away. My inmates teased and laughed at me. They asked me how many years I had got and I said 'five'. They said that I should not cry because five years is like five days and that I should not cry for five days. Then I was given prison uniform, which did not fit me properly because I am a big woman. I was given three blankets. I did not feel good for the floor was cold and there were many lice moving around everywhere.

I cried a lot, mostly for my children. I left my four children in the care of a housemaid who was also a young girl of seventeen years old. I did not believe that I would go to prison. I thought I would pay the fine and go home. So I did not organise any food for the children. My youngest was then one year and ten months old. I was still breast-feeding him. My eldest was the girl. I worried about the youngest. I complained about this to the prison warden and I was told to write a letter. But a letter could take a long time. I even mentioned about the children when I was in court but nothing was done for the children. My body was in prison, but my mind was out of the prison with the children. When I closed my eyes at night I could only think of the children. Every day I worried about them – what happened to them, have they got food and so on? Some of the prison inmates were young girls who committed offences like baby dumping and abortion. These inmates added to my worry about my eleven-year-old daughter's safety.

I told the prison officers that I was worried, their only advice was 'write a letter'. I was given paper and pen. I wrote the letter. What happened with the letter one could not tell. It may reach its destination or it may not. It could also take a long time to get to the receiver. You see, when I was in the prison, the people outside the prison forgot about me. To them I was as good as someone who was dead. This was why all my things in the house were taken away. I do not even know who took the beds, wardrobes etc. I had even started to build a house and I was told that the whole house was burnt down.

I wrote to my sister who was the only helpful one. She replied to my letters and gave me the news about the children. The news was not always good. For example, my youngest boy had lots of medical problems. The first problem was when he was treated for six months for malnutrition. The second time he was admitted to hospital for burns. He was burnt with hot tea. All the children stayed with my husband's mother. She was too old to take care of the children. They hired a young girl to take care of the youngest boy. The third problem involving hospitalisation was when he ate soap soda and his tongue was badly burnt and he nearly died. When he was in the hospital, the doctor asked for the mother of the child and he was told that that she is in prison and no one knew how long she would remain there. The father did not care for the children: he was busy with his girlfriends. The same doctor looked after this boy for the past two times when he was admitted to hospital. So the doctor recommended that the child should be sent to the orphanage. That was why I was very miserable to hear about these stories. I had no visits from my husband or from members of my family, except the one sister and a friend.

We were allowed visitors once every month for only five minutes. Visitors were allowed to bring Vaseline and *pata pata*. I think this was because the government did not have the money to give these things to the prisoners. Visitors may bring food only on Christmas Day and Independence Day. We could send only one letter a month but there was no restriction as to the number of letters you could receive. We wrote the letters and gave them to the prison warden who then put the stamp on. Sometimes there were no stamps readily available at the warden's office, then the letter could not be posted. Sometimes the letter could sit in the warden's office for a whole month.

I did not like being in prison for I was very worried about my children and nobody cared to visit me. I promised myself that when I get out of prison, I would not do silly things that would put me back in prison. I also learnt many tactics from the inmates who had lots of experience in committing offences. Some of them were once in the police force. There was an inmate who was working in the Commissioner's office. She was convicted for stealing files and selling the information for money. I learnt a lot from them. For example, I did not know that I could have denied the offence charged instead of saying 'yes' to the questions asked. I did not know that when I was brought before the magistrate. I could change my statement and deny the charge. I was informed that the rhino horns I carried should have been brought before the magistrate as evidence. In my case they were not brought to court and I could have used that to support my case. The absence of the rhino horns may have meant that the CID himself could have sold the rhino horns and pocketed the money. The inmate from the Commissioner's office suggested that I could have run away and avoided arrest. Some shoplifters showed me how to steal and hide the things between the legs and how to walk out of the shop without being noticed.

I also realised that when one comes out of prison, one comes out with a prison scar. This scar will remain with you for life. When I left the prison, I felt lost. There was no help from any one. With the prison scar, it was very difficult to get a job. I tried for a long time and then I got a job in a private nursery school in Mutare. I was in the scullery, washing dishes. This was in 1992. I was paid Z$600 per month and later increased to Z$900. Life was difficult. I lost everything when I was in prison. I wanted to buy them back.

Some of my friends who were in prison with me encouraged me to join them in their illegal deals. They said that my husband had left me and would not care for me; that I have learnt a lot in the prison and I should have the intelligence to get into deals successfully. I was afraid to be arrested again but at the same time I thought to myself that I know better how not to be imprisoned again. Economic hardships pushed me again to try and I was persuaded to do just one deal. Meanwhile I also kept my job. I did my deals during the weekends. I made sure that I was off-duty at 2 p.m. every Friday afternoon. This deal was the smuggling of JB Whisky, which was a very expensive item at that time. We worked in a group consisting of both men and women. We were informed that we could get as much as one million dollars for this deal. This was very tempting. I had never had a million dollars ever, so I joined the deal. We did not get arrested, so I thought I am clever. I then got on to another deal smuggling of drugs. This time I was arrested.

Then a certain woman brought drugs sometimes from Nigeria and sometimes from Tanzania. We were not told much about the details. We were just told what to do. We were told to collect three million dollars from a certain medical doctor. He came from Brazzaville and he usually stayed at the Sheraton for two or three weeks. When I went and collected the money from him, the police caught me. This time we hired a lawyer to defend us but he could not save us. We were remanded in Chikurubi, Harare, for six months before we went to the Court. The maximum penalty was twenty years but I got only twenty months. But I served only eight months. I think God had a hand in this.

This time I was much stronger. I did not like to go to prison. I thought I was experienced and clever enough not to be caught. When my inmates, saw me, they cheered and welcomed me back with them. I did not like it. I did not cry and I did not feel pain. I did not think about the children. I cannot explain. Sometimes I even beat myself to give pain to myself. The thought of committing suicide also came to my mind. I felt something spiritual within me. Even the prison officers who knew me during my first imprisonment also commented that I had changed. I used to shout and talk rudely to them. In my second imprisonment I was calm, silent and I prayed a lot. Somehow God intervened in my life and I decided to go straight to the Lord and I began to repent for my bad deeds.

In prison, women become friends quickly. They talk and share their problems with each other. It is a rumour that women have sex with each other, because it is not common among the female prisoners. I think it is more common in the male section. We talk about how to get money, about our children and husbands, about our in-laws. We comfort each other. Sometimes we gossiped and lied about each other and we got into fights. We also stole things from each other like soap, Vaseline and even uniforms. Some stole Vaseline to sell or barter in exchange for other things. For example, for one teaspoon of Vaseline I had to give up my two pieces of bread. Those lucky prisoners who have visitors to bring things for them can sell these things for food to those prisoners who have few or no visitors.

Life in prison is not good. There are strict rules and set times to do things. You are not free to do things as and when you want. It is a very constrictive life. You are let out of the cell at about 7 a.m. to do some jobs like washing the prison grounds, your clothes and work in the garden. By 3:30 in the afternoon you are back in your cell. On Saturdays and Sundays, you are allowed to go into the yard and play games and do your exercises. There is a netball court and you can play netball.

The food is also not interesting and you have no choice. You eat what you are given. Generally, in the morning you will get a cup of tea and a piece of plain bread. At lunch, you will get boiled leeks or cabbage and sadza, and for supper a small piece of meat with sadza. The meat can be pork or beef or chicken, but cooked in lots of water, so you get more gravy than meat.

The prisoners come from different backgrounds. Some of them are mentally disturbed. The more violent mentally disturbed prisoners are given injections to calm them down, but we still have to bear with their funny and dirty ways. For example, when they get their monthly periods they do not know how to keep themselves clean. The blood drips everywhere. Other prisoners have to try not to step on the blood especially if they do not have tackies. Even some of the normal prisoners have problems getting pads to use. We find other ways like cutting a corner of the blanket and reusing it by washing it. Some of us used newspapers by rubbing the newspapers to make them soft and absorbent.

When I left prison for the second time, I did not want to see anybody, not even my children. I went straight to the Prison Fellowship principal and asked to be allowed to attend the Bible School. I was not given admission partly because the principal thought that I wanted to join the Bible School as a way of escaping from the usual problems that an ex-prisoner faces, that is the feel of being lost; and partly because I did not have the basic educational requirement. I did not do Form 4. Anyway Lyn consoled me and tried to get me admission in other Bible schools.

Eventually, I got admitted to the Harare Theological College. I was called for an interview and the requirement was very basic — just to be able to read and write basic English. By then, I was forty-six years old. In fact I was the oldest student at the college. I was put on a special course where I had to do all the subjects with the other students. A certificate is obtained at the end of the course. I completed the course in July 2001. I am now doing my diploma and will finish it next year.

In 1998, when I went to Bible College, my family thought I was mad and I'll never learn anything. My own brother went to the college principal and told the principal about my prison background and how my husband divorced me. He did it to undermine me. He did not know that I was quite open about my prison sentences. When he came to see the principal, he did not even have the courtesy to visit me even though he was in the college compound. That was my own brother.

My sister is keen to know what I will do to be financially all right. Without money, she knows that the chances of going back to prison are real. She was not happy that I become a pastor, because a pastor has no money. I told my sister that I would never go back to prison again.

Now, at last, my brother and sister have accepted me. They have invited me to their homes. Even my husband's relatives have welcomed me back to their families. Everyone has accepted me. I think God has again intervened in these matters.

My husband married me under customary rights. Although he left me, he did not divorce me in the traditional way, which is that he must send me back to my parents or relatives. He refused to send me back to my relatives. He kept me as part of his family, but we do not have husband and wife relationship. Now we meet each other and we are on talking terms.

Now I want to work with the prisoners. My heart is there with the women prisoners. I hope to take the word of God to them. Now we have a small Bible school in the prison and we are sending bible materials to the prisoners. The word of God will encourage prisoners not to be tempted to do bad things when they come out of prison.

I want to work with women in prison so that they do not go back to prison again and again. This can only be done if women are taught the words of God. It is important to talk to prisoners and make them aware how important families are. For example, when I was in prison I could not look after my daughter and she had many miscarriages. I want to bring Bible classes into the women's prison so that they know the words of God. It is best to keep out of prison and only the Lord can help you, so listen for the word of God.

27

Auxilia

interviewed by Chiedza Musengezi

My name is Auxilia. My father and mother lived in a village in Nyajena in Chivi District. We were nine children in our family. I do not know my date of birth. We grew our own food; peanuts, groundnuts, maize, *rapoko*, sorghum and watermelons. We grew a lot of food. Our home was near the road to the local hospital. Passers-by on their way to visit sick relatives at Muchibwa Hospital would stop by for a drink of water. My mother always offered them food: *mahewu*, boiled groundnuts or boiled pumpkins. Beer attracted many people to our home, mostly men who were not well behaved. They fought over women and urinated on our kitchen wall. I did not respect them. My parents were traditional, they did not believe in sending girls to school. This is why I only went up to Standard 3, which was about half way through primary school. My mother brewed beer for sale to raise money for school fees.

My ambition was to find a decent man, get married and have children. I desired a warm and happy home with a lot of food. Then I met Francis T., who later became my first husband. He had come from Buhera to visit his grandparents, who lived in the same village as us. The courtship was long, about five months. I agreed to marry him and I went to his home to meet his family. My friend, Rhoda came with me. His family gave me a warm reception. His parents were nice people with an open and happy home. Relatives and neighbours came to see me when I got married. Francis and I lived in the same village as his parents. In 1972 we had our first baby, a daughter whom we named Chipo.

Then Francis and I decided to move to Gokwe. We built our new home at the bottom of a hill near a large flat rock – something that we regretted later. We had two more children, Stanley in 1973 and Lyton in 1976. We got caught up in the war of liberation. The hill close to our home provided shelter for the soldiers. Often there was gunfire exchange between ZIPRA and Rhodesian soldiers. Sometimes people died and the soldiers from either side would display them on the large flat rock very close to our homestead for everybody to see. It was their way of instilling fear and discouraging us from supporting the guerrillas. We felt especially insecure because we lived far away from our relatives. So we decided to go back to Buhera. We had another baby girl, Shylet in 1982. After her came Mary in 1986.

Then I suffered a misfortune, Francis died in a car accident. He had got a job as a temporary teacher. He asked for a lift to Chivhu from one of the teachers who had a car. The car overturned and Francis was badly injured and he died in hospital soon afterwards. I was now alone with five children. Two of my children died later. According to tradition they gave me Francis's brother to care for my children and me. He was a young man and I did not like the arrangement, I went back with all my children to my parents in Nyajena. It was at this point that I started selling gold.

There was a gold mine in our home area and I paid people from the mine to bring me gold. I would give them a goat in return for crushed gold-bearing stones. I used a magnet to pick out the tiny gold particles which I then cleaned, using an acid. I sold the gold and I would use the money to send my children to school. I went to Gweru and Kwekwe and exchanged the gold for second-hand clothes, radios and sometimes cash. Sometimes I exchanged a radio for a cow that I then sold for cash. This went on for quite some time until I met some people from Harare. They told me that my gold could fetch more money in Harare. They instructed me to go to Sheraton Hotel and ask for Mr M. I met him and he showed great interest in what I was doing. He looked like a good customer so I gave him the gold but I did not get the money. He told me to come back later in the day to collect it. I went back to Sheraton Hotel on several occasions but they told me that he no longer worked there. It was the last time I saw him. He disappeared leaving me stranded in Harare. I could not report him to the police because I knew that what I was doing was illegal. So, I looked for a job and got one with Coca-Cola. I used to pick up empty crates in their yard. Then I met Bernard who was also working in the same area. I told him my story and he was sympathetic. I moved in with him and we stayed together in Majubheki, Mbare, from 1987 to 1996, when I got arrested.

My children stayed at home in Nyajena with my brother, Bernard did not want me to bring them to Harare. He was against it: he only wanted his, the ones he himself had fathered. You see I had four children with Bernard, and three from my previous marriage to make a total of seven children.

Sometimes, I would get my son from my first marriage and I would stay with him for some time, but Bernard would soon complain and I would send him back to Nyajena. With time I made women friends in Mbare. They advised me that I could make money and look after my children. They introduced me to new ways of making money – selling 'tobacco'. In Mbare *mbanje* is commonly referred to as tobacco. I started selling tobacco in 1993, and I did so until 1996, when I got arrested.

I made doilies and chair-back covers. I took them to Mozambique. I usually travelled in a group because there were a number of women in Mbare who lived on selling tobacco. At the beginning I used to give my dolies to other women who brought back a bag of tobacco for me. With time I got a passport and travelled with the group. Bernard found out that I was selling tobacco because a lot of people used to knock at our door and ask for it. Bernard did not approve. He warned me that I would end up in jail. I did not stop. It seemed an easy way to make money: giving it up was difficult. As I got more deeply involved in the business, I brought larger quantities of tobacco, twenty to thirty kilograms. I made good money. Depending on how fast it was selling, I would make Z$150,000 to Z$100,000. I took some of the money and sent it to my children. My brother in Nyajena was looking after all of them. The rest I used it to buy food and household goods: beds, sofas, a sewing machine and blankets.

My husband advised me many times to stop. He said I was being greedy. He said I did not need that many things in the house, but I was hooked on it. In Mbare I became well known for selling tobacco. My customers gave me a nickname, 'Sister Masvingo' because I came from Masvingo. They would come at any time of day and knock at my door. 'Ko, ko, ko, Masvingo *hanzvadzi* [sister], I need some tobacco.' I would open the door, take out the bag of tobacco and weigh the amount they wanted. I had bought a pair of scales for accurate measurement. That way I made more money. I had become very efficient at sourcing and selling tobacco. I would buy radio cassettes, soap, blankets, second-hand clothes and exchange them for tobacco in Mozambique. I would catch a bus to Mutare early in the morning and arrive at midday. Then I would take another bus to Nyamaropa and then cross into Mozambique on foot. I exchanged my goods for tobacco in no time at all because the area is rich in tobacco and most of the people spoke Shona. It was quite a brisk trade. There were also young men on stand-by to carry any heavy bags. I could be back in Harare the following day. I built a network of customers of all races. I had a group of whites from Gweru. They bought large amounts for resale in Botswana. I would phone them to come and pick up their order as soon as I arrived from Nyamaropa

The police got to know about me. They set a trap. So one day when I was already in bed I heard a knock. As usual I woke up, opened the door and served the customer. Just as I was packing away my bag of tobacco another man appeared at the doorway. He held up his identity card. He was a plain-clothes policeman.

I asked the policeman to allow me to change into a proper dress, I had thoughtlessly served the customer in my nightdress, but he refused. He only allowed me to wear my tennis shoes and to take my identity card. My husband who was asleep woke up. The police said they had nothing against him, he could go back to bed. Bernard pleaded with them, asking them to arrest him instead of me so that I could look after our child. (I had had a child with Bernard. He was already going to school, in Grade 1.) The police refused and they took me to their car which they had parked a distance from my house. They drove me to Mbare Police Station where I stayed the night. I slept in their reception room, they did not put me in a cell.

The following day they took me to the Central Police Station in town. When I appeared in court, I admitted my crime. They asked how I would take it if my next-door neighbour had sold tobacco to my teenage children. I said I would not like it. Little did I know that I was incriminating myself. I was sentenced to seven years in prison. Two years were suspended which meant that I was going to be in Chikurubi for five years. I was numb. I was as good as dead. I asked myself many questions: what was going to happen to my child in Mbare and my other children in Nyajena? What was going to happen to the many relatives that I was looking after? Why did I do it?

When I arrived at Chikurubi, inmates had already been locked up in the cells. I was put in C-class. C-class prisoners saw me through the window they waved and jeered at me. Inside the cell I met some, who, like me, had been imprisoned for selling tobacco. When I entered the cell I was crying. Some of the inmates came forward to comfort me. At their request I told them about myself: my name, my husband, my home and what I was in prison for. Anna, who was in for murder, was a great comfort. She talked to me, encouraging me to be brave because five years was not such a long time. Some, who were in prison for the same crime as mine, had longer sentences. Some gave me clean blankets. Gradually I learnt that my situation was not too bad and that my fellow inmates did not want me to be sad and miserable.

Sleeping time was to be worst for me. There were six of us in the cell. The new arrivals slept by the door so I took my position. I slept on the hard cement floor with my head to the door and my feet pointing at the centre of the cell. The waste bucket was also placed next to the newcomer so it was near the door next to my head. The other inmates arranged themselves so that the feet met at the centre. This is where the waste bucket was most of the time. I could not sleep for several reasons. First of all, the floor was too hard. Secondly, I did not have a pillow and I developed a stiff neck. Thirdly, the space was too small. I sat up and cried but the others encouraged me to lie down because if the prison guards found me sitting up when they did their rounds of inspection at night, I would be punished. I tried to sleep on my stomach but it was equally uncomfortable. I tried all sorts of positions but none of them invited sleep.

The following morning I was called to the office. The prison guards wanted personal information from me to put in my file. They told me that if I observed the prison regulations I would only serve for three years and five months, which meant that I would go home on March 10, 2000. I was informed that all the women in green uniform were prison guards and I should address them as *ambuya*. They had a right to send me on errands. They gave me the meal times and they told me it was my duty to observe them. Later they said I could join the sewing group. I told them that I could not do so because I was hopeless at sewing. Even though I had a sewing machine at home I had not bothered to learn to use it. Tobacco money had spoilt me. They insisted that I attend the sewing classes. It was important that I left prison with a skill that I could use to earn a living. I did not do hard manual work.

Prison life was monotonous. Every morning after we woke up, the prison guard counted us to see if we were all present. I did not see the point of it because we were locked up all night. How could we escape when we spent the night under lock and key? I soon learnt that prison is not a place of respect and dignity. A grown woman like me could be called to fetch water for the prison guard to drink even though she would be sitting next to the water tap. I did things for them that I did not do for my husband at home. Sometimes two prison guards would be sitting and talking to each other then one of them would thrust a foot forward and order me to clean her shoes. I would take a cloth, kneel and clean the shoes. They would be talking about the prisoners as if I were not there. I wanted to protest against such things but I could not, I kept everything in my chest.

I developed high blood pressure in prison and I put it down to my inability to say the things I did not like. Sometimes one guard would bring a bag full of dirty clothes for me to wash and iron and one would bring a bag full of doilies for me to starch. I had no choice but to do it. I did many things for them: sewing buttons on their children's clothes, sewing name-tags on their children's uniforms, and making peanut butter. I was particularly good at making peanut butter. I could fill a five-litre tin. At times two guards brought peanuts for me to make into butter. I could make butter for one at a time, the one who approached me first. They argued between themselves and made it appear as if I was the one at fault. I suspected that it was one of the reasons that led to my transfer to Bulawayo. They accused me of disobeying some of the guards. My blood pressure rose because I did duties that I was not supposed to do. I went to Parirenyatwa many times for treatment.

Basically, I found it difficult to get along with the prison guards. They sent me on errands outside prison duties. For instance, one guard used to give me the keys to her house and a lot of home chores to do. I did her laundry, swept, polished the floors, I cooked too, boiling the meat so that when she went home all she had to do was brown the meat and add onions and tomatoes. Sometimes the guards asked me to carry stolen food, usually sugar and meat, to their houses. I knew I was not supposed to do all these things, but I could not refuse to do as I was told. I bottled up everything. I was trustworthy and a hard worker, and they took advantage of me. Menstruation time was uncomfortable. They gave a person two sanitary pads per day, one in the morning and another in the evening. That was

210

all. They did not give you any if you asked for more. They said we were being wasteful.

My daughter, Chipo, used to visit me in prison and so did my husband, Bernard. However, from April 1998, Bernard stopped coming to see me. Earlier on I had got wind that he was staying with another woman at home. Now I was convinced it was true or else why would he stop the visits. It also meant that this woman was sleeping in my bed, cooking in my pots and using my plates. My blood pressure rose higher at these thoughts. I could not breathe. The last straw was when I saw a woman from Mbare in remand prison. I spoke to her, inquiring after my family. The prison guard told me that I had broken a rule and for punishment I would be transferred to Bulawayo. My condition got worse but that did not stop the transfer. The car that took me to Bulawayo broke down in Shurugwi. I had to spend the night in there. They put me in a room with a tiny window. I could not breathe. The officer-in-charge at Chikurubi ordered that I be taken to hospital because I was not well, he thought it would be better if I could be sent to a prison where my relatives could easily come and see me. He was a kind man. I had a brother in Kadoma, so instead of Bulawayo, I ended up in Kadoma. I was happy to be in there, it was close to my brother. In fact I was better off away from Harare because my husband did not care about me any more.

In Kadoma Prison, I had light duties to do. I worked in the prison clinic labelling medicine bottles. I was not educated enough to do such a job but I worked under strict supervision and I did the job well. I stayed in Kadoma until the time of my release in March 10, 2000.

When I left Kadoma, my brother gave me the bus fare to go to Harare. He offered to come with me to meet my husband. I thanked him for the fare but I refused his offer to come with me. I could manage on my own. When I arrived in Harare, I went to Bernard's young brother's house. I found his wife at home. I asked her many questions about my husband. Where was he? Did he have another wife? Was he working? Where was my son? She did not give me any answers. She said my husband was at the beerhall, it would be better for me to wait for him to come back. He eventually arrived, and after an exchange of greetings, I asked him why he had not come to fetch me from prison. I had written to him advising him when I would be released and I would appreciate it if he could wait for me at the prison gate on the day. He gave a lot of lame excuses: he was unemployed, he

211

had no money, he had another wife to look after and so forth. I asked after my son. (Bernard and I had a child together, as I told you.) He told me that our son was under his sister's care in Mabvuku. I slept at his brothers' and he went home to his wife. The following morning we went to Mabvuku to see our son. When he saw me he cried. He wanted to come home with me. He had already started school in Mabvuku. I told him to stay behind and go to school. I promised to fetch him as soon as I was settled.

When I got home I was shocked to find an empty house. My television set was gone; and so were my sofas, my sewing machine, my pots and plates, stove, kitchen unit, electric fan and my clothes. The wardrobe was empty and the bed had no sheets. He explained that he had sold my property to buy food and to pay hospital fees for his pregnant wife.

I was upset but I was careful to keep my anger under control. I did not want to go back to prison. I went to report him to the police. The police helped me list down all the things he had sold. They asked me if I wanted him arrested. I did not want that; I wanted my property back and I wanted him out of my life. The police advised that they did not handle divorce cases but they could assist me to get my property back. They made my husband sign a statement that he would give me back everything he had sold. When I got home I was angry again, I drove Bernard out of the house along with his wife. He went to stay with his brother. He never gave me back a single item. I went back to the police several times but nothing came out of it. So here I am now. I am out of prison but with no husband nor property.

Bernard visits me now and again but he lives with his other wife.

28

Rosemary

interviewed by Chiedza Musengezi

My name is Rosemary. I was born in Marondera in 1969. My father is self-employed. My mother lives in the rural areas. She does communal farming. She usually grows vegetables and keeps a garden just to sustain herself. Our rural home is in Chihota Communal Lands.

I was born into a family of three boys and three girls, but one of the girls died. I am the first-born. My father has two wives and his younger wife has two children. My father and my mother are no longer together. They separated while we were still in school. I was in Grade 4 when my mother was thrown out by my father – he simply told her that he no longer loved her. So she felt there was no reason why she should continue to stay with someone who did not love her anymore. She then decided to leave him. She went back to her parents in Chihota. She cooks on her own.

My father remained here in the city, living with his second wife in Kuwadzana. He could not have cared less for us. Not even a jot. My stepmother did not look after us. We were looked after by our paternal grandmother. It was not easy: we would sell all sorts of things, go into town, through to the suburbs, such as Borrowdale, selling apples, bananas, Mbare bags, groundnuts – to enable us to make a living, sometimes we made three to four thousand dollars. Usually we would not even have shoes to walk in, not even tennis shoes. To ask *ambuya* to buy you shoes was always a nightmare. Aah, she would scream at you first, really abuse you verbally. Then she would release the money. We would buy *pata patas* but they did not help much, especially during the winter season. Sometimes you would not get anything at all.

We were about fifteen living in the house. My grandmother and my eldest aunt bought groceries for the family. When my aunt died, my grandmother could not cope on her own. I then became a vendor, so I could help with the groceries. The other aunts were idle.

Sister Illuminata from the Catholic Church assisted me with school fees, especially when my grandmother did not give me enough money. This sister was later transferred to Kutama Mission, so there was no one to help me. As for uniforms, I had senior friends who gave me their uniforms after they completed their Form 4.

Then, when I was in Form 2, I fell in love with a certain man who was at school, at St Ignatius. He was doing Form 6. I was at Harare Secondary School in Mbare. I lived just opposite the school. So I thought this man I had fallen in love with would perhaps marry me, and maybe it would change my life for the better.

So I nurtured our relationship and really enjoyed being in love. One day, he told me that his aunt wanted us to go and see her in Glen View. She wanted me to assist her with her school-work, her mathematics, because I was an above-average student. So he pleaded with me to give her a hand. I asked what level of education this aunt was, and he said Form 3 but, he said, 'I am sure you can help because the syllabi do not differ much.' So we went to Glen View, and I did the maths with the aunt, and sure enough, I could crack the problems. It was not so difficult: it was almost like the work I was doing in Form 2. When I had thoroughly relaxed, teaching my fellow scholar, he sent the aunt on an errand. I did not know that my partner, this man, Elvis, would abuse me. He took me, and I immediately fell pregnant. Then he went back to school and I went home.

People at our house took me to the doctor because I was constantly throwing up. They asked me if I was pregnant and I kept saying no, so they decided to take me to the doctor. He simply said, 'Ha, this girl is pregnant!' So then they wondered what to do next.

Well, I kept going to school. I always wore a blazer that matched my maroon uniform that I had got from a friend, because *ambuya* had refused to buy us uniforms. So we both kept going to school, this man doing his Form 6 and me doing Form 2. I was constantly writing to him, but he said, 'Hey leave me alone, I am about to write major exams, so quit disturbing me.' I also wrote my ZJC exams.

I then delivered the baby, who looked identical to him. I named the baby Belinda. When he heard that, he said that it was his mother who had been against the whole idea of him having fathered a child, and being in a relationship with me. He claimed he loved me and acknowledged that he had found me 'innocent and intact', and all that talk. However, I could not live with his mother, and they could not take the child from me. So I continued with my life, having resuscitated the peddling business again. It was not easy, not at all easy. My aunts were no longer contributing anything to the house: I was having to do everything.

I continued to go to school, I was now in Form 3 at Harare Secondary. You see I went into labour on a Thursday and I delivered on Friday morning. I had a safe delivery, though I had thirty stitches, and I was discharged on Saturday and on Monday, I went back to school. I had difficulties in walking but I had to act as if everything was normal. I endured the pain because I still wanted to go to school.

But aah, the teachers often argued with each other and could not accept that I had a child. (My friends who knew I had been pregnant spread the news at school.) The teachers got to hear of it. They did not believe it. You see I had a very small frame. I was really very small. One day, I was actually summoned to the headmaster's office, to verify if I had a child or not. At that time I was very religious. I went to church a lot, to the Roman Catholic Church. So when I was asked I just said to myself, what will I lose if I tell the truth?* The headmaster was a big white man. So I told him everything that had transpired. He actually cried in front of me. He told me I had proved I still wanted to continue with my education. Because of my determination he told me to go ahead with school. Many of the teachers could still not believe it: they would gaze at me in disbelief.

I was a very quiet person, too quiet, in fact. I was also very smart and particular about how I looked and presented myself to the world. I always did my best to look the best I could as a school child. I was also very intelligent academically, so that

---

* There has always been a strict rule about pregnant girls attending school. They are usually asked to leave.

really upset the teachers who heard the allegation. At one stage, even before all this questioning, I had wanted to confide in my home economics teacher about my problem. Somehow I could not bring myself to it, as she did not have the time, so I had just decided to keep quiet. I just wanted to go to school without disrupting anything ... I was producing milk but it never stained my clothes. I would always pad my breasts with cotton wool and changed the dressing often. I kept a little plastic bag together with perfume. I would take fragrant soap like Choice to wipe my breasts and wash in the toilet. There would never be anyone to see me there. Sometimes I would slice an orange and squeeze the juice into the water I used for cleaning myself up, usually in the toilet cistern. I would nicely squeeze the face towel and put it away with the spray perfume; and I would wash the breast-milk pads and pack them in my plastic bag. I would then go to class and sit confidently among others. That is why it was difficult for people to accept that I had a child.

I left the baby in the care of a girl, my aunt's maid, when I went to school. My aunt, who used to work at Air Zimbabwe, had stressed that I should continue going to school because I had really disappointed her. That aunt had always been kind to me. I just told her that I was sorry. I had really thought that that man would marry me and give me a better life than the one I was living with *ambuya*. This particular aunt did the best she could to make me comfortable. She was genuinely kind and generous, but *ambuya* had absolutely no care about us.

So I wrote my O-levels and I passed with an A in English, an A in maths. I think I had five As, and three Bs. I wanted to do my A-level but there was no one willing to pay my school fees. My aunt, the one who could assist, was ill. She then passed away after some time.

At the time, my young brother and I stayed with grandmother. My other sister stayed with one of my aunts, and the other two lived with my mother. They were still young. Then, my grandmother told me and my young brother to go and get money for my baby and for my brother's school fees, from my father. When we got there, my stepmother took my O-level certificates and burnt them. She was annoyed that nothing had been done to me when I fell pregnant. Also, I had passed my O-level while her daughter refused to proceed to Form 1. (Later, this girl became a commercial sex worker and now has six children, all with different fathers.)

So I went with my mother's brother and he collected copies of the certificates for me from the Ministry of Education. But then my stepmother repeated the same thing, she burnt them, and on a third attempt to get copies I did not succeed. The officers said this was too much, they were not going to even try and look for the results for me.

By then the father of my child was paying maintenance to help us. What happened was that when we found that I was pregnant, we reported the matter to the police, and they told us to return after the baby was delivered. Then some people told me, 'Look dear friend, things are not so smooth for you financially, why don't you apply for maintenance?' So I just went to the Charge Office with the baby. There was hot-seating at school, so we always started at 12 o'clock and finished at 3.00 p.m., and I just needed to report to the Charge Office between eight and nine in the morning, so I carried my baby on my back after having bathed her properly. It was easy. I went with the child, who was then four months old, to Harare Central Police Station.

[The process] took about three months. At first the father was denying paternity of the child. Both of us had been summoned to the Charge Office, so that our story could be heard from both sides. The officer that attended to me noticed that the child was identical to its father and was even the first to ask me if it wasn't his child. I said 'Yes, it is.' He asked, 'How can it be that the man is denying responsibility for a child that is his spitting image?' We then went to court. Unfortunately, afterwards, the father only paid maintenance for six months and then he stopped. It was a problem.

I then found a certain friend who decided to share her secret with me. She told me that a certain uncle of hers was coming to town, bringing tobacco from Mozambique. She suggested that if we sold this tobacco together, it would give me money to buy soap for my daughter. She said, 'Look your *ambuya* cannot help you any more. You have nothing. Your certificates were burnt by your stepmother.' So I asked, 'How do I sell it?' She said, 'Oh, you just twist it into little balls like this. And those interested in buying for retail, you just measure out a cupful, wrap the contents properly and give it to them.' I asked if we would not have the cops after us. She replied, 'Yes, we could be arrested, but what else can we do? Just find somewhere safe to put the tobacco because you can't keep it in the house.' At first I was scared, but when I saw my friend doing fairly well, I decided to try it. So

217

when her relative came, they gave me quite a bit, about ten kg. Ah, then I got busy, selling that tobacco.

We kept it separate, outside, near the hedge inside a bucket. That's where I kept mine, after twisting it. The rest I kept in a plastic [bag] in the toilet cistern. I sold a lot – it was good money. But I had not quite finished selling my ten kg, when my father's wife, the same one who burnt my certificates, started asking where I was getting money to buy my daughter all sorts of things. She asked if it was clean money. She talked to someone who said, 'Oh, maybe she is selling tobacco because her friend is in that business.' She then sent a policeman in plain clothes to see me. I had no idea that he was a policeman or that she had done this.

So I took out a little tobacco for him and he said to me he wanted much more, even up to five kg. I told him to wait while I collected it. It was then that he declared me under arrest and took out his credentials. I did not refuse him. I was interrogated about where I had got the tobacco. Because of my quiet nature, when our neighbours saw me answering those charges, they did not believe that I had done anything wrong, they felt I was being unjustly treated. But I acknowledged that I had been caught with *mbanje*. They wanted to know where I had got it. I told them I had bought it from someone who was passing through my area, someone I could not identify. I was really beaten up, really beaten up, in the hope that I would reveal other names. My face was swollen, my arms also, I was unrecognisable. It happened just over there, at that police station. They then took me to Mbare, but I still said that I did not know the person, I had just bought the *mbanje* without taking special note of the seller's features or identity.

I was tried in March 1984 and I was sentenced, after I had stayed in custody in Chikurubi for a long time. The child stayed with my aunt and she looked after her and sent her to school. You see we had a good relationship because her younger sisters were very naughty; they were not helping around the house with work or anything. But if she asked me to go to the market early, I would always oblige. I would wake up at 4 a.m., shower and though I did not have a jersey, I just used to go as was required. I used to follow instructions. So I helped her, and she liked me.

I stayed in prison a whole year. Initially I was given thirteen months but they said that I had not committed a major crime so I was just to serve a year's sentence. We were about twenty arrested for selling tobacco, because others had been caught with consignments as large as 50 kg. Aah, mine was really nothing.

We would share experiences. A lot of them would say, 'Look, I do not have a husband. This is what I have to do to earn a living.' I would then ask them where they got their tobacco. One said that she used to grow it in her garden, but many said they got theirs from Mozambique. A lot of the dealers are based in Mutare and most bought it from there. Only one person said she grew it in a maize field and was only later sold out by someone. The police had found fifteen kg of the weed. I would then ask why they had got into that business and most said that tobacco sells like hot cakes, because people love it. Just as alcohol brings high sales, so does tobacco. Cigarettes such as Madison and Kingsgate sell fast, but how much more *mbanje*? Most said they were sending their children to school with tobacco money and were still affording to look after themselves.

There were those prisoners that you got along with and could share jokes and stories with. But a lot of people in prison are very coarse and take advantage of you especially if you are small. Sometimes after dusk, you may even be ordered by an inmate to take your fingers and use them as though they were the male organ. If you refuse, you can be severely beaten up. One can even say I want you to eeeh … eat me … in my private parts. If you do not have a friend in there to rescue you, you will be doing that so much that by the time you leave, you will be ill.

Sometimes all the food and cigarettes that would be brought in for you by your visitors would be snatched by the bullies. Usually you would have nowhere to report because the bullies rule the roost. In some instances, it was the prison guards that would torture us. One could come up to you and say, 'I want you to polish my shoe, lick it and make it shine,' you would be left with no choice but to lick it until it was glossy. And we would do it. Then there are some guards who would say to me, 'Hey child, your relatives irk us by their constant visits. They bring food and you do not share it with us!' I just said that I was sorry, I did not know they wanted any. So one of them would go to the toilet and call me, telling me to clean the toilet with my bare hands. Especially one called *Ambuya* … . She would say 'Clean, lick my shoes and make them glossy'. Yes, she would say, 'Lick'. You have to acknowledge and truly feel that you are not at home: you are in jail. This is not a place where you live well with your relatives coming to visit, giving you all you want.

If you go to jail, I do not think you will come out all right. And the lice you find there, hmm, those bugs are something else. It is terrible! I went in with a heart problem and tonsils, but they did not care. The way the injection is administered is cruel. Should you be given tablets, it is just a fraction of the dosage. You are given just four tablets and told that is enough for you, keep them and drink when you get water. Sometimes you do not even get the water, or the tablets are snatched away from you by other inmates, just to spite you. Sometimes they just crush them right before your eyes, to remind you that you are a small fish. If you dare say, 'I get food from my visitors because I have ulcers,' they just grab that food and eat it. They then smoke away their cigarettes, like Madison and Kingsgate. You see, when you are in the remand, you actually get everything that your visitors bring you. So when you are junior, those that have been there for quite a while will harass you. They are the ones that snatch everything away. That is the problem.

My friend, the one who had introduced me to *mbanje*, never visited, for she was afraid that maybe I had told the police that she was also involved in drugs. She always sent her regards though. When I came out I told her it was not her fault that I had been arrested. We continued to be friends. She is late now.

The relatives that would bring food to me in prison were my mother's brother, my mother, my aunt, and my friends, yes. They brought me food because the food in prison, ah, it is difficult to cope with, but I had to get used to the prison diet where the vegetables are cooked with no oil, even spinach. So much so that when I got out I was overly used to impoverished food. My aunt was very worried about me. She would take me to restaurants, hotels and so on, in the hope that I would change, but it did not help.

When I left prison, *ambuya* asked me to move out of the house because she could not stand living with an ex-convict. She admonished me for not having told her about the tobacco. But I told her I did not think it necessary because I had not envisaged such an outcome, and I apologised. So I rented a flat. I was doing different part-time jobs. That way I was able to pay the rent. I worked as a part-time maid for different people. By then, the child had been taken by her paternal grandma. The latter was very fond of her only grandchild from her only son. She is the one who was living with her in the rural areas in Murehwa. So I could only do what . . . wait for the holidays, that's when she would stay with me, during school holidays.

So in 2000, the child only came two weeks before schools opened, and I was wondering why she had come so late. I was at my kiosk (by then I had a kiosk) when the child arrived. I was amazed at the way she was rather toned down, not excited about drinks from the kiosk as she usually was. She did not want to eat. She was coughing. I then bought cough syrup, Vicks, and many other goodies that I expected to excite my daughter, still there was no change. I then decided to take the child to Naidoo's: he was a doctor. I knew nothing. I suspected nothing. I did not know that she had been raped. Yes, she was raped in the year 2000.

She was just seven years old. I just asked myself what to do. The child had no interest in food for days, a week. She washed her own panties so clean that I could never have guessed. So I really quizzed myself why the child was behaving thus. Then a few days later, I sat in my kiosk and I saw her coming towards me from the toilet and I noticed her walking with a limp and I asked, 'Kumbirai, what is the problem?' She just said it was urine, and I let the matter rest. However, my mind did not rest. I worried but I did not think of rape. I bought rice, which I knew to be her favourite food, Mazowe, drink, apples, fruit, potato chips, everything, and gave to her. But, ah, she still did not eat. I asked myself what it was with Kumbirai.

That night I fell into a deep sleep after a long day's work. When I woke in the middle of the night, she was making noises like someone crying in her sleep. I woke up because of these noises and noticed that she was restless in her sleep. I then thought of inspecting her private parts to see what it was that made her limp.

So I decided to examine the child's pubic area. Wasn't I shocked! She was discharging some thick stuff. Her panties were full of it. I tell you I really suffered that night. I could not sleep. The following day I took the child to the clinic, thinking that going to Naidoo's was not such a good idea. They then referred me to Harare hospital. The child was examined by one white sister. There was also a young man and woman, and they asked, her if she wished to be examined by the man and she refused.

They pleaded with her, but she would not talk. She was just naming her aunt's son, who is currently in Grade 4, Tonderai. So she was claiming Tonderai had done that to her. They pleaded with her saying surely it can't be Tonderai, speak and we will give you what you want. They then told her she wasn't going to have to go back to the village but would live with me. Still the child would not open up.

After a while they called me in and told me that the child had been abused anally, so her back was really damaged, but it was very clear that she had been abused by

221

an adult, not the child that she was naming. I then asked Kumbirai who she sleeps with at her granny's place. She said it was *gogo*, and sometimes also *sekuru*, the grandmother's boyfriend. So I asked the child if she ever spent time with this *sekuru* and she said, 'Yes'. The sisters asked me to plead with her further. I told her she would never go to the village again. The white doctor also stressed that I should *never* send the child to the village again.

Schools had opened two days earlier. I was asked to collect her clothes so that I could transfer her, then we could have the *sekuru* arrested, but she still kept naming that young boy. His mother had died recently of that common disease we have nowadays. We really pleaded with the child in all ways we could think of, but she would not budge. I then said, 'Okay, suppose I get the culprit arrested, will my baby's innocence be restored?'

The child was discharging thick mucus-like stuff and the doctor pointed out that the child had been abused anally, whoever had done it had left just but a wink, to rid her of her virginity. She then ordered that I take full custody of the child from then on. She gave me tablets to assist with the discharge.

That is when my aunt, my father's cousin from Masvingo, came to see the child. She is a qualified nurse. I told her I wasn't settled, the medication had finished but the child kept discharging. I just needed this to finish, so this aunt negotiated with the doctor and was given the injection, which she asked me to administer. I guess it was out of hurt that I injected the child with a double dose – ten mls and it was an overdose, a dosage for adults, so the child spent the day sleeping. She only awoke after nine.

This aunt had shown me what do, but I just was helpless. The child was also being examined for any other infection so I was desperate to get her cleaned up and I underrated the power of injection. At the hospital she had been given tablets but we had also got a prescription for tablets, which my aunt said were not available but could be substituted by the injection. It was only then that the discharge stopped. It took almost two weeks.

I spent two weeks going to the hospital with the child for more persuasion, but she still named the young boy, Tonderai. Even today, she still says the same thing. When you ask her she actually cries so you end up saying to yourself, I might as well let the matter rest. I went to the grandmother and related the child's ordeal and how she was naming the boy as the culprit. The granny then took a rod and started beating Tonderai up, but I told her it was not right. In any case the issue was history. I told her I did not think it could be Tonderai because in any case his mother died and he is just a lonesome orphan. Leave him alone.

Tonderai's grandmother is this old woman's sister. So he would come to play at his elder granny's. So my daughter would claim she slept, ate and played at Tonderai's. That must be what she was coached to say. She is in Grade 4 now. She is so good in class and she is always coming out number one.

Now I have another stall. I had left the first one because of constant harassment from the old women who belonged to ZANU (PF). They were not pleased that I was not attending their meetings anymore. They labelled me a sell-out. I was asked by one of my neighbours in Mbare, during election time, to participate as ZANU (PF) secretary. I told her I did not think I qualified given the number of older women in the area but she convinced me. So when the MP was introducing projects for women, I was given a kiosk to run adjacent to Rufaro Stadium. Initially I hesitated to take it but I had already been made chairwoman. You see the Coca-Cola people were helping the MP to campaign, by offering loans to all those who wanted to start projects selling soft drinks. They gave me 30 crates for a start. So I had to take the credit Coca-Cola was giving. I worked and paid back the debt.

By now I had moved and I was renting a cottage in Greendale. I lived with my child. Then talk began in Mbare that I had deserted the township and therefore did not deserve to be running a tuckshop there. It was some older women that approached me one day and tore the keys from my kiosk door and told me in no uncertain terms to make my way out.

I went to Coca-Cola to report, because by then I had invested about fifty thousand dollars in the project. They said they would help me start up if I could find a place to run another kiosk. So I began the search, that's when I met an uncle who used to work at Express Driving School in Mbare. I told him my problem. He was ZANU (PF) councillor for Ward 6 in Mbare. So he gave me a corner to start immediately. It was right near the post office and opposite the bus terminus. I invited two young women to join me in the project. The older women once again came to challenge me and chase us away. Since I was now staying in Greendale they said I was invading their territory. Also I had ceased to attend the ZANU (PF) meetings.

They asked how I had got this new place. I told them, the same way as I got the previous one. I asked them if they had any idea what I had gone through to get it, since they were just hijackers. They then wanted to know how many we were and I told them three. The women claimed that my partners were supposed to be working with them, so I said I did not have a problem with that if they did their duties prior to going across. They tried to be impossible, countering my every suggestion, till I told them that I simply respected them as mothers in the community, so I did not understand their desire to see my projects flop, but whatever they wanted was okay with me. Only then did they leave me. It was not easy but I persevered. I went to Coca-Cola and paid all the money they wanted. They then gave me the soft drinks and their shelter. They also made a commitment to defend me if ever anyone harassed me again. I was told I had the choice of running the kiosk myself or renting it out, they just wanted the account kept up to date. I was also to ensure that it was operational at all times, come rain, sunshine or thunder. That is where I am working to date.

Now we order the drinks on our own. We do not get anything any more. It was just during the first days, to see us get on our feet.

What I wish for in my life is for people to appreciate and understand other people. It is a pity that if you have never had serious problems, it is difficult to comprehend them. I think a person should never go to jail, because it is not a nice place. The health conditions are bad – people actually die there. If only we could just keep away from crime, be it theft, or whatever. It is better to ask kind people for assistance with soap for washing and other things. It is certainly better than to be caught and sent to prison because that is just creating another problem. If only people would just live together in harmony. As for me now if I really run out of basics, should I be offered a job as a domestic worker, I would gladly take it. Better than going back to prison.

The child is now my major problem. I only wish that I get something better or that someone could assist me so that I can send her for regular medical examinations and treatment. I just wish to be able to fully provide for her because she is really an intelligent girl. Now she is at home, she is better: she is very jovial. She loves playing with other children. She also helps out at the kiosk diligently, she conducts sales just the way I would. If it is Z$1,600 I get in a day, that is exactly what she produces. But one thing she does not do is eat at other people's homes. She would

Dangerous drugs — Rosemary

rather starve, than eat elsewhere other than home. She will either say I have eaten or I will eat at home, something that I never taught her. This sometimes worries me and that is when I wish I could get help to enable me to sufficiently provide for her.

It is now very difficult to save money. The nature of the job in the kiosk takes a lot of money because I have to think of storage for the drinks at the local cloakroom as well as ensuring a constant supply of drinks. The starting point is quite a challenge. I am just grateful that I at least get bath soap for the child, the required school fees and books, and of course decent food for her. It is difficult to save, the nature of the job makes it so.

If only God could help me get a better job with better remuneration so that I can at least fend for my child. I would also like society to constantly advise people in a constructive manner to discourage crime. We must also always point out that jail life is not good. If I had not gone to jail, my daughter would never have been raped. My desire for quick money with tobacco shoved me down the worst pit ever. I should have thought of better ways, legal ways. But I wanted money quickly. Now look at what it cost me. Sometimes we commit crimes and think we will get away with it, but that is not true. It is better to seek assistance and share your problem than commit a crime.

29

Joyce

interviewed by S. Ncube

I am Joyce and I am aged fifty five. I was born on 1st January 1947. I am not sure how many we are in my family because my parents divorced when I was young: then, there were three of us. I am the first born. My parents lived in South Africa, which is the place of my birth, but they are from Malawi. They left for South Africa soon after they got married.

My uncle wanted me to be a minder for his child. He asked my parents, who agreed. I came to live in Zimbabwe with my uncle's family at the age of nine. Since then I have never been in contact with my family. We immediately moved to Zambia. These movements disturbed my education. I thought life would be better in Zambia but to my surprise and disappointment, the situation was very bad. My uncle's wife started to show her true colours. She hated me. She told lies about me to my uncle. As a result my uncle did not believe whatever I said. I was ill-treated. I used to have one dress only, which made it impossible for me to go to school. Fortunately, I had an aunt from my father's side who happened to be living in Zambia. She is the one who came to my rescue. She learnt about the ill-treatment that I was receiving from my uncle's wife, and she managed to find a polite way of dealing with the situation without causing more trouble. She would ask my uncle if I could spend a few days with her. I used to enjoy the days I spent with my aunt because she treated me well. Then I would hear that I was supposed to go back to my uncle's. I could not understand all this but I later discovered that my uncle's wife said she had a claim over me because her husband was the one who had brought me to Zambia. If anybody else wanted to have me, they would have to ask my parents like she did.

My aunt wrote to my father telling him about the situation I was in. It did not take long before he came for me. From Zambia, I came to Zimbabwe with my father. We stayed with his brother and family. The brother thought it was a good idea for me to remain in Zimbabwe with his family when my father went back to South Africa, because it was going to be hard for my father to look after me since he had divorced.

I was about twelve years old when my father left me here in Zimbabwe and since then I have never heard anything from him. His brother would write him but there would be no response. I took my uncle as my own father. I managed to go to school up to Standard 1. The wife of my uncle made it clear that she was not prepared to waste money on someone who was not her child. The treatment she gave me was no different from what I was receiving in Zambia. I had nothing to do and nowhere to go except to bear whatever hardship I was facing.

My other aunt from Zambia happened to visit us and was shocked to find a situation similar to the one I was in before. She thought the solution to my problems was to get married. The surprising thing is that no one argued. They all agreed, and it looked like my uncle had already someone in mind. The man was working with him at the farm, where my uncle was a cook and he was a waiter. My aunt was the one who was tasked to tell me about the arrangements they had made. I did not like the idea but there was nothing I could do. I tried to protest by crying, knowing well that I was wasting my time. No one paid attention so it did not help.

I got married to this man and he paid twelve pounds* as *lobola* to my uncle. He was from Mozambique.

I had my first child in 1961. I was fifteen. During my second pregnancy I suggested he must leave his job and look for another one away from my uncle's family, as they used to bother us a lot by demanding certain things be done for them. So we left the farm and came to stay with my husband's nephew in Bulawayo while my husband was looking for another job. Before long he got one at Burnside in Bulawayo, as a cook, a job he held until his death.

---

* The currency at the time.

Our life was not that bad: my husband was taking good care of the children and me. We had six children. We got a house in Njube and we left Burnside. I had my last born in 1986. The whites my husband used to work for left the country but they got him another job at Hillside. My husband died in 1989, three years after we had our last born.

My husband and I had nine children, five girls and four boys. Unfortunately, one of my sons passed away at the age of six, and one of my daughters passed away last year – she was born in 1970 and she was a twin to one of my boys. She used to do business – buying and selling. She would buy clothes from Botswana and resell them here. Two of my daughters are married. My first-born son joined the army, though he left after getting a job in Victoria Falls. He is the one who looked after us after the death of his father. Myself, I used to buy clothes in Bulawayo for resale in Hwange. I started doing this before the death of my husband after realising that our family had grown big and my husband's meagre salary was not enough.

In Hwange we met people who were dealing in *mbanje* and fish, and we used to bring fish to Bulawayo. So we decided to bring fish and *mbanje*. We discovered that by doing this we made more money than selling clothes. People used to buy clothes on credit not with cash. Sometimes they would take about three months to pay the whole bill; unlike fish and *mbanje*, these are paid for in cash, up front.

A friend suggested that I forget about dealing in clothes and start dealing in *mbanje*. She also advised that I stop getting the drug from Hwange and source it in Mozambique because it was cheaper. My friends and I decided to go and buy *mbanje* from Mozambique. I asked them if we were not going to be in trouble. They gave me confidence and assured me that there was nothing to worry about, we only needed to be careful.

We managed two trips successfully and I was so happy with the profit we made. During our third trip, we ran out of luck. We were caught red-handed. It was in May 1995. The CIO know all the tricks that people play to smuggle things into the country. And another thing that contributed to our arrest was the language barrier between us, and the people in Chipinge. They do not speak Ndebele. When you reach Birchenough [Bridge] you wait a long time for transport. This makes it easier for someone to spot you.

There was a morning bus to Zimbabwe which left the border around 3 a.m. It was often used by smugglers. The CIO knew this, and when we boarded the bus, they also got in. I could tell that there was something fishy going on because of their behaviour. One got in front of us and the other came behind, so that we were in the centre. When the bus started off one of the men went to talk to the bus conductor. I could tell they were talking about us. They were looking at us with talking eyes. I smelt a rat and tried to warn my friends who thought I was a coward. There was nothing to do because we were already trapped. Before long, the man who had been talking to the conductor started shouting, instructing the passengers who were sitting at the back to move to the front. My friends and I were ordered to carry our bags and sit at the back. At Chipinge terminus they flashed their police identity cards ordering us to drop off. We were under arrest. We did not say anything, we just did as they said. They got us inside the Chipinge municipal building and opened our bags to find what they already knew was inside.

After 30 minutes a police vehicle drove in and we were pushed inside and taken to the CIO department. Here they said our drug should be weighed first and our fingerprints should be taken. We were taken to the post office to weigh the drugs – the sentence depended on the weight of the drug. From there we were taken back to CIO department for fingerprints. After this we went to Chipinge Police Camp, where we were locked in a cell for three days. We were unlucky because it was a holiday. It should only have been for one day according to the law. There, in a cell, we were given two blankets for the three of us, one to spread on the floor and another to cover ourselves with. It was terribly cold and smelly. The cell was so small and had a built-in toilet. During the night people would make the floor dirty. It was dark and hard to see the bowl.

They used to open for us in the morning at 8 a.m. for a breakfast of porridge. We would be put back again at 12 o'clock when we were given sadza for lunch. We had our supper at 4 p.m. From there until the following morning at 8 a.m. we were locked up. On the third day we were taken to court after breakfast. We were remanded from 25th May to 26th July. We were taken to Chipinge Prison. There, life was tough. Our clothes were taken and all our belongings. We were given prison clothes – two prison uniforms each and used pants. It was disgusting to wear pants that were worn by someone else. I was afraid of contracting diseases. It should have been easy to refuse and do without, but we were forced to wear them especially when we were menstruating. During menstruation one was given a small piece of cotton wool that got wet quickly. To avoid soiling our clothes we used to tear pieces off the blankets to use as sanitary pads. We made sure that we were not caught tearing them.

Food here was better. We were given tea and porridge in the morning. Tea had milk but we had no bread. The food was there but it was not prepared properly. In the remand prison we were not locked in all time. Here, we were always outside knitting with the prison guards monitoring us. We were mixed with those who were already serving their sentences. Those on remand were made to carry out light duties such as picking up litter in the yard and cleaning prison guards' toilets. I am sure that they were taking advantage of us, making us clean their toilets, for I do not really think we were supposed to do that. The prison guards used to order us around and we never protested. We all knew that once we opposed whatever they demanded we would be inviting trouble for ourselves. I remember one day it was raining and we were ordered to sit down in the mud with nothing to protect us from the rain. No one had the guts to tell the prison guards that what they were doing was unreasonable and unfair. We all sat until we were told to get inside our cells.

My trial was in July 1995 and I was found guilty of being in possession of *mbanje*. The magistrate slapped me with three years in jail: one year was suspended on condition of good behaviour. I was then left with two years, which was again reduced by the eight months I had already spent in prison, so I was left with one year and four months to serve. I spent three days in Chipinge prison before moving to Chikurubi after my sentence was passed. I was in A-class, as prisoners are put in classes depending on how long your sentence is. A-class is for those serving one year six months and below. There is B-class up to D. The number of years one is serving and the nature of your crime determine your class.

My first days at Chikurubi were difficult. We were given torn old clothes for three months. Afterwards we were given new clothes. We were also given blankets and one nightdress. We had tea in the morning at 8 a.m. and lunch was served at 11 a.m. and supper was at 4 p.m. On Monday, we would have sadza with vegetables. Tuesday we would have sadza with beans and the following day we would have sadza with a small piece of meat. The food was always badly prepared and not enough. For example, tea used to be served with a thin slice of bread. Sometimes it would be black without milk and tasteless, as there would be no sugar.

One bar of soap was to be shared by two people for the whole month and you were expected to use it for both bathing and laundry. It was not enough. This forced us to wash blankets without soap at all to serve it for bathing. In Chikurubi we were allowed to put on tennis shoes and we were advised to put on slippers when visiting toilets to prevent the spread of tuberculosis, which had hit the prison. You had to buy your own slippers for the prison did not provide any. We faced problems during winter, as we did not have enough blankets. Each prisoner was given one blanket. So what we used to do was to come together, maybe three of us, so that we could share the blankets. That really helped, so it was important to make friends that you could share the blankets with.

We used to work hard, digging, cultivating and weeding in the garden. You really have to be strong because you do all sorts of jobs, even those that we usually regard as men's jobs. The prison guards differed: some were cruel and some really understood what we were going through. The horrible ones used to scold us for no reason. Sometimes you were told you were a witch, yet you would have done nothing wrong. It is surprising that they used to say such things and get away with it. I know it is against the law to tell someone such things. This made the relationship between prisoners and the prison guards very sour.

Prisoners sometimes fought each other but in my cell we told ourselves that prison was not a place to be fighting against each other. We used to hear reports from other cells of prisoners fighting amongst themselves. To avoid fights, some prisoners were chosen from each cell to monitor others. Such prisoners were called 'staff'. We heard that there were cases where prisoners killed each other in their cells. One would close your mouth using a blanket so that you would not be able to cry for help and then beat you to death. Fortunately, because of my age, I was asked to take care of the babies of other prisoners while their mothers were working in the fields. You were supposed to do everything for the babies like changing napkins, bathing and feeding them. It was very hard especially to calm crying babies, although, it was better than digging the garden. The mothers used to come and breastfeed their babies at 11 a.m. and at 3 p.m.

Anyone who fell sick was taken to hospital for treatment in the company of a prison guard and would be handcuffed until they were sure that you were not faking your sickness in order to escape. The prison guards used to have shifts. Those who started in the morning dismissed at 1 p.m. Another team would come and dismiss at 4 p.m. and then another team would spend the whole night on duty. There were lessons that were carried out in prison. The lucky ones managed to sit for Grade 7, ZJC and O-level examinations since all these were on offer. One had to pay examination fees and those who had money did not have any problems at all. Some courses were free, so I joined sewing. We did not work on Saturday and Sunday. All we did was our laundry and attend a church service every Sunday. Church was compulsory. We had a pastor who came to preach. The service was from 9 a.m. to 11 a.m.

Visitation was once a month. My children visited me, but not often because of the distance between Bulawayo and Harare. I knew life was difficult for them and they used to confirm that during their visits. They decided to rent other rooms and squeeze themselves and their property into one room. This helped them to get money for food from the rentals. My sister had to accommodate some of my children. The painful thing is that they were disturbed in their education because they had to stop going to school as they could not afford food and school fees at once.

In prison we used to hold meetings every month. In these meetings, everyone is expected to stand when her name is called in the register. You would be told the day you started serving your sentence, date of your release and your bag number where your belongings are kept. So you are always aware of your release date. A day before your release, you would be given a piece of soap to wash so that you would go home clean. If one did not have money for transport you would be issued with a warrant and would be accompanied by a prison guard to board the bus. It was on 26th November 1996 when I was released. I was given Z$500 by the prison, but it was not enough for my fare to Bulawayo. Fortunately my son had sent me transport money and new clothes to use on my release but I was very unfortunate as it arrived after I had left. The prison staff was very helpful as they posted back everything to Bulawayo.

On my release, I was issued with a warrant to use and I was accompanied by two prison guards to a bus. I was so happy as I was looking forward to being with my children. Likewise they were also delighted to be with me again. Unfortunately, when I arrived home, I received sad news about my grandchild who passed away during my absence. I did not stay even for an hour in my house, I had to proceed to Entumbane suburb to see my daughter whose child had passed away. She was so pleased to see me though she was still mourning her child. All the rituals that are carried out after death in a family had been done.

I wished I had been there to be with my daughter during this difficult time but because in prison we are not allowed to attend funerals, they decided to tell me about it when I was out. I hope one day they will change the law. It kills the hearts of many people who have lost their loved ones and are not able to go to the funeral. It is very hard to reconcile with the fact that you will never see that person again.

Another thing I would like to appeal to lawmakers is to be lenient with prisoners. They must consider the factors that would have led an individual to commit a certain crime. They must also look at the consequences that might result from the arrest. The food quality and quantity should be improved. Can there be someone who monitors the way the prison guards treat prisoners? I remember one inhumane thing that we were asked to do one day by one of the prison guards. We were going back to our cells after the daily routine. She ordered us to stand in a single file without our clothes on. We were naked as we got inside our cells. I could not believe my ears when I heard the prison guard saying 'everyone remove your clothes' only to see people removing their clothes.

I stayed about five days in my house after my release and I left for my rural home. My son gave me money to go and spend time with my children. Afterwards I started running a shebeen in my house but I've since stopped, as it is illegal and too risky. You are always playing hide and seek with police. Sometimes they confiscate all the beer and you run at a loss. Another problem is that people usually damage my property when they get drunk. They start fighting and vandalising my furniture and almost killing each other. At present I am not engaged in any business. My son who is in London is taking care of me. My future plans are to buy material and start sewing and selling clothes since I now have the skill. I learnt sewing during my imprisonment. I would like to urge other women not to engage in illegal dealings when they are in trouble. It is better to look for alternatives.

Section 7:

Shoplifting

30

Nyaradzo

interviewed by Keresia Chateuka

My name is Nyaradzo. I was born in June 1969 in Mutare. I am the last-born in our family. We were six girls in our family, four passed away. My remaining sister works at a bakery in Mutare. Both my parents are alive but they separated long back. My mother left my father's house when I was three days old. My grandparents brought me up. To date my father is a sign writer at Coca-Cola. He completely cut all ties with us. He never came to visit. My grandparents took him to court where he publicly handed us to them. They accepted us.

I had no problems with education since my mother worked. She managed to educate us from Grade 1 to Form 4. When I was in Grade 6 my mother was retrenched from work, so my mother's young sister took me to Honde Valley to complete Grades 6 and 7. I then did my Form 1 to 4 at a secondary school in Mutare. I was an average student. I never got enough time to study because of the market. (After my mother was retrenched she became a vendor.) It is that which sustained us after my grandfather passed away in 1980.

I only passed Shona at O-level. There is a subject, Food and Nutrition, which I was very good at but I used the wrong number for my practicals, it was a colleague's candidate number. I did not think anything would be amiss, as such. My teacher was shocked, when I did not pass. I finished school in 1987 and I spent two years doing nothing in particular. Then I got married.

I met my husband, Misheck, at the Salvation Army Church. We had a wonderful wedding. My husband worked temporarily at a board-and paper-mill. Then he was retrenched. I was staying with the in-laws. They told us to look for our own place and we did. I started selling vegetables at the market, making sweets from brown sugar and roasting peanuts. The money I got was not adequate to pay for rent, water, electricity and food. I had not enough money to look after my child.

Then I met some people who introduced me to shoplifting. It was my friend who had her family and a husband who had been retrenched. She had problems like me. We tried it out and it worked for a while. We were unaware of the gravity of the offence we were committing. We were able to send our children to school. We paid rent, electricity and water bills. Two years passed without us ever getting caught. We travelled to places like Marondera, Rusape, Chiredzi and Wedza. We would act like people going for a trip. We had a timetable and planned our activities well. This really paid us well. We brought bags full of goods that we sold in the townships at cheap prices until we got arrested.

My husband knew and at times he barred me from making trips saying we had enough money to use. But because we were addicted we would just go anyway. At times, we ended up getting arrested. The first time I was arrested and sent to prison was during one of our trips to Chiredzi. After accomplishing our business on that fateful day, we boarded a bus that was coming from Birchenough Bridge. We were expecting to reach Mutare at around 4 p.m. When we were almost in Mutare, we were stopped at a police roadblock. The police searched us. They did not expect to come across shoplifters. They were looking for a woman who was alleged to travel with lizards. They had had a tip off. The grapevine had it that the woman had once been arrested for misusing them. I am not sure how. All the bags were unloaded. They pinpointed one of our bags but no one stood up to claim it. They became suspicious. They searched the bus and found more stolen goods. My friends were ordered to disembark. They searched the bus again. They removed our bag from the bus. My colleagues said that it was mine and I disembarked. We were taken to Chiredzi Police Station, under a CID. They told us that they wanted to find out if we had previous convictions. They found out that I had one and I had got away with a fine. This time I was sentenced to a month. My friends got longer terms than me.

We were sentenced in Chiredzi. We served our sentence in Mutare. We realised things were hard. Our husbands came to get all four of our children. They cried terribly but we knew we had taken a good stance. There was no porridge, no food. When we were in prison, we woke up each morning and stood in a line. We all said good morning to the female jail guards and our children had also started doing so. It really pained us. We had to wake them up when it was not yet time and we were not allowed to carry them on our backs, though my second-born was only one year eight months old. They did not receive proper attention, hence our decision to send them back to their fathers.

Life in jail was hard. I used to wake up and think to myself that really it was all because of poverty. I had no other way out except shoplifting. It was painful. I thought if there were other means apart from shoplifting, I would try them. We had supper at around 3 p.m. and then we were locked up. We could never walk freely because we were under guard. The food – my foot! It did not matter if we came across cockroaches, ants or aphids; we had to eat the food like that. I had problems with my ulcers and they refused to give me light food. I had to force myself to eat the thick sadza. Even now, I am in pain because the problems got worse.

If you were sick in the cell, the nurse came and if you had no medication you would tell her so. She would always say that the medication would come the following day. At times nothing was done. The prison guards never took you to the clinic. They said we would run away. They calculated your chances of escape merely by looking at your face. Once I had such a terrible stomach ache that I ended up in tears, kneeling, pleading with the female guard to take me to the clinic. When this happened for the second time, I was taken to Chiredzi Hospital.

At times the guards say that you want to run away from work. So if you are in the cell during working time you do not say a word but adhere to all the rules passed to you. We never knew how they were going to treat us. It is worse when they came in a bad mood. You knew it would not be a good day at all. We were made to work without rest. We were made to run with buckets, watering the garden. In Chiredzi there was a female guard who considered herself senior to the other guards. On her bad days she made us carry buckets full of manure. The officer-in-charge knew of this, and she would tell us to leave such work for the male prisoners. The female guard got angry though. It looked like she planned to make us run and suffer.

When we were in prison there was a time when tyres were burnt in the pits. There was a prison guard who wanted to get wire to put on her chicken run. She instructed us to get into a pit with a lot of pieces of broken bottles although we had no shoes on. We lifted up the tyres, which made our uniforms black with soot. We did not even have enough soap to wash them. So we had to put up with the dirty uniforms. The officers saw the situation but were silent about it. Instead of resting during the weekend we removed the wires from the tyres. We made them into bundles. Some got pierced but we never got prevention from tetanus. The guards brought their milling stones so we could make peanut butter for them. We questioned if the officials at the gate did not notice this for you could throw and kill a person with the stones. We did their laundry, polished their shoes, even those for their children at school. We washed and ironed their linen. We had trying times. It was not the law.

At the time when the Zimbabwe Prison Fellowship people came, we could say our grievances, and I asked if I could be transferred to Mutare, so my relatives could visit me. The law allows you to serve your sentence near home, but they said that I had to serve my sentence in the place where I had committed the offence. So I finished my term at Chiredzi. Then I asked for a travel warrant to return home, which they denied me. They said they would give me one to Birchenough Bridge. So I got the warrant to Birchenough Bridge and paid the remaining fare to Mutare. I vowed never to commit crime again. I went back home. My family was happy. They knew of my deeds but started telling me to quit. So I stopped. If I see anything on the floor I never pick it up. My husband's family once talked saying that I was tarnishing their name. They knew we were in a tight situation with money, but they said I had to put a stop to shoplifting. His brothers were the loudest as they and their wives worked. They said a lot of things.

I have since stopped shoplifting but we still cannot make ends meet. We ask you if you can offer us help, so that maybe we can start projects. Right now there are some people being given land. Some are looking after pigs or keeping chickens for eggs or planting paprika. We have not been given a head start though we wish we could do something worthwhile. I am eager to work. When we did shoplifting, life was not as hard as it is now. We ask God to guide us. We used to pray for God's guidance even when we went shoplifting.

I want to tell the public that life can be so difficult at times such that you have nothing to hold on to. But all ways that give fast money are dangerous. If you go to prison, you would not have set an example to your children. My first-born could not talk to me. His grades dropped and I had to be called to school. The teacher asked if I had been away and I said, yes. Even at home, I do not get respect. The society labels you a thief all your days. So I say that going to prison is a bad thing. It is poverty that drives us there but it is not good at all.

31

Tildah

interviewed by Keresia Chateuka

My name is Tildah. I was born in Soza in 1945. We were twelve in our family but now only four are alive. Two of my sisters are employed as housemaids, my brother is retired and I am unemployed. I learnt at Mutanda School. My father passed away when I was in Standard 4. I could not continue with my education because of financial constraints. There was nothing I could do since my father had died. Things were not well in my family such that even if I wanted to do anything, the situation would not permit it. I was the eldest girl, but I could not help my siblings.

I then got pregnant and married Gilbert. This man used to do sign writing. I stayed with him for six years because he had paid *lobola* for me. Eventually he started being a nuisance. He became unfaithful and started cheating on me. He was seeing a schoolgirl. In those days it was said that if you spoiled a school-child you were not allowed to leave her.

The girl had been staying with her mother, so my husband left to stay with his girlfriend and her mother. I realised that he was not coming back home. By then I had two daughters, Barbara and Anna. (Both are married now. Barbara is working while Anna is unemployed. I have grandchildren.)

So, after I left Gilbert – or rather after Gilbert left me – I went to stay with my mother in the rural areas. Life was unbearable: nobody helped me to look after my children. I thought of becoming a commercial sex worker but then I thought otherwise. Being a prostitute had its dangers. I then had another baby.

In 1969 I started working at Sunflower. We packed beans and jam. While I was there some ladies introduced me to shoplifting. They taught me how to steal cooking oil by safely placing the gallon-tin in between the legs. I practiced until I could walk without difficulty. When Sunflower closed down, I resorted to shoplifting until 1998: by then, I had sons-in-law and grandchildren and I feared that if I continued shoplifting, I would lose their respect.

With shoplifting we could spend one week in town and in other places like Chiredzi, where we were not known. I got caught in Chiredzi where I had to pay a Z$200 fine. In Chipinge I got arrested and paid a fine of Z$150. The fine varied with the amount of goods stolen. After paying the fine you had to leave the goods behind.

I left for Rusape but was caught with an item between my legs. The guard in the shop held me by one hand, which left my other hand free. That was my chance, I used my free hand to remove the item from my legs and dropped it down. So, when they took me for body search, they found nothing. I denied I had stolen anything. This is how I escaped the wrath of the law that time. On another day my luck ran out. I had returned to the same shop but was caught red-handed. I paid a fine.

I decided then to change my profession, as it looked as if I was getting caught all the time. I resorted to selling *nipa* or *kachasu*, the illicit beer. This beer is prepared with sugar. It is very watery in nature. I bought my sugar and gave it to an old lady in the rural areas to make the beer for me to sell. When selling the beer I got arrested once and paid a fine. The second time, the arresting officer informed me that my previous cases were just too many. So I ended up at Chikurubi Maximum Prison, where I served a year.

My stay at Chikurubi was horrendous. The treatment was bad. But let me first tell you about the treatment in Chiredzi prison. The female jail guards were so cruel: they would tell us to polish their shoes, reminding us that despite being older than them, we were serving a crime and had to obey every order they gave us. They told us we could do nothing, for we were prisoners. I never answered back for fear of the unknown.

One of my sons-in-law knew about my crime but the other was oblivious to it. The former once came to Chipinge to pay a fine for me. I realised that I had to stop as this was humiliating me.

My stay at Chikurubi was worse. We had to crawl instead of walking. Even the toilet could only be flushed after a struggle; they simply told us prisoners that we had no choice. At Mandikisi, where I was on remand, they gave us tins in which to excrete. These were not usually emptied when they got full in the night. We put up with the odour until morning. It was terrible.

Looking back at the way prisoners are treated, I would rather be poor staying with my family. I never liked the treatment that I received in Chipinge. In prison they gave us pig fat to smear on our bodies instead of Vaseline. If your totem is a pig, you are supposed to revere the animal, but we had to eat it to survive. One has to be thankful that one made it out of prison alive. Some people died in prison. All diseases were present: you could go in there healthy and come out in a critical condition.

When I left prison, people questioned why I did all that, but I told them it was out of poverty. They were particularly amazed at my acts considering I was now old. People confronted me at times and I felt embarrassed. It was just like being accused of witchcraft, you could not deny anything when you knew you were engaged in doing it.

My mother suffered a stroke, so now I am looking after her. I am the first-born and others are working. At the moment I buy and sell sugar and tomatoes. The police raid us at times but that is life. One day you make profit and the next day all your goods are taken away from you. The tomato business is low, especially during the summer season.

I am staying with my young daughter at my brother's house in Chisamba. He has since left for Bulawayo, where he is working. I no longer want to steal.

Presently I need to start sewing. If I can be helped financially, then I can make a start. I do not mind being offered help, especially if I end up doing something that is profit-making. Even if I only get Z$500 out of the work, I would not mind, as long as I survive honestly. This is all I want.

What I can share with people about prison life is that it is hard. I find it fruitless to say any more to someone who has never been to prison, for he might not believe me. It is the same with AIDS: if one is not affected, it is hard for people to believe it is there. Since I have been to prison, I know it is a bad place to be in. You eat things you would never eat under normal circumstances. A cat can walk over the sadza that is meant for you to eat. The guards do not care one wit. In Chipinge, I once asked to have my sadza with water because the stew was totally out of this world. One had to be strong to survive.

32

Priscilla

interviewed by Shumirai Makasi

My name is Priscilla. I am the first-born child in my mother's family. We were four girls and I am the eldest. My mother and father divorced, leaving my siblings growing up under the care of a stepfather. My father wanted me to be under his custody but my mother was against that. As a compromise, my maternal grandmother looked after me. I left her when I was doing Grade 5, to stay with my mother. At first, my stepfather paid my school fees. He had to stop because his first-born also needed to be sent to school. The money was not enough for both of us. So I only went to school up to Form 2. Both my mother and my stepfather tilled the land – their only source of income.

Later, I was married. My husband worked at a brewery. I got divorced in 1997. I have two children, two boys and a girl. The main reason for leaving my husband was that he was a heavy drunkard. Whenever he was in that state, he made so much noise that it affected our neighbours. He made a nuisance of himself. It became so bad that he would pick fights with anyone he bumped into. One nasty incident was when I had just given birth; the baby was three days old. My husband came home one night so drunk that he became violent. He started breaking our furniture, and he shouted that I leave there and then. I felt so humiliated that my only hope was to go and report this to the police and I went that same night. What came out of my police reporting was that I could go to my relatives, and I did, I sought refuge at my father's place – by then he had remarried.

Now my husband pleads with me to return to our matrimonial home. I don't know what to do. He no longer works for the brewery. He has stopped drinking unless he does it secretly. He is now self-employed. He has a vegetable stall.

After I got divorced. I had to look for a job. I was a housemaid. I worked for one year six months. I was arrested in February 2001, and I was released in June of same year. I stole clothes. The woman I worked for was into buying and selling merchandise. She had a system that whenever her children were not around she would not leave me any food. On other occasions, she would take her children with her and not leave any food for me. In a bid to redress the situation, I decided to take some of the clothes so that I could re-sell them in order to get money to buy food for my children and me. Moreover, I was not getting enough to support my family.

After I separated from my husband, my mother looked after my children. In fact, just after we separated, he took the children claiming he would look after them, but once when I went to visit them, I saw my five-day-old in bad shape with a runny tummy – white stuff was coming out. I discovered she was being fed with yoghurt and some other stuff that I could not figure out. Obviously this was just too much for a tiny baby. I did not expect the baby to live when I saw that it was sick. So I took all my children to my mother, and she also stayed with them whilst I was in jail.

My employer never visited me in jail. She never did anything. All what I stole from her I returned. She was satisfied; she had all her goods back. However, when you are in court your accuser is the one to decide whether you should pay a fine or be convicted. I should have paid a fine since I had returned all that I had stolen – all that was not mine. She refused to allow me to pay the fine, even though I had asked for forgiveness. I explained how I did it and why I did it. I justified my stealing hoping that she would understand why I did it, but she still insisted that I go to jail. Up to now I have not seen her.

I was not satisfied with the sentencing. I thought it would be very minimal, since I had returned all that I had stolen. Four months was real punishment. There was no reason for this at all since I had returned all.

I found prison life difficult – unbearable. It's unfortunate that people take it lightly to have those who wrong them convicted. What the accuser overlooks is that the accused can come out a hardened criminal instead of a reformed person. The prison wardens are mainly responsible for this situation – their language, their behaviour, their instructions leave a lot to be desired. They send prisoners to steal for them. If one is not disciplined one can end up being a habitual criminal. It's amazing how the wardens encourage prisoners to steal.

I was in for four months. I met this girl who was arrested twice during my stay in there. She was so used to committing the same crime of stealing that she appeared to be enjoying it. What I mean is only that one became used to committing crime because there is nothing enjoyable in prison. You are cared for inhumanely. You will be amazed to hear that the wardens take part of the food allocated to prisoners. They asked prisoners to steal for them. I am talking of mealie-meal, tea-leaves, cooking oil, sugar, etc. So by the time it was our turn to queue for food there wouldn't be much food left. Sometimes you may be given food that is not properly cooked, i.e., no cooking oil added, yet that share of oil will have been taken by the wardens. As for the bedding, when you are a first-timer, normally you are given dirty smelly blankets, especially those used by inmates who wet themselves at night. Sometimes you are given blankets soiled during menstruation. It's unbearable. For you to get detergents or plain soap to wash those blankets ... it's something else.

As an inmate, you are regarded as a person who is not normal, or a moron. You might do something good or deserve a compliment, instead you are blamed for doing something wrong. What happens is that first thing in the morning you are counted. Thereafter, you prepare yourself for the day. Sometimes, you are given tea but the milk will have been stolen, so you take it black. The slices of bread are something else; even if there was an allocation of margarine to spread on the bread, there won't be any because it will have been stolen. I have never eaten such food ever, not once, since I was born. The tea was warm. You know when tea is prepared for lots of people, by the time it is served it will be warm, not hot. The milk poured in the tea is such that you feel like throwing up. Of course this is different from breakfast at home. You can actually have a hot cup of tea with milk and bread at home. You may not have much but at least, it is well prepared. This is different from being an inmate. When you are at home, you can have a nice bath when you feel like it, whereas in jail they give you a short time to bath. Sometimes the bell rings when you are in the middle of a bath. You are not given time to finish up. Instead, they punish you for not bathing in time. Sometimes you are beaten up for not finishing bathing on time or for no apparent reason at all.

I used to do kitchen duties. Those of us who were assigned to the kitchen were not allowed to perform any other duties. One day the bell rang for those who worked in the garden to rush for their duty. Those of us who worked in the kitchen remained behind. One of the wardens on duty called us. She wanted an explanation as to why we had remained behind. In no time she beat us up. We knew we were supposed to remain inside and work in the kitchen. Whilst we were trying to explain this, the warden was busy beating us up. The argument was that warden was the one to tell us what to do and not for us to tell them. You end up appearing to be an insane person or a moron. You begin to wonder why.

Some wardens use canes to beat you up. Some use whatever comes their way, be it a large stick or whatever and wherever they like. It could be on your face or back. Some will hit you on your palms or feet. They just do what they like. It's different from how you spank a child: you know what places to avoid, so you don't really hurt them. In our case, the wardens just beat you up wherever they liked. You are treated like a child and you fail to understand why.

Of course, you can report to other authorities, but your reporting can aggravate trouble for you. Whichever way you look at it, the wardens always end up ganging up against you. You may be supported, or even get sympathy from the officer-in-charge but the others end up ganging up against you, blaming and accusing you of all sorts of things. You end up being labelled insane. This whole issue evolves around the guards. You can take your problem to the officer-in-charge. If she asks why I have been beaten up, other guards quickly claim that I am a problem. It becomes difficult to defend yourself because you are labelled as problematic. But you know about the other's behaviour such as beating up prisoners, stealing and other such behaviour. You end up with no one to support you. At the end of it all, the officer-in-charge believes that the guards are the ones telling the truth.

Again, when you are called you are addressed as a 'bitch'. I had never been called that before because I am not a prostitute. There are guards who call you that name. Instead of using dignified language or behaviour, they use derogatory language. Sometimes when you are in the queue for a meal of sadza, they will shout, 'Here you are queuing for sadza, what have your children eaten at home?

You are late for your meal. You come walking slowly as if you are admiring your garden.' Whatever you do, you are regarded as insane. It is an unbearable way to live. Whatever you do, good or bad, you end up beaten or scolded. The language used is so bad it cannot be repeated: obscene language is used. If, say, you are not feeling well and you go to seek medical treatment, you are mocked. They ask whether you came to be treated in jail. They ask, 'Who, during your absence, takes care of your children when they are not well?' You are then left without receiving any treatment. Worse still for those who are convicted for baby dumping. The warders ask why they want to be treated [by the doctor] when they threw away their babies. They are told they should die, just like their babies who have died. If you are short-tempered you get angry.

Amongst prisoners, there is a mixed bag, each having committed a different crime from the other, but one ends up getting along with someone, because there are different chores to be done. And after a time, you can identify one you can call a friend. It's just the same as out here, you can identify one you call a friend. On the other hand, there are others to whom you are never close and you cannot discipline or advise them, and you have no right to do that to them. When relationships are superficial a lot happens. There is stealing – of all kinds food. The loot is hidden. If you try to report such activities to the guards, the inmates are quiet. They wait until it's evening time. They gang up against you, they cover you with blankets and then they beat you up. They tell you, 'We are beating you up because you are not co-operating.' If you report them to the guards they deny that accusation. Come evening time, they beat you up again until you never report them.

The stolen food will be cooked in the kitchen. Guards do not steal the food themselves. They send the prisoners to steal. Then as time goes on, prisoners end up stealing the food and hiding it: food such as sugar, margarine, tea-leaves, cooking oil or, when they go out to work in the garden, vegetables. Those who are asked to work in the kitchen cook enough stolen food for themselves using plenty of oil, and then they sell the rest to other prisoners. By 'selling' I mean they exchange food for a piece of bread or meat – they get vegetables in exchange for a piece of bread the following day, and so on. Soap, lotions, or whatever brought by those from outside is used for the barter dealing inside. Every day you are given one piece of bread. So, if you barter for vegetables, the following morning you will not get any bread. Sometimes you feel it's better to have a variety of food such as sadza with oiled vegetables, so you forgo tea and bread. In fact it's much better.

Each person sleeps on her mat. We are each given three blankets. Personally, I never had any problems. But each one behaves differently. Some end up being a nuisance to others. Whenever we received our monthly ration of half a bar of washing soap, a bar of Lifebuoy, and sometimes a tube of Colgate, there was this girl who used to sell her allocation. However, she never had anyone coming to visit her so she never got anything from outside, and as a result she would steal from other inmates. She would do that for a whole month. Such people are the ones who end up being beaten up or being locked up in solitary confinement. Sometimes this girl would sell her underpants to an inmate who was having her periods. She herself did not need panties because she was pregnant, but then she stole a panty from a mentally ill prisoner and was caught red-handed. Apparently another inmate who felt pity for her had given the mental prisoner this panty, but the warders had not given her any: (you were lucky if you got underpants from the warders). So, when this girl, the thief, was caught we reported her to the officer-in-charge. She was beaten up and transferred to a cell with expectant mothers.

I may not have much in my life, but I cannot stand untidiness. When I came out of prison, my blankets had not been aired during my absence and they made me sneeze. If I breathe unclean air, I sneeze. You can therefore imagine the difficult time I had when I was in prison.

A lot needs to be sorted out about prison life. Everything should start from the prison wardens. They need to learn to communicate with everyone else. Is it not that people are in prison because they have committed offences, but to help them reform, and to do this they need to be talked to, issues need to be discussed? They do not need to be disciplined by the warders as if they were children.

What I learnt in jail is that anything can get you arrested. If I swear at you and it pains you, I can be arrested. If my accuser decides that I have to be locked up, I get locked up. Anything can get you arrested. There are some in jail because they picked up something that had already been stolen. It starts off as a trick when a stolen item is thrown away or hidden somewhere. The victim thinks that she has picked up something and then she gets a rude awakening when she gets arrested.

My advice, therefore, is that one has to be very patient. Had I decided to be patient, I could have left my job rather than miscalculating and ending up doing the wrong thing. Instead of analysing my situation I felt like fixing this woman, my employer, by stealing her goods. In the end, I am the one who got into a fix. My advice is that if one is provoked or wronged don't take it to heart. The best thing to do is to pray. Cast all your burdens to God.

I have now been separated from my husband for five years. During the first days, he asked me to collect money from him to support our children. As time went on things changed. Once I got there and he began to behave strangely, as if he was seeing a strange thing. He ran away from me. Immediately after that, I started praying. Ever since we separated I have never done what other women do: such women use witchcraft or seek the advice of sorcerers. I continued praying until he got back to his senses. Before we separated we did our things together, we communicated, we planned and all was well. After we separated he never progressed.

After a time he realised that our children needed school uniforms. Right now he is staying with our eldest child. He is doing everything for that child. He is now talking of us reconciling. I think that maybe I made an unwise decision or just acted on an impulse when I left him. Perhaps I blocked what God had in store for me. When I separated from my husband, my baby was only a few days old – anyway, I could not carry my baby on the back, it was too small.

You can tell the difference between my children: the ones who grew up before we were separated, they ate all that is expected of babies – Cerelac and other baby foods – and you can tell the difference with their growth. Afterwards the children were deprived. You can tell the difference in environments in which the children grew up. That's what I saw that God makes distinctions in different situations. In addition, I saw that it is better to let God revenge on our behalf. If we are to do it ourselves, it does not make an impact.

Now my last-born is still staying with his grandmother. He goes to crèche. My mother and stepfather look after him well. I cannot stay with him for I do not earn enough to feed him and myself. I sew garments that I sell. I am now based at Prison Fellowship. My children visit me during the school holidays. They are both happy where they are.

My husband married another woman. When I left my matrimonial home, he found another woman. He has since separated from her. They have a son who is now staying with the mother. She attempted to poison him because he continued to support the children belonging to a woman from whom he had separated. She would have preferred him to do away with me completely. As I see it now, it was all in God's plan that she had to make such moves so that my husband would throw her out.

Section 8:

Wrongful arrest

33

Joyline

interviewed by Keresia Chateuka

My name is Joyline. I was born in Chivhu in 1956. We are six in our family, three boys and three girls, and I am the first-born child. I went to school up to Form 2 and then my parents failed to get money for school fees for me to go into Form 3. I am the only one in our family that did not make it to O-level. I did my primary education at Maware School and I did Form 2 through correspondence here in Harare. I feel my parents discriminated against me as they sold cattle to educate my brothers and sisters while they found it a waste of money to send me to secondary school.

I left home to find work in 1981. I came to Harare and stayed with my aunt. I started working for Mrs Z. in Mabvuku as a housemaid. She was married and she and her husband both worked. I was not ill-treated but sometimes I cried when she commented on how poorly I performed my daily chores. It was not bad but I felt that she could have been kinder to me. I left when my mother fell sick in the rural areas. I later came back and started working in Chitungwiza for a teacher, my aunt's friend. She had a husband and two children. I worked and studied with the Rapid Results College. I worked for this family for two years. I left after the teacher told me to go with her to her rural home during the school holidays. I refused, saying that while she was going to rest, I would not be on vacation like her. So, when she came back, she brought another maid and told me that I was fired. I left to stay with my aunt in Mufakose. I used to look after my pregnant cousin while my aunt made her trips to South Africa. I think I stayed with her for about three months. It was during this period that I met the man from next door who was to be my future husband.

The whole courtship process went as follows. The neighbours approached my cousin and she told them that I was her mother's niece and that I was looking after her. They asked where her mother was. She told them that she had gone to work but would soon come back. When I got to hear of it, I wanted to say 'no' because I was not looking for a man to settle down with. Marriage was out of the question. I wanted to sort out my life and make it better. My aunt and 'mother-in-law' finally met and later I heard my aunt telling me to go next door where I was wanted. I did not like it. I felt as if they were pledging me into marriage – *kuzvarira*. I refused the arranged marriage and I told my aunt that if it was a polite way of throwing me out of her home then she had to tell me directly. I did not like to have a husband for I was still young.

At that time I had not seen the man but I told them that I wanted to see him. This man stayed with them but he was usually at work. He had once been married but separated from the wife who did not get on well with her in-laws. When I heard about this, I was scared because I feared the same might happen to me. I asked my aunt about it but she comforted me saying that my future mother-in-law liked me very much. I had no reason to fear.

One day this man came to my aunt's place and we were given some time to get to know each other better. I repeatedly asked him about his former wife but he told me he loved me and I need not worry about his former wife. His name was David. He was from Rusape. He had two children from his previous marriage. His parents stayed with one while the mother had the other baby, she had left when she was pregnant.

We got married in 1984 and had our first baby in the same year. It was a girl. I lived with my in-laws, and everything was fine. David seemed a hard-working and trusting husband. But, after we had had three children, things took a turn. His parents told him they no longer liked me. We had already married in court under Chapter 238 and our preparations for a church wedding were at an advanced stage. The reason for their change of mind was not clear but they said I had refused to go to their church. At the time I was not going to any church, but when we got married we were going to the Apostolic Church. This church helped me through the birth of my second baby when I had complications and gave birth to a premature baby. Anyway the difficulties and disagreements persisted until the church wedding was cancelled. Then the relatives decided how they could get rid of me. They told David to look for his own house. We were no longer wanted in their home. While David was looking for a house for us, they took me to my family in the rural areas. We had tried to move out to live on our own, but my in-laws refused. They wanted their son to live with them and he agreed with them. That is how I was left at my parents. It was done under the pretence that they would come for me later. My husband never came for me. After the separation my husband married again with his parents assisting him.

I sought legal advice and he started paying maintenance for his three children. I think he did not like to pay any money without going to bed with me. He then started visiting and spending some nights. He would tell his wife that he was out on work duties. It was under these circumstances that I fell pregnant. David was retrenched in 2000; the company was not doing well. I could not get maintenance any more so I went back to the courts. My husband refused to have a portion of his pension taken at one time. He settled for a monthly payment. I received it for a while and then, one day, it suddenly stopped. I looked for him but nobody could tell me where he was, not even his family. I did not have school fees for the children and I gave up after a hard, fruitless search.

It was during 2002 that I heard from his relatives in Kuwadzana 6 that David had died at Easter. I knew nothing about it. His relatives did not allow me to see where he was buried, but the children were allowed there. They are conspiring with the wife so that I get nothing for my children from his estate. I am seeking legal advice so I can get a share, so that I can look after our children. At the moment I am looking after them through my own efforts.

I once worked as a security guard. My relatives helped me find the job. I had trained as a security guard and I have a certificate. I went to work for a big company in 1993. I worked for five years. It was during this time that I had a temptation that I will never forget.

I worked at OK and Bon Marché.* My work was commendable, even the managers praised me for my good work. I arrested many people who stole in the shops, including employees. Because of this I was not popular with the OK employees.

---

* Two supermarkets.

In 1996 when I was working at OK in Avonlea, I had a stroke of bad luck. It was in the month of September when a thief came into the shop in the afternoon. I was unaware of this because, at the time, the other two security guards had gone for lunch. The shop stocked food and clothing. There was a fitting room for those who wanted to try on clothes. I kept the key to the fitting-room. While I was patrolling the shop a woman approached me; she wanted to try on some clothes. I did not know she had stolen shirts and pairs of trousers. However, a till operator, had seen it. The woman went in and out of the fitting-room and returned the clothes she had tried on. I locked the fitting-room and returned the clothes.

When she walked out of the shop, this till operator followed her and arrested her. He put her in a little room where we detained suspected thieves. I was surprised when I was called to the manager's office. I saw this woman and the goods that she had stolen on top of the table. I forget how many items there were but they were all men's clothes. They asked me how the clothes had been stolen. I was shocked. I told them I had not seen anything at all. I explained what had taken place as well as I could but they were not convinced. They thought I had connived with the thief. They called the police and my employer. My seniors from the company arrived and I told them the story. They were not convinced. The suspected thief, Grace, was thoroughly beaten as they forced her to say that I had helped her to steal. Her back was very sore. She refused to be intimidated and confessed that she had stolen because she knew I was alone and that I would not notice anything. She cried, telling them to take her to the police, so she could confess. Still they were forcing her to say I had given her the clothes.

The police failed to turn up, so we were handcuffed and taken to Avondale Police Station by the officials from the company. They told the police that we had stolen property. They left us in police custody. When asked how we had stolen Grace told them she had stolen the goods for her husband. I was asked how I had assisted her and I stuck to my statement. They were *not* convinced as they had already been given a statement from OK and my company.

The police took us to a cell in Avondale. I refused to enter the cell because it was dark inside. I was afraid of the dark and there were no lights. It was full of people and I could not figure out who they were. Furthermore, I had left my baby at home who was still breastfeeding. At first they thought I was lying. I squeezed my breast for them to see the milk. They let me go to get my baby and I came back to the police station. Because I had a baby, I was told I could sleep in the charge office where there were some policemen. Grace slept in the cells. The following morning the OK officials came suggesting that I must have my house searched. The police did not refuse but said they would conduct the search. They trusted the police to recover goods but they found nothing. Still OK officials were not convinced. They said they wanted the case to be taken to court. We went to court the same day of the search. They took us to Rotten Row. It was on a Friday. The magistrate informed us there were no hearings on Fridays. He told us to go back to Chikurubi Remand. I felt pain because I feared for my baby that I had left at home. I tried to plead with the officials but they refused. They scolded me; they said I should have known [what I was getting into] before I committed the crime. I got out of the courtroom heading for the prison vehicle, crying. We left for Chikurubi. We were mixed, both men and women, even those with children. Since I had been denied permission to get my baby, I had to involuntarily wean her. She was a year old.

When we got to Chikurubi, we got off the vehicle and were counted. The women were taken to their prison while the males went to the male prison. They told us to remove our clothes and hand them over for safekeeping. Even watches and money had to be surrendered. They gave us prisoners' clothes to wear. They took us to a remand prison as we all awaited trial. I was surprised at the huge number of women inside. All along I thought that I was the only woman because I thought that only men committed crime. The people inside were happy for me to join them. I got a warm reception. They asked to know about my crime. When I told them, they dismissed it as petty. Since they described my crime as petty, I was curious to know about theirs. One said she was in for murder. I was completely shaken. I thought only men committed such crimes. I never slept that night.

They gave us small blankets, like the ones meant for children. Only those who had stayed a long time in prison were used to them, not me. I was really scared. I never liked the environment. It looked like I was in a hospital or a mortuary; it was so bleak. I could not eat. I also failed to sleep. I hated the place. The following morning I woke up and went for roll-call. They asked if there were people going to court. I, along with others, were put aside and told to prepare. They gave us food and we were told to eat all of it. They did not want prisoners to faint in court. I was feeling better although I was frightened at the thought of coming back without being tried, as had happened before.

After our meal, we left for Rotten Row, still in prison uniform. It was on a Saturday. During the session I was the first to be questioned. The judge asked if I accepted my offence but I denied it. When asked why, I narrated the event as I had done previously. Next was Grace who accepted her offence. She was asked to narrate her story. She then told the judge that she had been badly assaulted by the OK officials. She told the court that the till operator beat her forcing her to say that I had helped her to steal the goods. When she said her back had been badly bruised, a female jail guard was told to inspect her. It was true she had been injured. She was asked if she had been taken to hospital. The police had already taken her there.

The judge said I was free to go in peace for I had not committed a crime. The judge warned the OK officials, that they had no authority to assault people. We looked for our own transport to Chikurubi. When we arrived we got our clothes back and removed their uniforms. I weaned my baby for my breasts were already dry.

When I went back to work, they did not permit me to resume my duties because I had no letter from the prisons to confirm that I had been cleared. It takes a while to get that letter. (I still have it.) The letter authorised me to go back to work. I was back at work and I worked for three months before I left. My employers no longer had faith in me, though they knew I was a hard worker. I used to get rewards for my hard work from the Bon Marché authorities in Borrowdale but they had since left. I was never free at work any more. I thought it was better if I looked for a job elsewhere. I was afraid they would set a trap for me that could land me in jail. I had family to look after. I resigned from work and filled a form stating that I was going to school but would come back after completion. This is how I left work at that company in 1997. I was hurt to leave a job that I loved.

Sometimes I visit the shops where I used to work but I know the officials think I may steal their goods. I decided to seek revenge for the wrong accusations laid on me. I got a lawyer. He assisted me with my case. When it was heard in court the judge declared that I did not have strong enough evidence. I was disappointed, and so was my lawyer. He volunteered to take the case to court all over again. That is when the OK officials and lawyer reached an agreement. They paid me Z$5,000.

I am staying with my children. They are going to school. The social welfare is assisting me since my husband died. I hope those who read this will learn that it is not good to blame others for something they have not done. People should learn not to use their positions to manipulate others.

Section 9:

The experience of officials

34

Ollyn Rudo Nzuma, Regional Magistrate

interviewed by Irene Staunton

I was born on 28th September 1965, into a family of six. I am the second born. Both my parents were teachers and religious people, so they were very strict with us. I did my primary education in the Honde Valley, which is where we lived.

During the war my parents came to Harare and taught at Lochinvar Primary School, which is where I completed my Grade 7. I went to Monte Casino Secondary School for my O-level then to Gokomere High School for my A-level, and then I proceeded to the University of Zimbabwe to study law. At that time we had to complete two degrees in law. I first did Bachelor of Law (honours) and then I did the Bachelor of Laws. Nowadays they have just one programme [the latter]. At the time with Bachelor of Law (honours) you could join the magistrates' section and practise as a prosecutor but you could not practise as a lawyer – with a Bachelor of Laws you can do everything.

I decided to do law because I used to watch programmes on television like Los Angeles Law, which I enjoyed very much. When we had finished the LLB, we did practicals. We would go to the High Court and observe the procedures. So we acquired a knowledge of practice and would always refer to the rules of procedure in the High Court and the Magistrates Court. Later, I joined as a magisterial assistant to do my locum and learn the processes. From the clerk of court, you learn how you enter the court record book, open the files, the records for the litigants, and so on. From there you go to the civil courts and learn about applications and procedures. Then you go to the prosecution and you prosecute for not less than three months. After that, if you have done everything properly, you are sworn in as a magistrate.

When I became a magistrate, there were two departments: the criminal court and the civil court. I well remember my first experience in the criminal court. I felt overwhelmed because I had to deal with a case which was classified as a 'serious offence', so my only sentencing option was to send that person to prison. I was overwhelmed. I thought, 'Oh no, this is too much. I can't send this person to prison.' The offense was stock theft. The minimum sentence is three years. You can suspend sentence, but effectively that person has to serve in prison for not less than a year because from a three-year sentence you may suspend maybe one and a half or even two years depending on the circumstances. But there is no option of a fine. So I just had to send this person to prison and I felt overwhelmed. Then with time I became used to the process. Things were easier. I was able to interpret the law and I would say, 'Okay the law says this, so this has to be done, that is the position.'

My worst case was one of rape. It was the most dramatic case I have had to deal with. It was a father. He had a daughter who was nineteen years old. She had a boyfriend, a married man, a neighbour. The father told her, 'I do not want you to go out with this married man,' but she kept on going out with him. Then the father took this child, he tied her to the bin, both legs and both arms. And after removing all her clothes he started assaulting her; he assaulted her the whole night. She had scars all over her body. The following day he took this daughter and placed her in the bedroom. He raped her four times. He said it was a punishment: 'You want to have sexual intercourse with other men, so I have to do it to you. This is a punishment, I have to sleep with you.' He raped her four times and after that he brought some chillies and he inserted them in the girl's private parts. He said, 'I am doing this as a healing thing, so that you will not be in a position to feel desires for men. I want to kill the desires.' That girl was traumatized.

It happened that the uncle came and he saw that the girl was badly battered. She had bruises all over her body. He tried to find out what had happened. She simply said that she had been assaulted by the father, and the uncle did not report the case. Then she escaped from home – because the father used to lock her in the bedroom, and leave her. He didn't want people to see her. But she escaped. She travelled all the way from Harare to Mutare and she reported the matter to her elder sister. Then the sister came back with her and they reported the matter to the police. This is how the case came to light. That was the worst case I have had to deal with. You cannot believe that a father would behave in such a manner.

Obviously, the father when facing trial simply denied it. He only accepted that he had assaulted the complainant, his child; he also accepted that he had stripped her naked before he assaulted her. He said that he had kept her in his bedroom because he wanted her to heal. He did not want the police to know that he had assaulted the child, but he refused to accept that he had raped this girl. However, the doctor's reports confirmed that she was raped. She even contracted an STD.

It was so traumatic for the girl. She will need a long time under treatment and counselling for her to recover but it will be difficult for her to do so. Maybe she will try to forget but it will live with her for the rest of her life. Rape is something that you will live with for the rest of your life.

For such an offence we are looking at the maximum sentence that there is. The maximum jurisdiction where there is no HIV infection, is ten years per count. Now he has four counts because he raped her four times, so we are looking at about 40 years. Then you may suspend part of it on condition of good behaviour, so perhaps he will get fifteen years. But if there has been an HIV transmission the maximum sentence per count is twenty years. The court must weigh the circumstances of the case.

Now I am a regional magistrate and eighty per cent of the cases I deal with are rape cases. About ten per cent are for armed robbery, robbery of motor vehicles. The remaining ten per cent are for theft, big fraud cases and big theft cases: house-breaking with intent to steal; cases where a lot of property has been stolen from companies or shops, or departmental stores.

I try to understand the mind of the people I convict, and in my experience most of them will tell you it was because of evil spirits. I do not know where that comes from. Sometimes a person will tell you that he went to see a traditional healer, because he wanted to start a business or he wanted to become rich. Sometimes, he says that the traditional healer has advised him to sleep with anyone, sometimes with a minor, a child. It is the medicine. Some of the explanations are horrible because a person will give so many reasons for his behaviour. Some will say it just came over me because I found her naked, bathing maybe in the river. They find a woman naked and he says, 'It just came to me that I had to sleep with her and that is how it happened.' They give us so many reasons why they did what they did. From their point of view, they are seeking mitigation. They are trying to persuade the court that, 'I am not wrong. It is this woman who is wrong because she was naked and bathing.' Then you wonder how someone can talk like that because every individual has a right to privacy. Why would you go to the river, see a woman bathing and intrude into her privacy? They always give excuses. They have to find someone to blame. They do not blame themselves. Rather they say, 'the woman was naked' or 'there are evil spirits' or maybe 'there is a traditional healer who has influenced me' to do so and so.

Most of the time, in criminal cases, men try to find an excuse. They point at something as the cause of a crime but usually women readily accept responsibility. Even in court you find the procedure, the process, the trials with women are shorter because they quickly accept responsibility for their crime and the trial is shorter. But if you are dealing with men, they bring all sorts of excuses and explanations. The case can go on for hours or days or months. At the end of the day he will be convicted but when you ask him to mitigate, he will still say in mitigation, 'Well I did it but it was not really my fault, there was this thing…' I have noticed, however, that many women readily accept responsibility.

Women are rarely involved in armed robbery or big fraud – maybe about one per cent of women are involved. The offences which women commit are generally those petty offences like theft: shoplifting, or going to someone's fields and stealing some maize or stealing something during a funeral or during a church gathering. The offences are very petty when compared with those of their male counterparts.

If a survey was conducted properly, I think that you would find that most petty theft is committed because of starvation. Most women depend on the husband and often the husbands are neglecting them or he does not earn sufficient to sustain the family, or because of famine such as we have these days when there is no mealie-meal, and the most common commodities are hard to come by. So you find women going into the shops and stealing cooking oil or going to someone's field and stealing farm produce. Hunger drives the women to commit these petty offences.

When there are petty offences, the court avoids sending women to prison, as it makes the situation of the family even worse. Normally there is a fine to pay. If she does not have the money to pay the fine we look at the other option – community service. If the offence is very petty and if she gives you a reasonable explanation in her mitigation, you can even just give a warning and discharge her. You find that if you caution such a person, she will never come back to court again.

Of course, women should be imprisoned for armed robberies, big fraud cases, and the importation of drugs like cocaine or mandrax; and we now also have cases of assisted rape. We should send a message to the community that if you assist your husband or your brother to rape someone it is very, very wrong. These are serious offences and the perpetrator should go to prison.

From my own experience, female magistrates are more compassionate over gender issues. For example, we have cases where a wife beats up the husband's girlfriend and then comes in court as an accused person. She is facing a case of an assault with intent to cause grievous bodily harm. Maybe she has thoroughly bashed this girlfriend who has lost a tooth or something. When you try to discuss the issue of sentencing, a male magistrate will say, 'No, she had no right to beat this girlfriend. An assault case is an assault case, she deserves punishment.' But when you are a female magistrate you can see that this woman was wronged – perhaps the husband came home with the girlfriend. The provocation is high, so the woman could not just resist beating this girlfriend. So you try to be lenient. Maybe you give a fine which is on the high side and suspend a portion of it on condition she does not do it again. But with men you find that they do not even consider imposing a fine. They simply send the woman to prison. So, if you look at the sentencing pattern, you find this variance. Similarly, when we deal with peace order cases, when women have been assaulted, if female magistrates are involved, the sentences are stiff because you do not want this man to return and assault this woman again: you want to deter him. But with male magistrates their sentences are light. They might just give a fine of Z$200.

Such inconsistencies occur because there is need to train magistrates about gender issues. We have already begun programmes with organisations like Zimbabwe Women Lawyers Association and Musasa Project that train magistrates. They pick on a specific topic such as domestic violence and look at the sort of cases we have to deal with. They try to sensitise both male and female magistrates to be

269

sensitive to the nature of these cases because women have special needs. They are different from men and they have to be treated differently. It is a fact that has to be accepted. In our department we have the Women Judges Foundation for judges and magistrates. We have training programmes. We train judges and magistrates on gender issues, on gender equality.

Everyone who is sentenced has the right to appeal, but you must appeal soon after the pronouncement of sentence. Whether this happens depends with whether you know your rights. Normally when you pass sentence you advise the person of his or her rights and tell them that they have the right to appeal within seven days. If that person is not represented by a lawyer, there are application forms at the prisons for bail pending appeal. The appeal is taken straight to the High Court. But sometimes – say a woman who is sentenced to three years – becomes so dejected that she may not even apply; and so she may end up spending all those years in custody. And her children suffer of course.

You find that when men go to prison, the families, the wife is there to support the husband. But when it is the woman in prison, it is the other way round because of societal expectations. Society does not expect a woman to go to prison. Consequently, you find that the husband may visit her at first and then he backs off, and the family members back off. They just leave the woman languishing in custody. I am sure there must be – or there should be – an organisation which would support this woman morally and emotionally. It really is a problem with the system. We deal with this person in the courts, they go to prison and you are through with them; they are forgotten, unless they make an application for bail. I am not sure to what extent the Zimbabwe Prison Fellowship Association is involved or whether the organisation is in a position to represent this woman in court. There is a gap that has to be filled somewhere somehow. We need people to look into this gap to see what should be done if a woman is sent into prison. Maybe we need to know more about her background; and there should more follow-up.

In Zimbabwe our statutes, most acts of parliament and the law textbooks are based on Roman-Dutch Law and this type of law applies equally to men and women. It has the same penalty system. If, however, you go to the chief, he tries to take a more reconciliatory attitude when he looks at this woman and what she has done. From the traditional point of view, the chief is quite sympathetic to the woman culprit. Punishment is usually based on compensation, even, sometimes, when it is a criminal issue. Usually she has to pay a fine, a beast or a goat as compensation and so she is not uprooted from society. She is easily accepted back into it. Once she pays compensation, the family accepts her. She will integrate well and she will reform. So, traditionally, the system is lighter for women. It treats women differently as opposed to the penal system, which metes out the same penalties whether you are male or female. It is only that the courts have developed a more sympathetic approach to a female offender. You have to be merciful, you have to listen carefully because of the special circumstances.

If we have a dual system of justice, legal and traditional, it would favour one section of the population – maybe those people living in the rural areas. So I would suggest that policy makers need to sit down and do a better job of grading offences. Most very serious offences: rape, armed robbery, big fraud, are committed by men – only a very small percentage of women commit such offences. So there is need to review the law so that the chiefs handle all the minor cases, and the bigger cases are tried through the penal system, as our law has to follow international standards. For example, I would not like a case of rape being settled by a chief, because obviously he will ask the man whether he is willing to marry the woman; and if the man says, 'Yes,' the chief will say, 'Okay can you pay the seduction damages and then marry her.' Such a sentence would mean that you are undermining the seriousness of the offence. What we want is a justice system that looks at other people's rights, and the infringement of other people's basic rights. With offences like rape, you are infringing someone's right to liberty, privacy, and so forth plus we have the hurt and the psychological effects of that case. I would not recommend that a traditional chief handles rape cases, but I would recommend that he handle petty offences like stealing maize in someone's field.

Imprisonment is not always the right way to punish an offender because you are trying to look at the reformatory aspect of this person – you want this person to be reformed. However, imprisonment can be so harsh that instead of reforming, this person will go in the opposite direction or maybe meet hardcore criminals. Imprisonment can destroy a person so when they get out, he or she will commit another offence and go back to jail. Sentencing should depend on the circumstances and what you want to achieve at the end of the day, as well as deterring other offenders. Reform should form part of the prison experience, and community service can help the person to reform.

There is a community service committee. The president of the community service committee right now is a judge, a chief justice, and the service is run parallel to the Ministry of Justice. When you decide that this person does not deserve to go to prison, you recommend community service and write it on the record. At every court, there is a community service officer, a person qualified in social work, you then stand down the case, you tell the accused person to come to court on some other day. You pass the record on to the community service officer. He or she will talk to the accused person, will visit their family, talk to the parents or the family and find out whether they are still willing to have the accused person living with them. He will then visit institutions near the accused's home so that he is able to walk there and do some duties. When everything is in order he tells the court. We then simply write on the sentence that the person has to do community service for so many hours at this hospital, or at this school.

What normally happens with cases like theft where you do not recover your property, or where there is damage or malicious injury to property, and in some assault cases where a specific amount is specified in a criminal court, you normally order for restitution. You suspend a term of imprisonment and tell the accused person that by such and such a date you should have paid Mrs. Moyo her Z$400,000. That is how we deal with restitution. We try to bring the victim to the same position he or she was in before the offence was committed. Unfortunately in cases such as rape, the only assistance we can offer victims is counselling. In a criminal court it is very difficult to make a financial assessment of how much the person should be compensated.

With murder cases you find – maybe because of our tradition and culture – the perpetrator is asked to pay compensation in the form of cattle. They are trying to prevent the avenging spirits, the *ngozi*, from retribution. So you often find that by the time the case comes to court, the perpetrator has already paid something, usually in cattle. If this has not been done, a criminal court is not able to order compensation in the form of money for a murder case. They will simply send the person to prison and the victims have to go through the civil courts and institute legal proceedings for loss of support or earnings against the accused person who is now in custody. Usually it is difficult because once the perpetrator is in custody, there is no way he can pay even if a judgement has been given that he must do so.

When people are not represented in court, normally the assumption is that they cannot afford a lawyer and the law is very clear. It is the court's duty to assist the accused person. Of course, you can do this, but there are limitations as to what you can do. You cannot tell the accused person what to say.

And there is discrimination between different aspects of society. In a petty case you might order a fine of say Z$1,000, but if the accused fails to pay, he goes to prison for twenty days. Those who can pay will escape the jail term. It is a problem, because we say the law applies equally to all people, but the anomalies exist: a poor person ends up serving twenty days in prison with labour, a rich person does not.

And if we look at the abuse cases, most children who are abused are orphans, or children who do not have stable backgrounds, many of them are stepchildren. I don't know why stepchildren are ill-treated — it is something that requires analysis by psychologists or social scientists. But it is true that stepchildren are often abused by their stepmothers. They assault or cause injury to the child — often even a two- or three-year-old child will have scars from being assaulted by the stepmother. You try to find out why she did it and she will simply tell you, 'I was angry.' In my experience we have never discovered the real reason behind such behaviour towards stepchildren.

I am not happy with the state of the prisons in Zimbabwe though it is a long time since I last visited them. But when I did, the situation was abominable because there were so many inmates in one cell. I am told there are even more now and it is not healthy. If a woman has a baby she uses the same cell as the other inmates. The toilet is in one corner. When they are asleep the child can crawl to the toilet. Should a child suffer because the mother is a criminal? Moreover, facilities for women in prisons are difficult because prisons were built for men. There should be facilities for babies: changing rooms, places for a mother with a baby to sleep, so that there is no health hazard for the child. Prisons are also crowded. Inmates have various diseases. Should we bring up a child in such an environment?

I see a need in Zimbabwe for a Family Law court that would consider issues such as maintenance, peace orders, domestic violence, adoption of children, the juvenile court, and so on, so that we ensure that cases involving women are handled by experts. I think we should look at women and their circumstances when we're dealing with sentences or punishments.

The law cannot make society progressive, but society is dynamic, so the law must keep pace with changes in society. The law should also be dynamic. But, if the law is ahead of people, it will be very difficult to apply it. What is important is to look at society's expectations and the changes that have taken place in order to extract or formulate appropriate laws. Laws should match the people's situation and expectations, you cannot try to fit people to a law that is ahead of them. Rather you should look at current society and decide what it is that you want to combat or to prevent in say, the next ten years, and make laws to suit the situation.

Civics should also be taught in schools from the early years. Civics should be included in the curriculum, so that children are taught about, and learn to discuss, the laws in the country. They should be taught about their rights as individuals. They should be taught about what the constitution says about them. Then they will have a broader perspective as they grow older, and we will have a better and more understanding society.

Let's say you get into a public vehicle and someone starts smoking. He may say, I have the right to do what I want. This is a free Zimbabwe. This answer means that the person does not fully understand what 'a right' is because a right comes with responsibility. If you have a right, you have to make sure that your right is not infringing other people's rights. People need proper education about individual rights, human rights, and responsibility. We have to respect each other as citizens of the same country.

No one, for example, has the right to use violence. Let us look, for example, at domestic violence, which is very prevalent. The man believes he has the right to assault the wife because he married that wife, he paid *lobola* for her, he thinks he is the head of the family and he assaults the wife. That is a misplaced right because you are using that right to justify your violence, which is something that is harming another person. It is not only harming your wife but it is harming the whole society.

Most of the magistrates in Zimbabwe are free. I haven't received any form of threat. I have been a magistrate in big and smaller towns but wherever you are, the community appreciates and respects you.

35

Mabel Chinyamurindi
Chief Superintendent

interviewed by Chiedza Musengezi

My name is Mabel Chinyamurindi. I was born on the 24th December 1961 into a family of four. I have a twin brother, Willie, another brother, Michael, and a sister. I went to school in Highfield. My father was a teacher and my mother was a housewife. My childhood was not perfect in the sense that we grew up staying with only our mother, whilst our father was staying with another woman. I did my O-levels and after that I spent a year and a half without working. Afterwards I worked as a clerk. It was not much, just writing down the names of people who came in with requests from districts and provinces. Then I got transferred to Bulawayo. At the time it was a challenge to go and work in Bulawayo. I ran into problems, I was a Shona working among the Ndebele. Some of the office staff felt that I should not have come from Harare to take over their jobs in Bulawayo. It was resolved that I would go back to Harare. The early eighties were a difficult time. Tensions were running high in the office. I did not go back to Harare. I opted to stay in Bulawayo because I had made friends and I had a flat. Then I started working for the Citizens Advice Bureau as a volunteer. I went two to three times a week and sometimes more if I had the time. I provided voluntary services such as typing.

Then I learned through the party office that there were opportunities for those who wanted to join the Prison Service, the Police, the CIO, the Army and the Post Office. I received a letter informing me that I could join the police in Harare but because I had not kept my appointment, when I came to Harare I was told that they had already filled the position. Then I was referred to the Prison Services. It was not my first choice but what I wanted was a job, any job. So I joined the Prison Service on the 5th March 1985. Upon joining I went through a training that took six months. The Prison Services are a paramilitary [force]. Training involved foot drills, how to handle prisoners and, most importantly, we were taught the prison books, the admission registers, and other books pertaining to imprisonment. Foot drills is physical training for the paramilitary. It is not as rigorous as training in the army. Foot drills serve to instill discipline. You learn to get orders at the stations, listen and operate according to the orders given. We were taught that the main duty of a prison officer is to prevent an escape. So at all times when you are with a prisoner you have to be very careful what you are doing and make sure that the prisoner in your custody does not escape. We were also taught about the importance of rehabilitation. We learnt to establish a talking relationship with the prisoner so that we could know about their problems, and if they ran away we would know where to find them. Some of the prisoners escaped from prison because they have problems, but if you talk to them and give them advice they may feel better.

When I look back at the training, I find that it was too basic. I think more is needed to be done such as making the officers know about human rights, especially the international conventions to which our government is a signatory. Trainees need to know what the conventions say with regard to prisoners. Respect for human rights was there in the training but not much attention was paid to see that we adhered to them. We did not care to ask prisoners if they had any complaints. Today it is an obligation. On admission, we have to ask prisoners if they have problems that we need to know about. We beat up prisoners even though our seniors always said it was wrong. Behind their backs we would do things they would not want us to do. I did things that I regret today: for instance, once in a while, I would hit prisoners. When you are in authority and you have five prisoners in your care and you want to make them see your point and they do not see it, you feel tempted. You are saying to them, 'Look, you are here because you committed offenses. You did not listen and I am telling you, you have got to do this and you are not listening again.' You are inclined to instil a bit of discipline in them especially if you met with difficult prisoners. You would not need to do it with some prisoners who were good; they are also the ones that you get emotionally attached to. When they lose someone in their family you would end up going to them and say, 'I heard you lost your mother, I'm sorry.' You would sit down and you talk to the prisoner. It all depends on the prisoner's attitude towards you, the majority of the prisoners are down to earth and obedient. Only a fraction of them are tough, so if you meet such a prisoner you have to be tough too.

I have a long service with Prison Services. Having joined in 1985, I was promoted in 1986 to the rank of Senior Prisoner Officer and then in 1987 I was promoted to the rank of Principal Prison Officer. In 1989 I was promoted to the rank of Chief Prison Officer. In 1991 I was promoted to the rank of Superintendent and in 1997 I was promoted to Chief Superintendent, a rank that I hold at present.[*] People have an attitude towards those who work in prisons. I remember when I wrote my brother to tell him that I had joined the Prison Services, I hinted that I was supposed to have joined the police but because I was late for the interview the vacancy was filled. He was taken aback. He advised me to wait for the next recruitment because the police force was better than the prisons. The attitude is the same when you meet someone and say, 'I am a prison officer.' They look down on me: I don't know why – probably, because before independence recruitment of prison guards was carried out without any selection criteria. As a result, the people who joined the Prison Services were those that had failed to secure a job anywhere else. But from the eighties, the Prison Services started recruiting people with O-level. However, for the people outside, it was difficult for them to understand that someone who had O-level could opt for such a career. At seminars we were overlooked and other people within the Ministry of Justice would make presentations on our behalf. They would get someone from the Ministry to speak on behalf of the Prison Services until we asked them why we could not speak for ourselves. It was only then that we started conversing with people who heard our views. Thereafter they assessed us and we began to earn their respect. Before that the general attitude was that prison officers were ignorant illiterates. I think the public equated us with Fawcett Security guards, the ones you hire to look after property. It could also be that our main function was preventing escape.

---

[*] At the time of the interview. Mabel Chinyamurindi has now left the service.

My job has also had an effect on my family. When I got the job I had children but I was not married. So at least I was happy because I had a source of income. I grew to like the job and because of the promotions my family started to accept and respect it. They started accepting the fact that I was a prison officer and I was reaping the rewards of being in a job through promotion. The promotions came with benefits such as a car and a big, comfortable house. The attitude towards prison officers has now changed for the better. People now understand that a prison officer can be a psychologist, a social worker, or someone giving security services. The old image is slowly giving way to a new type of prison officer who has professional skills. They are computer literate and can also be a trainer in computers and typing skills. A lot has changed.

I have some memories of my early days at work. I remember when I first came from the training depot, my first task was to take a pregnant woman to the maternity wing. I was in uniform with a prisoner in labour. The prisoner was about my age – quite young. She was on the floor, writhing in pain. She started to bleed, something that drew the attention of the nurses. They complained that I had brought a prisoner who was dirtying their floors. I was new and was afraid that the prisoner that I had brought to hospital might die. I was also afraid of upsetting the nurses. I cleaned up the floor. When I told my colleagues at the station what had happened they said I should have told off the nurses. I should have said that my job was to look after the prisoner so that she does not escape. The next morning I was really anxious to find out what had happened because when I left the hospital the prisoner had not given birth. I was relieved and happy when I found out that she had had a baby and was in good health.

It is difficult to be pregnant and in prison. I know so because I am a mother myself, I have been pregnant several times. There are times when a pregnant mother pines for a specific food. When you are in prison you cannot get what you want when you want it. There are times when you would want to lie down, you cannot do that in prison. Although there are no hard and fast rules about treating pregnant inmates in the prisons, we try as much as possible to make sure that they are well taken care of, but it is obviously not as free and comfortable as home.

We have a temporary prison for women in Harare, the Chikurubi Female Section. We also have one prison in Shurugwi. It is a small prison, which houses females only – way back they used to keep male prisoners there. Our prisons, I'm sorry to say, do not have any special facilities for women, especially for pregnant women and children. If we had prisons built specifically for women, they would have special features but these prisons were built initially for males and were not modified for the use of female prisoners. I would like to see better sanitation facilities for women such as incinerators for burning waste. In 1991, I went to the UK. I visited a female prison called Holloway, one of the biggest women prisons in the world. It has a baby-care unit and a drug-weaning centre. If the baby is comfortable, then the mother is rested. A nursing mother has access to her baby: the baby's cot is beside the mother's bed. In Zimbabwe we have nothing like that. However mothers do sleep with their babies, which is a good idea. During the day they would be doing prison duties without the babies but during the night they will be given the opportunity to be with their babies. At Chikurubi Female Section there is a system whereby older prisoners, the ones that cannot work in the garden, look after babies during the day. It is more or less the same thing we do at home. We leave our babies with our grandmothers when we go to the fields to weed.

During my long service with prisons women rarely commit crime inside prison except when they run away from us. Once in a while they escape. Usually they will be missing their children or a boyfriend or a husband or are simply afraid of being in prison. In the majority of cases, we find the prisoner with her family. They do not go very far away. Male prisoners do. For example, a male prisoner assaulted a prison officer and in the Chidumo case you read about in the newspapers two or so years ago, a prison officer was shot.

Prison officers are the people in the justice system who spend a lot of time with prisoners, and at very close range. The prison officer's job is not easy. For instance, take a person who is going to be in prison for fifteen years. The only person that the prisoner will rely upon is the prison officer. Whatever advice they give is really going to have an impact on the life of the prisoner. It is important for prison officers to be trained in social work so that they are able to interact with prisoners effectively. This will assist prisoners to prevent them committing further crimes. Now the training takes this into account but on a very low scale. The good news is that we are moving in the right direction. The training puts emphasis on social training unlike the time when I trained. Now with prison officers going to study psychology at the School of Social Work and the university, there will be some improvement in the running of our prisons. It will help prison officers to communicate with inmates meaningfully.

The majority of women inmates commit crime in order to look after their families. They are in prison because they were trying to fend for their families, especially the ones who are serving sentences for drug offenses. They peddled *mbanje* so that they would be able to provide for their families and so are the ones who shoplifted. A small fraction is in for infanticide and illegal abortion. These are women who are deserted in times of need. Even though they are in prison, because they need to look after their families, a custodial sentence is appropriate because some of them have come to prison more times than I can remember. The first time the magistrate gives them a suspended sentence and they go home. However, they come back two or three times. Some make it a habit of fending for their families through stealing. It has to be stopped.

Personally, I think it is not really necessary for a first offender to go to prison leaving her family behind. The prisoner will worry all the time because there is no one looking after her children. Because she communicates the problem to us, we run around looking for social workers to check on the children. Sometimes the trouble is not necessary. The introduction of the community service scheme has helped in that such women can be with their families whilst they serve their sentences. Sometimes those that steal small things are sent to do community service. As a result we now [only] have people who have fairly serious crimes coming into prison. Nonetheless, during the initial investigations before they [the first offenders] are sentenced they come into prison. Some of them lie, that's why they end up in prison. They do not give the correct address. So it is difficult for the prosecutor to locate them next time they want them. Such prisoners are not good candidates for community service.

On admission, prisoners are given a towel, toothbrush, toothpaste and soap. They are also allowed to get floor polish for their cell. Financially, however, things are not good. Where the relatives can provide these things they are allowed to do so. Even though we do not have enough money, we make sure on admission that each prisoner gets something. During their imprisonment women learn skills to enable them to get a job. At Chikurubi, for example, they have got a number of projects for this purpose. They sew, knit, type and make soap. After training we hope that they can use these skills at home or find a job and earn.

Depending on the type of crime the person has committed, prison can have a good or bad effect on a prisoner. For those who have committed petty crimes, I think the effect is bad as they are exposed to hard-core criminals and to the hard life in prison. They get hardened. But for those that commit serious crimes such as murder, or trafficking of drugs like cocaine, I think they should be treated accordingly.

Only a small fraction of the prisoners would have committed murder. They usually commit murder in anger. Their husbands beat them up and in self-defense they get a hoe or pole and hit back. Unfortunately in these instances the husband gets fatally injured and dies. But if we were to trace back their history, we would usually find that the woman would have endured beatings for a long time, sometimes up to fifteen years. She then got to a point where she said 'enough'. Sometimes women commit murder after finding their husbands with girlfriends and then they fight the girlfriends and in the end they kill their husbands. These are the kind of serious crime that women commit.

Prison routine sometimes encourages character building and sometimes it does not. We have had prisoners who have graduated from institutions for young offenders to prison. They are used to the type of life whereby they are told to wash and they go and wash. They do not mind living by instructions; they get used to it. But other prisoners say there is nothing as dehumanising as being told to wash at a certain time, eat at a certain time and have the lights switched off at a certain time. They say their lives are too controlled – they wake up at 6 o'clock in the morning and are told to sleep at 8 p.m. I would not want to be in a similar situation. There is no privilege, no choice. I remember a case where we had a child who was born in prison and because Mlondolozi prison has cement floors, the child never stepped on the ground from birth. The first time the prison officers took the baby outside to meet other prisoners the child cried because she would not walk on the ground. You can get really affected. You think, 'Why on earth am I putting my child through this?' Those that find prison routine dehumanising do not benefit much, but on the other hand they need to understand that they are there because they committed an offence and the law calls for them to be punished or for them to be in prison. If they do not want to come back, they must make sure that when they are out they avoid crime. So the ones that do not want this dehumanising experience do not re-offend. They do not come back to prison.

Although it seems as if every detail of prison life is regulated, it is not quite like that. It is not as if we say they have to 'eat now' or 'sleep now'. We tell them that the time for eating is between such and such hours and then we leave them. Some of them are so willing to co-operate with officers that we leave them on their own to follow the time guide. We do not always follow them behind. They can do things on their own.

Inmates can have an influence on each other. When a prisoner comes in, the first night she goes through a lot of questioning: what crime she committed, how long her sentence is, and so on. If she committed a big crime, such as stealing two million dollars, the others will make her feel important and clever. It all depends on the crimes. So the more serious the crime, the more respect she gets from her inmates at first. However, she soon learns that it is not something to be proud of because it means staying in prison for a long time.

From a distance it may seem as if the prison system has contradictory roles. On one hand, we are supposed to confine criminals and keep them away from the public and, on the other, we must transform these rejects of society into good citizens. The two roles compliment each other. Society still likes the criminals but for retribution purposes they have to come into prison. The wronged person must see that the criminal has been dealt with. Say, for example, you have your cellphone stolen. You would like the person to pay you back, but in the majority of such cases the criminals involved have nothing. Sometimes, they are given time to pay but they fail to meet the deadline.

I have had an opportunity to work in a male prison and a female prison and with regard to hygiene and sanitation, I'm happy to say that female prisons, are clean. Women are able to wash their clothes properly, iron them properly whilst the men will not bother with such things. The men are used to have women clean for them. There is a clinic inside a female prison and at night there is a nurse on stand-by. Problems like headache and other minor illnesses are attended to straight away, but where we have complications they are referred to hospitals. We have our own prison trucks for that.

Now we have HIV and AIDS, and the prisons have not been spared. If you can imagine that the ones that come to prison are some of the poorest of society, when this disease attacks them they cannot afford medication. The good thing is that at least we can look after them. They are given the medication unlike when they are at home. Although prison is not the best place, prisoners are given accommodation, medication, food, a balanced diet when they are not feeling well, and they are also allowed food from home if their families can bring them some. (I would advocate for women of forty years or more to have pap smears on admission because it is very important.)

No attention was given to the female prisoners in the past. The major problem is that if you compare the number of females with the numbers of males, you find women prisoners are just a fraction of the total prison population. By virtue of that fact, you find that investing in a very small number of people against a big number is not the normal practice. Maybe people were also not conscious of women's needs. I think it would be a real breakthrough if women prisons could be improved. If I were given the opportunity to make recommendations, I would recommend that prisoners who are pregnant be released from prison so that at least they are able to have their babies outside and prepare adequately for the pregnancy and the baby. Psychologically, it would help them because they need the emotional support of the family, particularly if they are not feeling well. Pregnant women need more attention; they need physical exercises. I remember when I was pregnant I went for exercises. In the courts, I feel magistrates and judges could be more considerate towards pregnant women when sentencing them, for the sake of the child.

Many spouses do not give support to their counterparts in prison. There are instances when husbands visit their wives, but these are few. Most do come on the first day to find out how long their wives are going to be in prison, so that they can give themselves as much freedom as they want. Some will write letters but some will not even respond to letters written to them by their wives. Many do not want to be associated with their wives during the time that they are in prison. When they are nearing the end of their sentences, the husbands will show interest in them again. However family members – sisters, brothers, aunts and parents – come to prison and they support their loved ones throughout.

There is entertainment in prison especially towards public holidays. Prisoners are allowed to perform drama. They also hold exhibitions for the groups that do dressmaking. Some have their own churches in prison in small groups. They get together and preach the word of God. They form choirs and sing. Prisoners do care about each other. You see it more when a prisoner has lost a relative, it becomes a concern for everyone. Sometimes if a prisoner has been in remand prison long enough for the others to discuss what sort of sentence to expect and she gets a longer one than expected, they sympathise with her. Even prison officers do. In the end, they are like a family even though they have diverse backgrounds.

We categorise prisoners. The D-class never mixes with the C-, B-, and A-classes. They have to be promoted to a lower class. The remand prisoners never mix with the convicted prisoners. They are a few women in the D-class. Once in a while we have prisoners who want to harm themselves because they are serving long sentences. One may swallow a needle when they are sewing. Usually they are seeking attention when they do such things, they want some attention or maybe they want to go to hospital and maybe escape.

Prison duties include cleaning the cells where they stay, doing courses and studying. If you come without any O-levels, you are free to start studying, then you write your O-levels. Others opt to be idle. I would like to see women take up more courses. Lack of equipment hampers such plans. We need a big workshop – a tailoring workshop with 500 machines for women to learn different aspects of tailoring and things. If we had more equipment it would really help.

I would also like to recommend a crèche for the children. If funds were available, I would have the children of the inmates play in a free and beautiful environment so at least the children do not have to feel they are in prison all the time. I would also advocate for female prisons to be built because the facilities that exist are not good enough. The majority of the women that are in prison are not hard-core criminals. They are fit to be in an open prison environment that allows semi-freedom; a place where they can do their own cooking in their own time with food they like. Women prisoners need an environment that encourages more social contact with other people from outside. It is very important for a mother to have contact with her children and it is equally important for a wife to have contact with her husband. When I see them seated quietly on their own and I ask what are you thinking of. They say they wish to speak to so and so, usually a member of the family. The open prison setting affords prisoners an opportunity for home visits to check on their families. Employment of more social workers is required so that each prisoner can talk to them on a one-to-one basis instead of one social worker listening to twenty prisoners all at once.

I have learnt from being a prison officer that your status as a person can change at any time. A prison is not a place for a particular group of people. Anyone can end up there. We have had politicians, doctors, bankers, lawyers, teachers and unemployed single mothers. I too have to be law-abiding else I'll be locked up. I listen to prisoners and sometimes I think to myself, I could have done the same. So I would not like to look down on prisoners because my own status can change. There is no class distinction. From my experience different groups of people come to prison. We have rural women, who, at the sight of a court room, will say 'yes' to everything levelled against them because they are afraid. Then there is another a group of people who stand their ground even if they committed the offences. They will appear in court denying the charges. The advantaged ones have lawyers and have good representation in court. The lawyer fights on their behalf; the client is alerted beforehand of the questions that are likely to be asked. The lawyer also knows the court procedure. The case will be heard properly. A rural person from Hurungwe charged with trafficking drugs is likely just to say, 'I'm sorry. I was caught with *mbanje* and I'm sorry.' She will have no lawyer to advise her on mitigating factors. Some people lack exposure.

I think women's organisations are not doing enough. I would like to see them providing more information than they are doing now because the most important thing is information for both the unconvicted and the convicted prisoner. Information on the rights of the arrested should be made available, even at the police stations. People should able to get a leaflet on essential information pertaining to our justice system. People need to know their rights: even leaflets on prison visiting times. There is no such basic information for the public. Women's organisations are not pushy enough. They need to get more involved with disadvantaged women such as prisoners. Relatives can pass messages through us to the prisoners, but the prisoners cannot phone back and say I want to speak to my father and things like that. Prisoners need strong organisations to stand up and speak for them.

36

Peter Mandiyanike,
Director – Prison Fellowship, Zimbabwe

interviewed by Irene Staunton

My name is Peter Mandiyanike, I was born in 1945 into a family of six and I am the first son. I grew up in Manicaland in a Christian family. My father was very involved in church work. I did my primary education up to Standard 6 in Marange and then I went to Hilltop School under the Christian church. After that I went to Weathrow School of Commerce in Gweru to be trained as a bookkeeper. The school was run by missionaries; and the course lasted two years. Then I worked under Rhodesia Railways for a year, before moving to Foulds Construction as the wages clerk. I was very mobile. I was looking for higher wages, and to climb up the ladder. After that I moved to Aluminium Industries as the first African production control clerk, a position which I held for eight years.

By then – 1977 – I was a leader, the youth leader of the United Methodist Church and also a youth leader with the Inter-denominational churches. One day when we were having a combined meeting at the cathedral, Bishop Paul Burrow, of the Anglican Church issued a challenge, he said: 'The missionaries have deserted the children at Goromonzi Children's Home, so is there anybody who would like to undertake a challenge?' I was challenged. So I left Aluminium Industries and I went to Bishop Paul and I said, 'Can I please take the challenge?' And he said, 'Here are the keys for the office, you just have to drive there.' When I arrived the children were alone with the nuns because the priests had run away as they felt threatened that they would fall victims of the war. The orphanage was about 60 kilometres from Harare, in the Goromonzi/Juru area.

When I first went to the mission, we had about 60 children, but as the war grew we got more children who had been under the custody of Chief Tangwena in Nyanga. He just fled to Mozambique and left 120 children on their own. These were brought to me. Within moments I found myself with 120 more children. It was a difficult time.

So I started from scratch, getting the children to settle, putting out my feelers as to who was operating in that area. I wanted to know who the terrorists were. By then there were the Muzorewas – the Pfumorevanhu, the ZANLAs and, of course, the Rhodesian Forces. I did my research well and I got in touch with these guys, and then I had to make my choice as to who I should be with.

Anyway, I chose to support the ZANLA forces under the leadership of Robert Mugabe though the government of the day expected me to be very loyal to them and I pretended that I was. When they came to the school I told them false stories about who was operating where and when these ZANLAs came, the *chimurenga* guys, I told them the truth. I even gave them the opportunity to teach the children. So when the Rhodesian Army Forces wanted to find out who the teachers were, I said: 'Go, talk to them. Ask them about the terrorists.' So they were actually talking to the terrorists themselves; the actual guys in the bush. I did that to defend myself, but eventually I developed a very big interest in the war and became seriously involved.

What encouraged me was that many youngsters, relatives from my home in Manicaland, went to Mozambique to join the liberation struggle. I thought, 'If we don't assist them then they will all perish.' So the only thing to do was join the ZANLAs. But I played very neutral. I didn't want people to know that I was at the forefront of the *chimurenga* movement.

I was the mission superintendent and I had about 28 teachers under me. It was quite a big school, the only one in Murehwa, Mashonaland East, that was never closed during the war. Eventually, in 1980, we had independence. We thought everything was over, and we wanted to celebrate thinking that independence is a time to mess around. So I tampered with the law, and I went on to squander all the school's money, and go about with the children, go about with the nuns. I thought nobody would catch me. I went drinking and womanizing. I looked at beautiful girls and I said, 'I want to go with you tonight,' and so on. I thought that was okay. It was this freedom that we thought we had – the freedom that a man can do anything he wants. You can take any woman you want, you can eat money, you can spend freely, even if the money was not yours: to me that was the kind of freedom I thought we had.

Of course, some teachers were not happy with what I was doing but because I had been at the forefront of the *chimurenga* war, they could say very little. They kept quiet. There was only one person, the headmaster of the primary school, who came to me and said, 'Brother, stop this. You'll find yourself in trouble.' But instead of appreciating him, I hated him. I wished he was not at the school at all. I said, 'You keep your eyes far too open and you'd better be careful.'

My wife did not accept my behaviour – although I didn't treat her as my wife, I treated her the same as my car: 'I bought you, so you've got no say.' You can imagine my feelings with a little *dhaka*, getting drunk every day, womanising, spending nights away. My wife kept quiet, she had no say, though once she warned me, 'Look, you are going to find yourself in serious trouble,' and I said, 'Don't worry about that, I will solve it myself.'

The nuns were not very happy with me because I proposed love to some of them, and then changed and went for school children, and then changed and so on. Anyway in 1985, when I was on leave, they decided to get me into serious trouble with the police. They reported that I was going about with the children and that I was squandering money.

So when I came back from leave, two youngsters, two very young police investigators arrived. They told me, 'We are from Harare. We have been asked to pick you up.' I was having my breakfast, I was in my morning gown. They said, 'Don't worry, don't dress yourself, you will be back soon. We are not gonna take time.' So they took me half-dressed to Harare.

When I got to the Harare Central Police Station, they said, 'Brother, we are charging you with thirty counts: indecent assault, stealing money from the school, rape, etc.' Thirty counts! 'What have you got to say? This is a police warned and cautioned statement.' Of course, I denied everything.

They never took me back, they threw me into custody in the remand. Then a friend, Mrs Dawson, heard about it because the story was on the front page of the paper. She came straight and paid bail for me, but I was barred from going back to school because I would interfere with the investigations with the children. So I couldn't see my family. Anyway I stayed in Borrowdale and if my wife wanted to see me, she would come at the weekend.

Two years passed, I thought the case was over. But in April 1987, I found myself thrown into prison – after two years out of custody on remand. The magistrate was very harsh. He said, ' I want to teach you a lesson so that anybody who ever takes your position will not abuse his rights. Such allegations should not be made by a father like you who was supposed to be responsible for the children and the staff.' And he threw me into prison for ten years. No remission – nothing.

That magistrate is now a high court judge. We sit together in the high court – I am on the national committee of community service. Once I reminded him, I said, 'Do you remember that you threw me into prison for ten years?' He had long forgotten but I never forgot.

So this was my first time to talk to a policeman, to appear in court, to experience prison life. I didn't know what to do. Imagine it: being the superintendent of a big mission school, to being in prison with a lot of different characters. I just had to adjust and fit in.

I remember after my first three days my wife came to see me, she said, 'Should I wait for you?' I replied, 'The choice is yours. I'm gonna be here for ten years, you either stay or go. Whatever you decide I will accept.' Luckily, she decided to stay. She was very loyal. She came to see me every month. She never missed once.

Then a very strange thing happened after three months of my incarceration at Harare Central. One night, at about midnight, something struck me on my head. I woke up. I looked at the other prisoners. Everybody was fast asleep but something had struck me on my forehead and it was a hard strike. The next day, I was unable to work in the tailor's shop. I just sat in the yard. I didn't talk to anybody. Then the officer-in-charge came to me and said, 'What are you doing here?' and I said, 'I am sorry. I am very powerless, I have lost control of myself. I don't know what has happened.' He asked, 'Where are you supposed to work?' I told him, 'The workshop'. Then, he said, 'What is your name?' He went straight to the records, looked at my warrant and said, 'You are in the wrong prison. You are supposed to be in the maximum-security prison. You've been given ten years. You have to go to Chikurubi with immediate effect.' But he could not find any transport to take me, so they had to wait for a truck and this came in the evening. I was given special escorts and taken to Chikurubi in the middle of the night where I was thrown into a cell in E section.

By coincidence that very same night a person who became a colleague of mine, Moffat Karambamuchero, was also transferred to Chikurubi from Mutare Prison. We were thrown into the same cell. The next day I found this handsome young man, crying: sobbing tears, and I felt pity for him. The rest of the prisoners were making a mockery of him. They said, 'Even if you cry blood tears you will never get out of this place.' I moved over to him, I said, 'What's your name? And what's your problem?' He shared with me that he had been a bank manager at CABS in Manicaland and that his family was left in Darlington in Mutare. It was the time of the FRELIMO war in Mozambique and he was very worried that he might not see his wife and children again because of the FRELIMO – in case they invaded.

I said to this young man, 'Brother we have no option, can I pray with you?' It was my first day in Chikurubi and my first day to open my mouth in prayer for a very long time. We prayed and prayed. Luckily, that afternoon his father came to see him. After the visit the young man smiled and said, 'Thank you for your prayers, my father was here with the good news that my family is okay, and they have moved to Marondera. Can we continue with the prayers?'

That was the beginning of God's work. I remember continuously praying on that same spot three times a day regardless of what other prisoners said or if they made mockery: 'Whom do you want to cheat? If you were Christians you should have prayed out there and you would not have been here.' We never took heed of them.

During the war Christianity went away. It was war and either you did what the guerrillas, the ZANLAS, said or you die. That is when I started drinking beer, smoking *dhaka*, and so on. I completely lost my direction. I was no longer a Christian but I was leading a mission school. I was supposed to be a Christian. I punished the children who did not go to church. I would go down the dormitory with a whip, and give the children corporal punishment, whip them and tell them to go to church

Meantime, I would stay seated at home, even though my house was only a stone's throw away from the church. I thought that during the liberation war we had no room for Christianity. My mind had completely changed. I hated the missionaries. I thought that we were fighting because of the missionaries who had cheated us. Christianity from 1978 to 1980 was not in my life. It vanished. I was a guerrilla, so to speak. I was involved in planting landmines. I could see people going over a landmine and getting killed because I knew exactly where the enemy was coming from. I can't even tell how many deaths I caused – but I was at the forefront of the struggle. I want to say that I was one of those that really caused people to die: children, nuns, I can't count. I could only repeat what Paul says in the Bible, 'If it was killing, count it on me.' All sorts of evil were surrounding me then because it was a do or die situation. If you don't do what I instruct you to do, you are just going to die. No reverse gear. So it was a tough situation. You know, people in town never saw what was happening out there. I was right at the forefront. I could not resign because my house was used as a storeroom for new ammunition. I would drive to Mozambique at night through the Mutoko border, pick stuff up and come back. We used to operate at night from 6 p.m. to 6 a.m.

Luckily Christ was very merciful, and he pitied me before the end of my life. Otherwise I would not be alive today. So you see when I began to pray with Moffat, it was my first time to pray for a long, long time.

In maximum security, you cannot meet with another prisoner. But when we received Christ, when the change of life came, the officer-in-charge saw the seriousness of our prayer, and he instructed the junior officers that on Sundays they should open all the cells: 'Let these guys move from cell to cell, door to door and preach the gospel,' he said. He himself as the Officer Commanding would sometimes join us during Sunday prayers and we felt that something was happening. This was when the vision of forming Prison Fellowship Zimbabwe came about. At the time, we were not allowed to write anything down, so we decided to put our vision, our dream, on tissues and luckily when Moffat was released he managed to smuggle out the tissue.

Then the Pope visited Harare and there was an amnesty. That saw us being recognised as different from the very dangerous criminals with long-term sentences, and we were classified C-class prisoners which was better. Moffat's sentence was reduced from five to two years. My sentence was reduced to three years, and instead of being kept in the maximum security, we were given gangs again. Moffat went to the kitchen and he was the prisoner in charge of the storeroom where the food was kept. I was put in charge of the laundry machine and I sat behind it doing the washing for all the prison guards and the prisoners for two years. Then I enrolled myself to study theology with the Zimbabwe Theological College and Moffat also enrolled with a Mutare College. We received our diplomas when we came out of prison: Moffat in 1988, me in 1989 – there were other amnesties.

So we came out of prison rejuvenated. We had read a book in prison, *Born Again* written by Charles Colson the founder of Prison Fellowship International. That book really brought our vision into reality. What we read in that book was exactly what we had put on tissue paper. Inside that book there was Charles Colson's address. So I said to Moffat, 'As soon as you get out of here, get hold of this gentleman.' And as soon as he got hold of that gentleman he was sent a ticket. He flew, I remember his first trip was to Costa Rica in the southern part of America. Imagine, from prison to America! When he came back to me, he came back with a smile and said, 'Oh boy, the thing is on. It's real brother, we gonna start a ministry.' He kept coming back to promise me a post. He said, 'You will make a choice if you want to become a chairman, you will be chairman or you can have whichever post you want.'

He did the running around, putting the organisation in place although he did not register it officially because it was difficult. The government was very suspicious of us ex-convicts wanting to register an organisation to do with inmates. But Moffat kept running around, finding people to join us.

I was released a year later, and the organisation was there but it was not official. And then, Moffat was earmarked to become the Africa Regional Director in Ghana. So, by the time I came out of prison he was operating from there. He kept phoning me saying, 'Brother take over from where I left off.'

But I only wanted the organisation to be a Manicaland thing, I didn't want to do anything with the Mashona people. To me they were a bit naughty. So I said I will start with Prison Fellowship in Manicaland. So I did and I was operating in Mutare, Chipinge, Nyanga and Rusape. I didn't want to go any further. But later Moffat returned to Zimbabwe because he couldn't obtain a work permit in Ghana. So, his office was transferred to Harare, and he came to Manicaland and he said, 'Brother there is no need for you to operate at regional level only.' He came to see me together with Ron Nickel, the vice-president of the international scenario and he said, 'Look, why don't you come to Harare and become as a full-time worker for Prison Fellowship, Zimbabwe?'

So in 1990, I moved from Mutare and became the Executive Director of Prison Fellowship. It took us four years to register the organisation – 1990 to 1994. That's when the prison department and the government said, 'Look, these guys are serious.' So we were officially registered, although the prison department would not fully open their doors: they would open one half-way and close the other. It went on like this until they had proved beyond doubt that we had no hidden agenda but really wanted to assist them with their rehabilitation programmes.

As we talk now, a lot has been achieved. Community service began with our assistance because of our exposure to the international scenario. We were also very seriously involved with the open prisons that the government is beginning to put in place. We were consulted about the budget relating to judiciary system. We keep our eyes very open in order to protect the rights of inmates because they are still human beings, though they are in prison. We have a lot of say and I must confess that currently we have a very good relationship with government, particularly with the prison department. They respect us and the issue of seeing us as ex-convicts has long gone. They now view us as very serious people who know what we are doing.

It is a challenge because society has a very negative attitude to prisoners. The mentality is that if a person makes a mistake, lock him up and punish him. Then we come in with a soft voice, a Christian voice to say, 'Look, human beings are human beings, whether they make a mistake or not they have to be introduced to their maker, God.' This is our philosophy. We say, 'Look this is an opportunity, many people like Moses were murderous, but God made use of them.' We can say, 'Look if God did what he did to me and Moffat, there is no reason why He can't change your life as well.' It's a life challenge: that's why we are still so excited about it.

I think the main weakness with our system lies with the judiciary. Government must come up with a new set of laws because we are using the Roman-Dutch laws that may not apply to Africans. For example, minor crimes in our culture never went before the chief. It was the family or the kraal head who dealt with them and compensation was the major issue. For instance, if I steal your chicken, it was not a big deal. At the family level, the kraal head would say, 'Look you've been caught with Taurai's chicken which was supposed to lay eggs and hatch chickens for her. Return that chicken to her plus another chicken in compensation.' What I am saying is that in Zimbabwean culture we are not interested in throwing people into prison. What they are interested in is compensation.

As for bigger crimes, if somebody murders somebody, surely they have to be eradicated from society; and they are supposed to stay in prison for their own security as well. But I think that if I raped your daughter, you must be consulted to say your piece of mind. In our culture anybody who has a daughter is expecting *lobola*. But in the judicial system now, once they apprehend the culprit, they don't consult the victim. It is simply a matter of the government and it decides what to do through the magistrate: the victim is not consulted. The parents are not consulted. I feel that if it is a rape charge, the parent must be consulted. I can bet you – three quarters of the parents would say, 'Look I want my *lobola*. I want damages, I want medical funds,' and so on. But if you put the culprit in prison, you have to feed him and the victim's parents are left with a diseased child. The parents are gonna pay for the rapist's food in prison as well through their taxes. They will continue to suffer and the culprit and government are not helping at all.

The incarceration of those who steal and stuff like that is not helping at all. When they come out of prison, they get into some other kind of trouble. So the government must go back to the drawing board and revise the entire judicial system and the classification of inmates. What we are doing now is grooming more criminals in prisons instead of protecting them and re-training them. If I go to prison as a rapist, that's a social and psychological problem. I'm not a thief. But if you place me with criminals then I come out having graduated from being a rapist to being a criminal. If I go to prison because of a traffic offence, why should I be put in the same cell with a murderer or with a real thief? It's a traffic offence, and I may be an upright person. The systems that we are using are wrong and they need to be re-examined.

There are mental patients in prison. The *ngozi* are spirits of the deceased, of dead people and the *ngozi* is there – in prison. If you steal things from somebody, it might not affect you now but sooner or later your children will see the results of your crime. The *ngozi* are there. The *ngozi* are what the Christians call the devil's spirits. If you go steal, you will feel the repercussions later.

Women are looked after by women guards and there has always been some kind of softness. Men and women prisoners are not treated in the same way. Women are treated better than men. For instance, women don't do hard labour, as the men do, working in the fields the whole day. If they work it will be in the small garden around the prison.

Women respect each other better than men do. I see a kind of softness even in the way the wardens speak to the ladies, the inmates. They speak well, but, if you go to the male prisons, harsh words are spoken. It's like a tug of war between the prisoners and the wardens. The prisoners want to beat the system, the warders want to control them: don't take this into a cell, don't talk at this time, don't eat now, etc. But if lock up is from 4:30 p.m. to 6 a.m., prisoners will be hungry and bored and they have to find something to do. The attitude of wardens is: 'You wronged society. We are the society. You must be punished.' So there cannot be a good relationship between a prisoner and a prison officer.

Society relies strongly on the officers to rehabilitate prisoners, but because of overcrowding and stress, rehabilitation programmes don't work. The warders can't talk to the prisoners one on one, and they can't open the cells because there are too many inmates. One officer is supposed to look after five prisoners but if he has twenty or thirty, security is weak. So he will keep everyone locked up. Rehabilitation will not take place until the problem of overcrowding is addressed.

The relationship between the prisoners and the guards is harsh. If you are not careful you will come out of prison a worse person than you entered it. No one speaks kindly. Instead of accepting responsibility for the wrong that they have done, prisoners teach each other worse ways. They have got too much empty time. Lock-up is when pastors and social workers should talk to the prisoners, preach to them, hold Bible study classes, so that their minds are occupied. These three factors: no programmes of activity, poor food, bad influences, are those which need to be addressed. There is freedom of worship in prison and those who seriously want to change their lives can do so.

Many people do not understand the court procedures and they go to prison for crimes they didn't commit due to lack of education. If you have no money you can't defend yourself. If I have money and I fail to bribe the police, then I have to bribe the magistrate; if I fail to bribe the magistrate, I have to bribe the prison guards for a bit of favouritism. If you are poor, nobody knows who you are and you suffer the consequences from the moment you are apprehended by the police. Very often people admit to crimes they have not committed because they are scared, or because they don't understand the procedures.

Prison is like death: the prisoner is buried. If you are incarcerated, then you will find out who your true friends are. Nobody will stand by you. I was a well-known person, the superintendent of a mission school, but nobody stood by me. When I was in prison my own brothers went to my wife and asked for my belongings. When I came out, all my possessions had gone. My wife could not resist their pressure. So I started again with nothing: no radio, no spoon, no cup – nothing. My wife and my four children had been left with nothing.

My children suffered when I was in prison. They will never, never forget it. Everybody pointed a finger at them, laughing and mocking them. When I came out they were barefoot, they had nothing. My own blood brothers did not take care of them. When you come out of prison, nobody wants to assist you. Instead they watch you with suspicion.

In America, for instance, if somebody goes to prison and his wife is not working, the children are taken care of by social welfare. But in Zimbabwe the government does not want to know. I currently have two cases where both parents were apprehended. Nobody wants to know about the children. This is why Prison Fellowship exists.

For example, in my case, I was the superintendent so my salary was not bad. The government should have found out how much I had in the bank, how much I stole from the school, what damage I did to some peoples' daughters. Then they should have said: 'You must pay back the school; pay damages to the families for their daughters; and provided me with rehabilitation. They could have looked back and asked what good did this man do? Well, he did this and that for the sake of liberation, I would say I deserved a maximum of three years. I was a first offender and I was thrown into a maximum prison for ten years. To me that was politics. The judge was a white man.

You think rape is a terrible crime, but we have to look at it in two ways. Yes, damage is done but sending the culprit into prison does not solve the problem. He is gonna come out and continue. He will be worse and rape more. Rape a is socio-psychological problem and the psychologists need to find out what causes this man to rape women. But in prison there is nothing. No rehabilitation, no follow up, nobody talks to you. You are just locked away. What are we achieving? In our tradition the chief would say, 'Look you raped my daughter, come and work for me for the next ten years'. If I rape your daughter, I admired her and I am wishing she was my wife, young as she is. And in my culture we will say: 'Marry her or pay the seduction damages.'

Some rapists must go to prison because otherwise they may do it again and again, but we need to educate these guys. We need to say: 'Do you understand the damage you have done to this girl? Who is going to marry the one you have damaged? Do you understand the stigmatization?' But to give someone ten years and lock the door …A rapist is a womanizer, he will come out of prison more vicious. You hear about guys being released and coming back the next day, because he raped somebody on his way home. Locking up a person, a man who is supposed to have a wife, locking him up for ten years. It can't work. That is why there is this homosexuality in prison.

It starts with the guys that are in for life, so their only option is homosexuality. It begins like a relationship between a teacher and a pupil, a niece and an uncle, as a relationship of trust. Homosexuality is done to youngsters, ignorant of what's happening in prisons. They go into prison for the first time, they don't get their fair share of food, and the old-timers say, 'Hey, youngster, you did not eat properly. I have a little extra, come, eat my portion. I will look after you. I will feed you,' and so on. These youngsters are very innocent, very trusting and now he has a protector. That is where it starts.

And there are drugs in prison. They get marijuana, it makes you sleep all night and before you know what is happening you are raped many times. I want to tell you that if the love I discovered in prison in terms of homosexuality, could be applied to our wives – there would be no divorce. These guys, who are called young little girls for purposes of homosexuality, they don't even bath. They just go into the tap and the guys bathe them you know. So, in prison there is homosexuality not by choice but by circumstances. Youngsters get caught before they realise what is happening. That is why Prison Fellowship has asked the prison department to give orientation to all first offenders, to educate them what to expect, what to watch out for, and so on.

If I was going to change the prison structure, my first request to the Minister of Home Affairs, would be for enough money to educate our police in crime prevention. Right now they just wait, and watch. Then they apprehend someone after they have committed a crime. They don't have to do that. I think we have to start with the policemen, educate them about their role, and about crime prevention. How do we recruit our policemen, what sort of interviews do we give them? Should we just look at height, strength, and certificates? To be a good policeman is a calling. Is your heart there? Do you know the implications? Are you called to be a policeman, are you called to save the nation? If you are just in it for the money and have other hidden agendas, then we don't want you. The police should understand their role and their importance. They should know who should be apprehended, who cautioned, who warned, and so on. We must put a stop to bribery, corruption and stuff like that, because if we don't get our police right, our home affairs right, then the judiciary will not be right. God-fearing people are what we are looking for. Once we have that then we are done. Good police are at the heart of the nation. And this depends on good selection and good training.

We need good systems in the prisons. The prison officers know that bad things are happening but they will never say it. They will say there is no homosexuality. When you are representing government you don't come out and say what you know, otherwise you will be victimized. Even the visiting magistrates know that when they go to the prisons, if the officer-in- charge, knows that they are coming, the place will be clean, the food clean, the floors swept. But come back without warning and you will see the real truth. So we need good systems.

Next on my list of priorities, I would want to persuade the government to understand that if a nation is *not* a God-fearing nation they are finished. I did not drop my spears, my guns, my *mbanje*, my beer by choice. Something struck me on the forehead. I don't know what that was, but it was the end of my *mbanje*, my beer. We have got to fear God, and we have got to respect each other. Now we are talking about the third *chimurenga* war, the *hondo yeminda* system, but I say, 'Tools down to all these evil deeds. Tools down, guns down.' We are all created in an image of God and seek God's guidance no matter what colour we are and we must respect each other. The white people must also understand that if they have a piece of land, it is time to share. Don't be too greedy. They did have a chance and now it is the black man's turn.

Maybe I would like to conclude by saying that from my experience with Prison Fellowship, if you are to combat crime in Zimbabwe or around the world, we have to get everybody involved. Do not destroy the good cultural structures that we have. Get parents involved. Now there are parents who sleep without knowing where their children are. In society it is the parents' responsibility to groom their children. If we are to eradicate crime in this country everybody must be involved: parents, teachers, church people, government, the policemen, everybody. Crime is an epidemic, a disease it is something that destroys a nation. Zimbabwe is now a country of burglar bars. We are fed up with these things and unless we put our heads together and work as a team, nothing will happen. Crime is not for the police, the magistrates, the guards, alone: no, no, no. It is for the nation and therefore if we put our heads together we can eradicate crime.

Who buys the stolen goods? Nobody asks this question. Who is responsible the thief or the buyer? By buying they are promoting crime. If people do make mistakes we have got no right to condemn them. Let us just pick up those that have fallen. I like the Jesus way of doing things. He said to Peter, who had the intention to murder someone, 'Peter that is not the way. Take the ear back,' and when this happened, Jesus did not say, 'Out of my team.' Let us not drop people because they have committed a crime. Let us help them out, help them to start afresh.

Remember people steal from poverty. They tell us, 'I was at the edge. I did what I did because I had to survive. My husband died. I have no source of income. I went to the Department of Social Welfare, they say I am too young,' and so on and so on. 'My only alternative was to steal.' As I speak, there are people in prison who are opting to stay there rather than live in poverty. We are now a poverty country. Where are we heading? We will eventually have no food for the prisoners.

Look at this country, we have a beautiful country, but the structures have broken down. There is nothing any more. So let's go back to the drawing board and humble ourselves and say God we are done, pity us. I am a Christian: no matter what you covered up, it will be uncovered.

37

Regina Kasavadyo, Prison Nurse

interviewed by Virginia Phiri

I am Sister Regina Kasavadyo. I have been at Chikurubi female prison since 1992. I joined the Prison Services in 1989 as a State Registered Nurse and I am a trained psychiatric nurse. I also deal in STD [sexually transmitted disease] management and I am a CONNECT-trained counsellor.[*] These qualifications have equipped me to deal with the problems that I encounter in my job. This type of work needs a lot of patience, one must be committed to the nursing profession, not just to earning money but one must have a humane heart to be able to deal with the cases I come across. I enjoy my work: it is quite challenging.

Women look after each other very well. They alert the guards if one of them is not well, even if it is at the middle of the night. Some women also get sick because they might be pregnant and they don't know it. When they are admitted to prison, we normally ask them if they are pregnant but because some women do not know their cycles, they usually say they are not pregnant. Such cases are not many. However, those who know that they are pregnant are the difficult ones. Normally, they would have had children before, but they do not bother to register at the anti-natal clinics in their home areas. We then have to register them and take care of them accordingly. Sometimes we have cases where women just keep quiet, even if they know that they about to give birth. That then becomes our problem and we have to deal with it here at our clinic. We are not equipped to

---

[*] CONNECT is an organisation which provides family counselling and support.

deliver babies but at times we end up doing so. We have enough gloves, but at times we find ourselves handling births without them. We try to be careful these days especially with this era of HIV/AIDS. A lot of blood is involved during birth, as we all know. We try to encourage the women to tell us when the birth signs begin to show. First pregnancies are normally tricky, we don't take chances with these, we send them to Parirenyatwa or Harare hospitals.

Let me talk about sanitation in prison. Few women know about their monthly cycle; these are the ones who come to me and request pads telling me that their time for menstruating is near and they want to prepare for it. The rest come when they have started to menstruate. It is never a problem because it is a right for every woman to have access to pads for their menstruation. We order the pads from the medical stores and these are provided as per request. There was only one time when there was a shortage of pads: the medical stores did not have them in stock. It was only for a short while. In cases like this, we normally switch to cotton wool, which is always available. No woman goes without anything when menstruating. For heavy bleeders we double the allocation and make sure that they keep dry.

Some time this year we had a donation of pads from Mr Stephen Margolis who owns a company that manufactures pads. This donation was very much appreciated, more so because it was coming from a man. He is a wonderful man. Women themselves have not thought of buying pads and donating them to us. I hope they will take the good example set by Mr Margolis.

We used to dispose of the used pads in the incinerator, but it broke down, so we now resort to using black plastic bags supplied by the City of Harare. Women are supplied with ordinary plastic bags [in which] to keep the used pads before taking them to the big black plastic bags. This is done for the heavy bleeders at night when they need to change their pads. For the normal bleeders they keep the pad on them until morning. This is the most hygienic means we can use under these conditions.

When it is menstruation time most of the prisoners realise that and they ask the wardens to tell the clinic authority that they need pads. We always meet their requests. There are few cases when patients do not know enough about their monthly cycle to alert the wardens, and then we move in to clean the patients and dress them properly. For menstruation pains, vomiting, headaches, backaches and stomach-aches, we give painkillers. For serious cases, we consult our doctor, who checks the patient and decides what to do. At times, serious stomach cases are threatening abortions or infections. Defaulting from the birth control pill, that is, just stopping the pill when one comes to prison can also cause bleeding. The cases that our doctor cannot handle are sent to either Parirenyatwa Hospital or Harare Hospital.

We also offer women underwear. It is a right for every prisoner to have underwear. We give one pair of pants per prisoner. That is what we can afford. Some prisoners have underwear brought from home for them, we do allow that. For those who cannot have underwear brought from home, they make do with what we give them. The ones we offer are normally referred to as *maparashuti* – parachutes. These are baggy type of panties made out of strong material, they last long and they serve the purpose.

We also have psychiatric patients. The causes of their conditions vary, sometimes hormonal imbalance after birth can cause confusion, other cases are related to drugs taken before admission to Chikurubi. Other causes are unknown since the accurate medical history of patients is not known. Appropriate medication is administered and most patients recover after treatment. Counselling also goes along with medication and the results are normally good. We have very few violent cases, when that happens we sedate the patient then transfer them to the Pari Annex Section where they are admitted and treated. Once any of our prisoners is admitted at any hospital, they are guarded by prison wardens for 24 hours a day, this is done in shifts.

We also manage STDs. On admission we ask prisoners if they have any sexually transmitted diseases that we can assist in treating, most of them are shy but a few cases volunteer, especially the ones with sores on their genitals, we give them antibiotics and the infections are cleared up. For the shy ones we press for information or other women tell us about their STD problems, then we call them to find out if the information received is true, we examine them and treat the infections. Some cases are really complicated but we do the best we can to ease the discomfort by giving medication and counselling. It looks like when they are at home it is difficult to access medication due to costs involved. They would rather use the money to buy food for the children; this is how far women sacrifice for their children.

Other health problems that I come across are cases of suspected tuberculosis. This is very common, the suspected patients are tested for TB, if found positive they get isolated in a special ward, they are given medication and special food. Milk is also important in their diet. We grow our own food, so there is no shortage of food; and we also have dairy cows, so there is no shortage of milk. The TB cases are treated successfully because the medication is supervised: there is no way a patient cannot take the medication.

There are a lot of children who stay here with their mothers. The population of children increases every day. This is due to petty crimes committed by their mothers. I think it is done intentionally by the parents because when they are in prison with their children they can be fed and have proper medical care. Economic hardships must be creating this situation. Children have normal child diseases like coughing, fever, diahorrea, and sometimes measles. These cases are treated normally as if the parents were at home. Appropriate food is given to the sick children and their mothers take care of them day and night, like they would do in a home environment.

Sometimes when mothers are admitted at Chikurubi, they bring with them children who are already sick, we term these 'failures to thrive'. We try to treat these children, but in most cases they die: we don't give up on them, we do the best we can. The children are also appropriately dressed in case of cold nights in winter. Clothes are donated. Prison Fellowship and other organisations help with children's clothes. Appropriate inoculations are also given at appropriate times. We prefer to keep only mothers in prison but most mothers say it is best they keep their children with them because nobody is prepared to look after the child of a convict. At times we ask the children's homes to assist in looking after the children when their parents are in prison. At the moment most homes are full, they cannot take more children from us.

Well-wishers can donate things like soap, Vaseline, porridge, clothes. Blankets would be very much appreciated, as the number of small children has increased: help from well-wishers can go a long way. For instance, we have a young mother with twins, one and half months old. She struggles to feed the babies; she does not have enough milk. We try by all means to give breast-feeding mothers more food than others, but still the children need more than just milk – porridge is essential. We have babies only a month old, born here. The oldest is a six years old boy. We are trying to place him in a home but the homes are full. Toys will also do for the bigger children, we have a nursery where the children play. Maybe you as writers and mothers can influence the community to help these children; that will be much appreciated. These women and children are my family; I care for them. I am like their mother, their health and well-being is my responsibility.

One more thing, two weeks before the women are released, we offer them a birth control [preparation] that agrees with them; they are not forced, most of them welcome the idea. We go through with them how the contraceptives work and what changes to expect. This gives the women freedom to be sexually active without having to worry about pregnancy. We also offer them condoms and tell them about the dangers of contracting HIV if they practice unprotected sex. The AIDS topic is normally discussed openly; women like to know about how it is contracted, they are also aware that it is incurable. Testing for HIV is also discussed so that one knows her status: the interest to know more about HIV/AIDS is there.

Prison is no place for a woman
Julie Stewart

W omen make up only 3.5 per cent of the prison population in Zimbabwe. Therein lies the dilemma. The female prisoner presents a problem to prison management but given their small numbers, one that is liable to be overlooked. Prisons in Zimbabwe, as they are currently constructed and run, are not suitable for women: their facilities and rehabilitation programmes (where these exist) are based on male needs. Until recently the particular problems of women prisoners were not articulated and, therefore, not addressed. Recently, however, there has been increased awareness as to the special situation of women in prison, and this has led to some improvements, for example, changes have been made in the availability of sanitary wear for women prisoners. In 2003, the Chief Magistrate gave a directive instructing magistrates that pregnant and nursing mothers should be remanded out of custody, meaning that while they await trial they should not be held in prison. Further, according to magistrates in Harare:

> We do not sentence women, who commit such crimes as infanticide, to prison. It is normally community service. They normally have lots of family responsibilities

Ollyn Nzuma, a magistrate is recorded in her interview in this book as remarking:

> ... [T]here is discrimination between different aspects of society. In a petty case you might order a fine of say Z$1,000, but if the accused fails to pay he is sent to prison for twenty days. Those who can pay will escape the jail term. It is a problem because we say the law applies equally to all people, but the anomalies exist: a poor person ends up serving twenty days in prison with labour, a rich person does not.

These inequities prevail: such a person should be sentenced to community service rather than jail. As according to Mabel Chinyamurindi a Superintendent in the prison service at the time she was interviewed:

> Depending on the type of crime the person has committed, prison can have a good or bad effect on a prisoner. For those who have committed petty crimes I think the effect is bad as they are exposed to hard-core criminals.... They get hardened. Prison routine sometimes encourages character building and sometimes it does not. We have had prisoners who have graduated from institutions for young offenders to prison. They are used to the type of life whereby they are told to wash and they go and wash.

Thus, these accounts of prison and the individual experiences of the inmates and former inmates present an opportunity to press for further reform and also to take steps to ensure that recent reforms are supported and maintained.

Women require female-specific spaces

Despite the various initiatives to reduce the number of women in prison and on remand – women are still in prison, children are with their mothers in prison. Realistically this situation will continue albeit, one hopes, with fewer women involved. As the stories in this book reveal, prison is a frightening, unsavoury and unsanitary place to be. If incarceration is to remain a form of punishment then a radical reform of the way in which women are imprisoned, their conditions and facilities, needs to be undertaken. The cells that women inhabit are usually long army-style barracks, de-personalised and stark. Women's physical realms are more 'intimate' than men's. Women need privacy to deal with their intimate needs – prison denies them this privacy and imposes embarrassment and exposure as an additional punishment.

The women in this book have spoken about their problems and from their analysis of these experiences it is possible to tease out some solutions that need not be costly and could be prisoner driven. More appropriate housing is needed for the women prisoners, individual space and personalised surroundings. Is there any reason why women cannot bring into prison such personal items as bedding and curtaining for creating private cubicles? Women who don't have the resources could make such items for themselves. Public appeals, even in these hard times, might yield end cuts from rolls of material. Why do women in Zimbabwean prisons still wear prison issue – in other prison systems women wear their own clothes. This reform could be a saving to the system and for most prisoners would raise their self-esteem. At the very least it would provide an opportunity for the women to do practical dressmaking. If women are to be in prison with their children and the children's developmental needs are to be adequately addressed each woman needs to have private space to be with her child, and to have the opportunity to play and interact with her child in a relaxed and calm atmosphere. Ollyn Nzuma (magistrate) comments:

> There should be facilities for babies: changing rooms, places for a mother with a baby to sleep, so that there is no health hazard for the child. Prisons are also crowded. Inmates have various diseases. Should we bring up a child in such an environment?

Appropriate surroundings are needed for these children to interact with other children and consideration should be given to opportunities for them to be able to interact with their siblings.

Mabel Chinyamurindi, a former Prison Superintendent, has clearly thought about what is needed:

> I would like to recommend a crèche for the children. If funds were available, I would have the children of the inmates play in a free and beautiful environment so at least the children do not have to feel they are prison all the time.

For the women with children who were left behind in their homes, their greatest stress was not seeing them and constantly worrying about their welfare. Alienation from their children is an added distress and an especially grievous punishment for women.

> I miss my children a lot, especially the one who is not so well. I hope he is being looked after properly. I am told that he is being looked after well but I cannot be sure about that. I am not there to see for myself. (Sheila)

Keeping babies and small children in prison with their mothers is unsatisfactory, highly stressful for the women and potentially prejudicial to the children. Finding a balance is evidently difficult unless the overall conditions of women's imprisonment are changed. Women are as capable as men in undertaking building work. Female prisoners can make bricks and put together fittings to provide suitable small units for two or three women with children to have separate 'cells' and some form of common facilities area. This would make it possible for children, who are not in prison with their mothers, to visit for short periods. A more structured approach to crèche facilities, with training for some women prisoners in crèche management and children's developmental needs, would enable a more appropriate space for the children to grow and develop.

Do open prisons provide a woman friendly solution?

Following the male-based pattern now established at Connemara Prison just outside Kwekwe, more open prisons have been suggested for women. For, given the nature of their crimes, the majority of women are unlikely to be a security threat to society. Thus, the open prison system would seem to be a practical and humanitarian way forward.

Mabel Chinyamurindi sums up the problems of women in prison:

> I would also advocate for female prisons to be built because the facilities that exist are not good enough. The majority of women that are in prison are not hard-core criminals. They are fit to be in an open prison environment that allows semi-freedom; a place where they can do their own cooking in their own time with food they like. Women prisoners need an environment that encourages more social contact with other people from outside. It is very important for a mother to have contact with her children and it is equally important for a wife to have contact with her husband…. The open prison setting affords prisoners an opportunity for home visits and to check on their families.

Rehabilitation or deterrence

One of the vexed questions that all the stories raise is whether prison serves any effective purpose? Certainly, the majority of women end their accounts with a vow never to be imprisoned again and to try and to conduct their lives so as to ensure that they never again commit a criminal offence. Thus, the conditions in prison would seem to have a deterrent effect.

What is unclear is whether they have been prepared in other ways to avoid situations that could lead to a repetition of their crimes, or the commission of new crimes. It appears from these stories that many women were driven to a criminal act out of financial and emotional desperation. Thus, unless those factors are addressed as part of the rehabilitation process, there is a significant risk that the same conditions may trigger another criminal act. Ollyn Nzuma, (magistrate) comments on the violence that often occurs between women and their step-children and the need to address the underlying problems:

> I don't know why step-children are ill-treated – it is something which requires analysis by psychologists or social scientists.

Such women clearly require expert counselling as do many others. Women who believe witchcraft is the cause of their problems and do not receive information and advice to help dispel these misconceptions remain at risk for a repeat of their previous actions should similar circumstances arise in the future. Regrettably the prisons service is very short of such expertise.

> Employment of more social workers is required so that each prisoner can talk to them on a one-to-one basis instead of one social worker listening to twenty prisoners all at once. (Mabel Chinyamurindi: former Prison Superintendent)

Social workers are in short supply and government-provided social workers are virtually non-existent. This, perhaps, is a challenge to voluntary organisations – for without rehabilitation many of these women will leave prison with their underlying problems unresolved – leaving them vulnerable to the commission of repeat offences. As one woman who was interviewed told us:

> I stopped shoplifting for a little while after I came back from prison. I went on trips to buy maize that I then sold in town. I found it hard and slow going, so I am sorry to say I am shoplifting again. I know it is risky. I do not want to go back to jail, but what else can I do to earn money?

The question remains would she have benefited from a more organised and focused training programme? Perhaps quick money will always be a temptation but effort needs to be made to ensure that there are real alternatives available when women leave prison, so that they are better skilled and equipped for a life outside. Rehabilitation does not seem to be very high on the prison agenda. The opportunities for a woman to learn new skills seem to be very limited. If social and economic problems are the root cause of many of these women's crimes, very little is done through the prison system to remove those problems and prepare the women for a better future. What seems to take place is that women who are on work programmes may gain skills but they have no proof of those skills as a former prisoner stated:

> Some did practical subjects like sewing but the disadvantage was that there were no certificates issued. It would be easy to get a job if they could offer such certificates.

The care and concern of some of the warders was significant for some prisoners, but this seemed from the women's accounts to be random rather than part of a concerted rehabilitation and counselling programme.

Crushing the spirit

Anyone who visits a women's prison in Zimbabwe is likely to be struck by the subservient behaviour of the inmates – they kneel or squat before any form of authority. It is quite disturbing to be interviewing a prisoner who spends her whole time on her knees during an individual interview; any suggestion that she might sit is usually ignored, or perhaps rejected out of fear.* The rationale behind the prisoner kneeling or squatting seemed to be intended to break her spirit and probably also create a greater degree of security in interchanges as a prone person has a restricted opportunity to attack someone standing over them.

Martha's experience in trying to provide for her baby is disturbing:

> Sometimes the baby food was not well prepared. So one day I decided to complain because my baby had diarrhoea and on checking on the baby food I found out that the porridge was lumpy and no egg had been added as was required. I went up to one of the prison guards and said, 'Look *vanambuya*, look at the poor quality of the food my baby is fed.' As soon as

---

* This happened to me during the 1999/2000 WLSA study. Perhaps I was especially disturbed as the prisoner concerned was of my own race, European, and this is not expected behaviour between such persons, regardless of status.

I said that they beat me up – they beat me up at lunchtime. … Oh they beat me and beat me… I was really upset and I told them I was going to report them to the magistrates who come to find out from us about our living conditions in prison. They threatened to extend my stay… if I reported them. It was too serious a threat. I did not want to stay a day more than necessary. I never said a word against them from that day… However, after this incident their behaviour towards me improved. They were friendly. They offered me Lacto for my baby… We got on better than before. Maybe the beatings were a show of their power over me and the other prisoners.

The hostility and verbal aggression shown to a woman who was a school teacher seems to have been directed at humiliating her and gaining power over someone who was perceived as having a higher social status – Lilian describes her arrival at the prison thus:

When I arrived the prison guards on duty were all out to humiliate me. "Here come the teachers who earn a lot of money. They have turned into wheelers and dealers." Another one said "Is she the one with the beautiful long hair? She'll have to cut it right away." Sometimes one would talk to me kindly, asking what happened, then another would shout, "Give her one of those yellow dresses full of lice! And a blanket to match! Teachers must learn that prisons have lice. Prisons are not classrooms."

Perhaps Fortunate sums up the experience of many:

You come out of prison worse off than you were before. It is impossible to come out with an improved character.

She attributes this to the way prisoners are treated:

I think prison guards need thorough training on how to look after prisoners. They never had a good word about us. Their language was vulgar. They shouted obscenities that I cannot repeat.

Nonetheless, as some of the stories indicate there are caring and concerned guards who do make a difference.

As Mercy states:

[Y]ou also meet born-again officers who remind you that you have a future.

Such encouragement should not be haphazard – prison and confinement, lock up, lack of normal freedom are the punishment. Humiliation is not required and needs to be addressed as a serious issue that detracts from effective rehabilitation.

Is community service a viable option?

One of the assumptions about the way to deal with the punishment of women is to promote the sentencing of them to community service. The policy is now to try as far as possible to impose community service as a substitute for custodial sentences of up to 24 months. None of the women in this book had done a period of community service, so the efficacy of this approach to women and punishment cannot be gauged. In 1999/2000, however, the Women and Law in Southern Africa Research and Development Trust (WLSA) carried out a study of women's experiences with the justice delivery system[†] and women undergoing community service were interviewed. Most of the work they were doing was cleaning and domestic work. This provided them with an alternative to prison and the opportunity to remain with their families. It did not, however, address the root cause of their original crime – social ostracisation, either real (if the girl was pregnant and unmarried) or envisaged – a perception that led to crimes such as infanticide and abortion. So our concern about rehabilitation remains, as community service sentences do not have an inbuilt rehabilitative and counselling component. Instead, like the women in prison, access was fortuitous; it depended on whom they met, and how they interacted with other people in the places they were sent for community service.

Community service relies on volunteer organisations to provide places. Managing the process, however, can be difficult. In 2000, during the study on 'access to justice' carried out by WLSA, a suggestion was made to the Community Service programme that the Women's Law Centre at the University and WLSA itself might be possible sites for women to undertake community service. The snag was that being based in a low-density suburb, commuting would be a problem for the women undergoing such punishment. Perhaps other organisations could take up the challenge. Certainly, the Women's Law Centre needs to take up the issue again.

[†] Stewart et al (2000) *In the Shadow of the Law: Women and the Justice Delivery in Zimbabwe*, WLSA, Harare (Weaver Press); Stewart et al, (2001) *Pregnancy and Childbirth: Joy or Despair: Women and Gender Generated Crimes of Violence*, WLSA, Harare (Weaver Press).

Another problem that seems to affect women who are eligible for community service is the way in which work is conceptualised in the sentencing process. Community service is intended to be structured around a person's normal employment or work activities. Thus, men in employment might do community service in the evenings or over weekends. Unemployed males might find themselves undertaking community service during the normal working week. Many women do not work in the formal sector, they may be buying or selling in the informal arena or if they are full-time home workers, they do not describe their daily routines as work. Thus a woman with small or school-aged children can be sentenced to community service during the normal working week. The problem is that she has a myriad of other duties to perform: child care, feeding the family, washing, cleaning, plus income-generating activities. Realistically, therefore, the woman also needs to be treated as an employed person: her hours of community service, and when they are served, should be calculated in the light of her pressing home-based duties. Concern has been expressed that women may be defaulting on community service not because they wish to avoid it, but because the pressures of daily life are overwhelming and women have to somehow balance the competing pressures in their complex days. Women do not fit easily into space constructed and designed for men. Prisons and punishment need to be reviewed and reformed from the perspective of women and women's reproductive, social, emotional and work-based lives. Sex and gender-based analysis of prisons and punishment is long overdue in the Zimbabwean system. The encouraging element is that judicial officers and prison authorities are willing to initiate change when the problems are brought to their attention.

Mabel Chinyamurindi's words challenge us all:

> I think women's organisations are not doing enough. I would like to see them providing more information than they are doing ... Information on the rights of the arrested should be made available even at police stations. ... They need to get more involved with disadvantaged women such as prisoners.

The code of silence around women in prison has been broken and surely change is now possible.

A Tragedy of Lives:
women in prison in Zimbabwe

Conclusion

Amy Tsanga

A *Tragedy of Lives* allows women who are or have been in prison in Zimbabwe to tell their own stories. As Ollyn Nzuma, the magistrate, tells us women accept responsibility for their actions, they do not try to explain them away or deny responsibility. Thus they tell us of the crimes that sent them to prison that include reproductive crimes, domestic violence, culpable homicide, fraud, dealing in drugs, shoplifting and assault. Their stories provide us with real insight into the social, cultural, and economic, backgrounds of the women that help us to appreciate their circumstances that led to them being judged 'criminals' although most are women with a strong sense of right and wrong.

As the women narrate their stories from childhood, we better understand the opportunities and constraints that shaped their lives, and how social, cultural, and economic realities often act in combination to reinforce women's oppression. These testimonials provide us with pointers for further analysis and exploration of the circumstances that can contribute to the vulnerability of women in so far as crime is concerned.

In terms of social profiles, the stories reveal a heterogeneous picture. Some women come from polygamous families with the attendant problems of competition for resources while others come from monogamous families. For instance, Maria, imprisoned for culpable homicide after hitting her husband with pole, tells a story of a difficult childhood as her father lived in Dangamvura with another woman and she grew up without enough clothes or food. When her father sent her mother back to her home after having an affair, Maria's problems intensified as the father refused to look after the nine children, arguing that he was not sure if they were his own. Maria only managed to go as far as Grade 6 before she married.

In cases where the parents separated, this impacted negatively on the children. Clara, imprisoned for abortion, tells us that her parents were separated and she was brought up by her mother who was very strict resulting in her being unable to communicate with her only parent about issues of sexuality. Similarly, Mercy, imprisoned for defrauding her employer tells us that her parents were divorced when she was still at University with the result that she had to become responsible for her mother at an early age. In addition, when her parents divorced her father sold the house leaving them homeless. Marina imprisoned for dealing with dangerous drugs also states that her father left her mother when she was pregnant with her and for a long time she did not know where her father was. Education was not a smooth process as she states that her mother and stepfather drank heavily. She reveals that she grew up under very difficult conditions with her stepfather, often having to resort to selling vegetables in order to raise school fees. She also ate from dustbins. She also reveals a background of family violence at the hands of her mother and her sister. The relatives who came to her rescue also over worked her. Not surprisingly when she met a man when she was in Form 1, she saw this as an opportunity to escape poverty only to have him deny paternity. Even later in her life, when she goes back to school to do tailoring, she has to drop out because of fees. She tries to break her cycle of poverty by selling drugs as a way of making an easy income. In other cases one or both parents died, often precipitating a period of upheaval as grandparents or other relatives assumed responsibility for them. Some had a positive experience of step-parents and relatives others did not. Some report a happy stable childhood, others were less fortunate. For example, Joyce imprisoned for dealing with dangerous drugs, reveals how her uncle took her in as a child minder after her parents divorced. She tells of a very unhappy childhood at the hands of her aunt who she says hated her and told lies about her. She later moved to Zimbabwe and was raised by another uncle. Her educational opportunities were limited because her uncle's wife was not prepared to spend money on her education. She only went up to Standard 1. The treatment she received was no better than that she had received at the hands of her aunt in Zambia. Sadly, her family also resorts to marriage as the solution to her problems. She tells how she was married off to a Mozambican man against her wishes. Surprisingly though, she reports that life with her husband was not that bad as he looked after her and the children and it was his death, which left her with a large family to look after, that precipitated her need to raise income through any means possible.

In terms of family background, what is striking is that the majority of these women come from large families. For example, Sandra imprisoned for fraud, states that she came from a polygamous family with a total of seventeen children. Her mother, the junior wife had ten children. She was not happy in her marriage as she was treated as a servant. Even though Sandra managed to go up to Form 4 her story reveals the continued pressure of looking after a large family. Family size sometimes acted as a constraint in terms of resources available. For example, Viola, a commercial sex worker, imprisoned for stabbing a man, states that she came from a family of ten and was the eighth born. Her sister who had nine children brought her up but could not afford to pay her fees so she only went up to Grade 7 even though her sister's own children went up to Form 4. Unable to continue with schooling, Viola marries at sixteen.

Some of the women such as Joyce who had a large family (nine children although two died) found herself in severely constrained circumstances especially after her husband died. However, in light of increased cost of living, even women with one or two children report having an equally hard time raising enough money for the upkeep of their families.

We also see a mixture of rural and urban backgrounds in the social profiles of the women. Yet, generally, whether rural or urban, most are underprivileged women who have had little opportunity to acquire meaningful education and skills that they can rely on for survival. The majority report coming from poor families while a few state that they were able to survive, at least in terms of there being adequate food for the family, even if there were few resources for education. For most, opportunities for further education were limited especially in cases where the father died or deserted the family at an early age. Several of the women managed to go as far as Form 4 but only Mercy has a university education. The majority of the testimonials indicate that the women are either primary or high school drop-outs as a result of there being no money to pursue further studies.

Others dropped out because they had failed exams, while in Clara's case peer pressure influenced her decision to drop out of school.

Education regulates access to certified skills training, jobs and access to credit. These stories reveal that most of those with little education were engaged in low paying jobs such as domestic work, vegetable vending, peasant farming, or were simply not in paid employment. For many, the first skills training they acquired was in prison. In a minority of cases, however, the women held very good jobs such as the case of the Mercy the administrator with a business studies degree, Lilian the teacher, and Sheila the secretarial trained POSB worker who all committed fraud. Clearly crimes occurs across class as each woman explains what led her astray in relation to her own personal circumstances and the pressures she encountered. In the case of Lilian, the teacher imprisoned for fraud, her personal circumstances changed when she had to support her deceased brother's five children as well as her own family.

From a social and cultural perspective, these testimonials also reveal the way marriage acts as an escape route for some women caught in a poverty trap. For these women Joyce, Viola, and Maria discussed above, early marriage appeared to offer a way out of the economic hardships that have shaped their lives. Yet, in some cases such as that of Maria who found herself in an abusive marriage, the very act of marriage precipitated the process that led to her committing crime that sent her to prison. With little education and no job, Maria had her first child at the age of 17. The story of her married life is one of abuse that involved being cut with a razor blade on her arms and thighs. In a story that betrays a continuation of a cycle of violence, she hit her husband in self-defence when he was assaulting her, and he died.

Maureen, who set a hut on fire resulting in the death of a child, also reveals some of the cultural constraints that women face when it comes to leaving troubled marriages. Although she once packed her bags and left she was told to return to her husband. She also says fatalistically that she thought that this was how marriage was supposed to be when her husband would take all the money from the sale of her cotton. These stories raise significant questions regarding custom and marriage and how women can be empowered to leave abusive relationships before it is too late regardless of the extended family's views.

We also see how attitudes towards marriage provide a constraining framework for women. From Elizabeth's story, we see how society's expectation that women should bear children leads her to steal a child. Familial pressure to remain in a marriage, even when it is not working, ultimately cause two women, Beti and Maria to kill their husbands in what is now called 'slow burn' a metaphor for the relentless pressure on a woman in a situation where there is little or no support. Of significance is that the women's view of marriage is influenced by what they believe society expects of them. Several interviews also reveal women's sexual subordination to men within a society where the man is free to have relationships outside marriage but the woman is not. On the other hand, we occasionally see how marriage acts as a supportive institution by making a woman less vulnerable to economic hardships as in Joyce's case where she reports that her husband when he was alive, looked after herself and the children.

These personal stories tell us that as long as women continue to have the primary responsibility for bringing up children, the pressures brought to bear upon them will continue to be enormous. Parent child relationships also emerge in the stories. Lack of communication between mother and daughter results in problems when a young woman, Clara, unable to communicate with her mother aborts her own child.

Another factor that emerges through the testimonies is that most women are generally ignorant of their legal rights under state laws making them vulnerable when confronted with a legal system with which they are not familiar. This is exemplified in the case of Sofia who is accused of assisting her husband to rape her niece. Some women, such as Loveness, who allegedly stole from her former husband appears to have been imprisoned for a petty case. Her story does not reveal how much she was said to have stolen but ten months in prison seems somewhat excessive. Such realities highlight the need to improve programmes aimed at increasing women's awareness of their rights.

Overall, these life stories show that a combination of life changes often acting in concert have been critical to the negative outcomes which led the women to prison. These include widowhood, turn-coat husbands who beat or cheat on their wives, desertion, over-stretched family resources, the pressures of supporting the extended family and frustration to mention a few. The stress accompanying such circumstances significantly increased the risks of negative behaviour that ultimately led to the commission of certain crimes. Many, as we have said before, were unable to continue with school or married young. Appreciating the multiple pressures on women is important if we are to avoid generalisations about which situations lead to crime.

Even though the circumstances impacting on these women's lives are multiple, they raise important questions about the issues around which women's rights activists need to focus their energy. Could, for instance, awareness about women's reproductive health rights have saved some of the women from prison? Some of the testimonials point to the persistence of strong beliefs in witchcraft, which led to problems for women in at least three instances. Could Ellen, for instance, not have benefited from knowledge of some of the gynaecologic problems that can affect women and, more significantly, would she not have benefited from better access to health care? Marina's story also tells of strong beliefs in witchcraft. For instance when she was involved in an accident where two people died her family went to a witchdoctor who said she was possessed of evil spirits. In Marina we see a woman controlled very much by her belief system. When she became involved in selling *mbanje* she tells us that she consulted a prophet before going on the trip that led to her arrest. What are the implications for action in terms of other key concerns raised by the women such as incest?

When looked at overall, the stories reveal that more often than not women from poor backgrounds and limited opportunities are the ones most vulnerable to imprisonment. We must, therefore, question the meaning of 'equality': is it just that someone who is privileged in terms of education and their ability to afford a lawyer, should escape prison while a person with neither is penalised more harshly? We must ask if the poor are more likely to be arrested by the police, because the latter feel less intimidated by poverty than wealth? and how social hierarchies effect both the attitude of both the police and the prison service. And we must try to ensure that prisons of the future serve a truly rehabilitative process in terms of both education and counselling.

Society often assumes a very punitive attitude to people, in particular women, who have served prison sentences. *A Tragedy of Lives* must enable us to have more understanding, more compassion, and help us to improve our system of penalties and retribution.

www.ingramcontent.com/pod-product-compliance
Lightning Source LLC
Chambersburg PA
CBHW031459270326
41930CB00006B/163